Human Rights and Revolutions

Human Rights and Revolutions

Edited by Jeffrey N. Wasserstrom,
Lynn Hunt, and Marilyn B. Young

ROWMAN & LITTLEFIELD PUBLISHERS, INC.
Lanham • Boulder • New York • Oxford

ROWMAN & LITTLEFIELD PUBLISHERS, INC.

Published in the United States of America
by Rowman & Littlefield Publishers, Inc.
4720 Boston Way, Lanham, Maryland 20706
http://www.rowmanlittlefield.com

12 Hid's Copse Road, Cumnor Hill, Oxford OX2 9JJ, England

British Library Cataloguing in Publication Information Available

Library of Congress Cataloging-in-Publication Data

Human rights and revolutions / Jeffrey N. Wasserstrom, Lynn Hunt, and Marilyn B. Young [editors].
    p. cm.
    Includes bibliographical references and index.
    ISBN 0-8476-8736-8 (alk. paper)—ISBN 0-8476-8737-6 (pbk. : alk. paper)
    1. Human rights.   2. Revolutions.   I. Wasserstrom, Jeffrey N.   II. Hunt, Lynn Avery.   III. Young, Marilyn Blatt.

JC585 .H86   2000
323—dc21
00-038741

Printed in the United States of America

♾™ The paper used in this publication meets the minimum requirements of American National Standard for Information Sciences—Permanence of Paper for Printed Library Materials, ANSI/NISO Z39.48-1992.

Contents

Preface

Over the past twenty years, human rights, variously interpreted, have been officially embraced by a wide variety of nation-states. Some countries insist on the primacy of economic human rights while they reduce welfare provisions; others proclaim their adherence to an international code of human rights, even as they violate its premises in the name of national security. These are the ordinary hypocrisies and contradictions of state policy and, while it remains important to track and expose such opportunism, the challenge they pose is primarily political. The essays in this volume, however, take on a prior intellectual task: to explore the origin, diffusion, and practice of human rights from their conceptual origin to the present. The editors were clear, from the outset, about the range of topics we wished to see addressed but we had no prior commitment to a particular point of view; nor did we expect (or encourage) uniformity in the approaches taken by individual authors. In the event, we were not disappointed: the essays diverge in their points of departure, their conclusions, their predictions for the future. They are united, however, by a shared conviction that the concept of human rights is of central importance in history and in contemporary politics and must be understood in the specific context in which it was developed and practiced across time and place.

The reader will at once note the numerous occasions on which the word "paradox" is invoked by the authors. Paradox, not contradiction. Contradiction allows for resolution, and indeed, in some philosophical systems, this resolution is the very engine of history. But paradox involves posing irreconcilable propositions of equal force. For Lynn Hunt, the very origin of human rights is paradoxical, while Michael Zuckert explores the paradox in a specifically American setting. Jeffrey Wasserstrom names a series of Chinese paradoxes that open one from the other like the proverbial boxes. Those essays that do not signal paradox in their titles address themselves to it in the bodies of their essays. So, too, paradox dominates discussion of the linkages between human rights and revolutionary movements, between metropolitan Enlightenment and colonial restrictions, between all the varieties of the universal and particular with which this volume deals. The expectation that social revolutions invariably repress human rights is countered by the observation that revolutions at the same time mobilize on the basis of the expansion of those rights. David Zaret addresses the issue in his discussion of the English Revolution in terms of the "uneven connections between human rights and revolutionary traditions." His essay introduces paradox at a different level from those outlined by Hunt and Zuckert. The Levellers, to paraphrase the poet Adrienne Rich, used what they had to create what they needed. Their approach, Zuckert argues, prefigures that of many modern revolutionary groups that reworked existing practices in their efforts to claim larger rights.

Pointing to a paradox does not end the discussion but rather expands it. Lynn Hunt observes that the paradoxes that surround the subject of human rights measure "the depth of the challenge" human rights pose to social hierarchies and privileges of all sorts. Yanni Kotsonis, in his discussion of revolutionary Russia, adds a note of caution. In Russia, as elsewhere in post-Enlightenment Europe, "the question of who was deserving of human rights and liberation depended in part on who was considered mature enough to accept the responsibilities of the citizen." Thus, to plumb fully the ambiguities of human rights, Kotsonis finds, it is useful to add to it the concept of citizen. The link between the rights all humans can claim and the responsibilities of citizens is strong, though sometimes only implicit. The question of human rights, then, depends on who is recognized as a citizen. One may be born human, but citizenship is ascriptive. Against the dominant view in both Russian and Western European historiography, Kotsonis insists that Russia was not exceptional in its embrace of Enlightenment values that were themselves paradoxical. From their inception, "human rights and liberation were dual." "Underdeveloped" segments of the Russian population, like "underdeveloped" countries in the eyes of Western imperialists, could reasonably be excluded until they had, under the careful management of the Party— or the imperialist state—matured sufficiently to warrant inclusion. The link between human and citizen served as a "terrain to measure all and exclude most."

In extending the consideration of the link between citizenship and human rights, Florence Bernault's perspective is that of the colonial state in Africa, which possessed many of the attributes of a nation in terms of territorial boundaries and central governing administration, while sovereignty and legislative power remained monopolized by the metropolitan government. Here the paradoxes of citizenship were multiple. In the British Empire, she points out, there was no assumption that Africans were eligible for British citizenship; in much of francophone Africa, by contrast, colonialism's ideological justification lay precisely in the possibility of assimilation to French civilization and thus the rights and responsibilities of citizenship. This did not make citizenship probable; instead it forced upon colonial administrations the necessity of developing exclusive categories that maintained the ideology without putting it into practice. The criteria for passage from one category to another was, of course, determined by the state. And when in 1946 a new French constitution proclaimed all former subjects of the empire citizens, the full rights of citizenship continued to exclude Africans through the manipulation of varieties of legal discrimination.

Bernault shows that independence did not resolve the difficulties. The requirements of nationalist movements meant the focus of struggle was collective political and economic rights rather than those an individual citizen might claim. The paradoxes and ambiguities of human rights in Africa recall, in a different key, those described by Kotsonis and Wasserstrom: the legitimation of authoritarian governments in the name of national unity; the exclusion of categories of people who fail to meet a standard for citizenship the government in power deems appropriate.

The essays by Timothy McDaniel and Alice Bullard raise fundamental questions about the concept of human rights as they relate to non-European societies. Bullard uses the example of the French penal colony of New Caledonia to argue the need to go beyond the common opposition of individual rights and the intrusive power of the state. Here again the way in which citizenship has been used to exclude is clear: ex-Communards, exiled to New Caledonia, were able to claim the rights of citizens. Neither their politics nor their class permanently banned them from participating in French political life. Moreover, their citizenship did not entail either cultural or economic sacrifices. The indigenous inhabitants, on the other hand, marked by their racial and cultural difference, could not "embark on the long process of acquiring 'civilization'" until they acknowledged the inferiority of their own culture and society. Bullard's conclusion is perhaps the starkest statement of the limitations of the language of human rights in "situations of radical cultural difference," and while not suggesting the abandonment of such language, she asks those who use it to acknowledge that it does not always nor everywhere work toward the empowerment of the oppressed.

Timothy McDaniel's essay on Islam and human rights directly confronts a subject whose contemporary charge is especially strong. Paradox is at the center of his argument, too. The concept of universal human rights, he finds, "gives rise to conflicts over civilizational values, particularly between Islam and the West," conflicts based more on ignorance of Islam's history and ideology than on anything essential either to Islam or the West. McDaniel's careful analysis stresses the combination of hierarchy and rights embraced by Islam. The Islamic hierarchy of rights, he argues, is based "on a rich appreciation of the individual in his or her socially defined roles." Rights, in this system, are not opposed to hierarchy, as in Lynn Hunt's argument, but rather are integrated into hierarchy. Christian universalism, on the other hand, creates a "greater danger of exclusion, for there is no subordinate place for the outsider." From this proposition, McDaniel moves to a discussion of contemporary revolutionary Islamic states, whose attempt to establish an ideal nation flies in the face of the history of Islam.

Alexander Woodside's essay on Vietnam, written, one feels, more in sorrow than in anger, reviews the meager results for the people of Vietnam today of the vast sacrifices they have endured. Like Bullard, he insists on a historical understanding of the "stunted" life of human rights in Vietnam. The question should lead us to examine "why they were stunted in the practice" during the French colonial period. And he concludes with a reflection that expresses a common conviction among all the essays that look at human rights in a revolutionary context: "[The Vietnamese revolution] has harbored what most revolutions harbor, and what may be an important right in itself. That is the right to hope."

Analyzing paradox is one thing; living it is quite another. Both Carlos Basombrío Iglesias and Adam Michnik offer what we should perhaps call field reports: the one of how an organization committed to human rights (the Legal Defense Institute of Peru, of which he is a member) proceeded in the face of a selectively repressive government and an indiscriminately repressive insurgent movement. From the ashes of the defeat of the Shining Path insurrection, Iglesias manages nevertheless to extract a possibility of hope. Adam Michnik, a significant actor in the Polish struggle, offers a striking analysis of dictatorships, their claims and arguments as well as their organs of repression. Any discussion of ending a dictatorial regime must pay attention not only to the freedoms dictatorships withhold but also to what dictatorships offer in the way of security, the promise of changed property relations, the establishment of sovereignty and independence. In this, although in a different key, he echoes Iglesias's comments on the way in which the violence of the insurgency created, in a majority of Peruvians, a sense of "frustration and desperation" so that it became "common sense that sacrificing democracy and human rights . . . were costs well worth paying to overcome the threat of Shining Path." Drawing on his experience in Poland to comment on the current struggle in Burma, Michnik urges the difficult course of negotiation against the absolutist politics of both government and dissident hard-liners. Negotiations and compromises are bound to disappoint, to foster a sense of injustice. But the choice to negotiate "is free of casualties— people are disappointed but alive." Still, negotiations are only possible "when a democratic opposition is strong enough to defend itself against dictatorship, and when dictatorship is strong enough not to let the opposition seize power overnight. The weakness of both sides becomes a chance for the people."

A final set of paradoxes concludes the volume. The recent war (and ongoing violence) in Kosovo is explored in two essays, one by Robin Blackburn and the other by David Rieff. Neither author believes the Kosovo war successful. But for Blackburn, it was a war whose strategic goal, the expansion of NATO, killed any possibility of a negotiated settlement and "precipitated a humanitarian catastrophe." Rieff understands the war as having been undertaken "more in the name of human rights and moral obligation" than out of any more traditional set of interests, but he is as dissatisfied with its conduct or result as Blackburn is. Rieff warns against the conflation of human rights and humanitarianism, which has plagued not just the intervention in Kosovo but those in Somalia, Rwanda, and Bosnia as well; against the conflation of war and crime; and most insistently against the pretense that, in the absence of world government, "international law can be upheld as strenuously as the domestic laws of democratic states." He urges instead the institution of a system of mandates and trusteeships administered by the United States and the NATO powers, a sort of "liberal imperialism" as the only alternative to "barbarism." Blackburn, who finds the prospect of the United States in the role of "global bully" deeply disheartening, would surely disagree. But he would probably second Rieff's observation that a "half a century of campaigning by human rights activists" has fundamentally challenged the old system of state sovereignty. What separates them is their evaluation of what that challenge has yielded.

This final section of essays seems to me to imply that it may be desirable to distinguish between notions of human rights within a polity, as variously discussed by all the authors, and the far more complicated effort to pursue them internationally. The contrast between the analyses of Blackburn and Rieff reveals the dangers involved in the challenges to state sovereignty Rieff says have become so common. The language of human rights, like language of revolution, may be especially vulnerable to universalist claims on behalf of very narrow interests.

The disagreement between Blackburn and Rieff brings us back to Lynn Hunt's essay. Hunt observes that declarations of human rights, contrary to their claims of eternal and universal transcendence, have a specific history and a "vexed relationship" in particular to the "concrete histories of revolutions" or, in the case of Kosovo and other self-proclaimed human rights interventions, to the concrete histories of international relations. Revolutions, in recent history the origin of totalitarianism, are also the context in which the claims of groups and individuals to human rights have developed. The context in which international claims to human rights have developed is, on the other hand, war. Most revolutionary movements, once in power, tend to present their popular basis and accomplishments in freeing the populace from oppression as legitimating their own acts of oppression: having first established categories of exclusion, they rule in the name of "the people," whose state-defined human rights they readily guarantee. Seeking a more just collectivity, in the process they deny those absolute individual rights upon which human rights logically rest. The essays in this volume suggest that the tension between human rights and established social organizations of all kinds may be structural. But, in Lynn Hunt's words, human rights pose a continuing challenge to "inequality, injustice, and despotic authority of all kinds."

A recognition and acknowledgment of the paradox, combined with the most careful consideration of the concrete historical situation, and, as Michnik insists, a preference for negotiation over absolutisms of any variety, is what constitutes the struggle for the further expansion of human rights worldwide.

Marilyn B. Young

Part I

Introductory Perspectives

1

The Paradoxical Origins of Human Rights

Lynn Hunt

Declarations of human rights always make universalistic claims that resound with brave confidence. In 1948, for example, when the United Nations adopted the Universal Declaration of Human Rights, it proclaimed that "recognition of the inherent dignity and of the equal and inalienable rights of all members of the human family is the foundation of freedom, justice and peace in the world."[1] Yet these confident claims rest on a series of troubling paradoxes. Human rights are supposed to be eternal and universal, engraved, as it were, in human nature. But not everyone believes them to be inscribed in human nature, and the notion itself of human rights has a distinct history; it entered into political discourse only at certain times and in specific places. What is imagined to be universal and above history turns out to be contingent and grounded in a very particular history. Does this paradox undermine their validity?

The paradoxes do not end with a vexed relationship to history in the abstract. Human rights also have a paradoxical relationship to the concrete histories of revolutions. Rights, especially property rights, have a long history in the West, but they would never have become *human rights* without revolutions. What political theorists take to be the chief dividing line between present-day democracy and totalitarianism—the guarantee of individual human rights—had its origins in revolution. Although the development of a legal tradition of rights and social contract theories helped shape the concept of human rights, without revolutions human rights would never have become a political reality. Revolutions, the supposed origins of totalitarianism, turn out to be the origins of human rights as well.

To understand these paradoxes, it is essential to be clear about the definition of human rights. Human rights depend on three related assumptions: 1) that rights are *universal* and *equal*, which means that all human beings have certain

3

inherent rights simply by virtue of being human and not by virtue of their status in society, whether that is defined by sex, race, ethnicity, a group of families, a social class, an occupational group, or even an entire nation; 2) that these rights are consequently imagined as *natural*, as stemming from human nature itself, and they have in the past often been called "natural rights"; and 3) that the legitimacy of any government rests on its ability to guarantee under the law the human rights of all its members. Although these assumptions sound abstract and universal, they only came to make sense to some, by no means all, people in the eighteenth century. Without the universalism of the eighteenth-century Enlightenment and the political shocks of the American and French Revolutions of 1776 and 1789, there would have been no concept of human rights in the West.

ATTACKS ON THE ENLIGHTENMENT

The now widespread denigration of the French Revolution of 1789 can hardly be surprising, given the political shifts of the last twenty years, but it is perhaps more surprising that the Enlightenment too has been the subject of sharp criticism. From the time of the French Revolution forward, liberals (defenders of constitutional guarantees of individual rights and of free market government policies) could defend the values of the Enlightenment even while rejecting many aspects of the French Revolution; indeed, in the nineteenth century, this distinction between the Enlightenment and the French Revolution provided one of the chief definitions of liberalism as doctrine. In the twentieth century, however, this distinction has been blurred as various critical schools, especially those now associated with postmodernism (and earlier those of the extreme right) have posited the Enlightenment itself as the source of rather than the solution to all modern problems.

Most influential in staking out this position has been Max Horkheimer and Theodor Adorno's *Dialectic of Enlightenment*, a book originally published in 1947 but only coming into its own in the 1970s and afterward. Recoiling from the Nazi horrors that had forced them to flee from their native Germany, Horkheimer and Adorno argued that mankind was "sinking into a new kind of barbarism" thanks to "the indefatigable self-destructiveness of enlightenment." In their view, the "Enlightenment is totalitarian" because it turned reason into fascistic domination. Through the development of the administrative state and repressive forms of capitalist industrialism, reason turned into irrational domination and even murder.[2] The Enlightenment led to Auschwitz.

This view has inspired a host of studies critical of Enlightenment rationalism and universalism. Dorinda Outram, for example, explicitly endorses the Horkheimer and Adorno position and uses it to explain the totalitarian nature of the French Revolution: "The history of Revolutionary bodies is the history of a self-image of rationality, reflexivity, universalism, autonomy, individuation and emancipation always containing the potential for transposition into its direct opposite"—that is, the massacre and dismemberment, even the extermination, of all non-normal groups (women, Jews, homosexuals, or the poor).[3] More recently, Lawrence Birken has published a book with the inflammatory title: *Hitler as Philosophe*. He argues that "Nazism—and especially Hitler's exposition of it—represented an attenuated and popularized form of the Enlightenment style of thought."[4] Birken's book is only interesting as a symptom, for it deliberately falsifies the past; in fact, Hitler repeatedly denounced both the Enlightenment and the French Revolution. Birken could not resist the temptation held out in Horkheimer and Adorno's book of blaming the Enlightenment for the rise of National Socialism.[5]

A long list of studies attacking the Enlightenment for its antifeminism, anti-Semitism, and racism would only serve to reinforce the point: it is apparently possible for scholars to blame the Enlightenment for every disaster of modernity. I do not deny that many Enlightenment writers held attitudes that we would now criticize as racist, sexist, or religiously bigoted. The priest Henri Grégoire, for instance, who was one of the most consistent and broad-minded advocates of rights for Jews and blacks, referred to the Jews as "parasitic plants who eat away the substance of the tree to which they are attached."[6] But to label these views "anti-Semitic" (and conclude, as some have, that Grégoire's actions led straight to Auschwitz) is only to anachronistically pat ourselves on the back for our own historical superiority. Even more important, this kind of labeling distorts the historical record because it covers over what was truly new and different in the eighteenth century; in the case of the Jews, for example, what was new was not the ubiquity of anti-Semitism, a feature of European life for centuries, but rather the fact that French revolutionaries like Grégoire felt called upon to discuss the status of Jews in a public forum and after such discussion felt compelled to grant Jews the very same forms of citizenship enjoyed by other French men. Nowhere else in the world, not even in the new United States, did Jews have full civil and political rights. In most of Europe, governments did not emancipate them until the late nineteenth or early twentieth century. In the United States, they gained rights on a state by state basis from 1776 up to the 1820s.[7] In France, in contrast, they gained full rights in 1791.

RIGHTS AND REVOLUTIONS

Since anti-Enlightenment critiques either overlook the notion of human rights altogether or, in a scholarly sleight of hand, blame it for the emergence of modern forms of bigotry, they cannot reckon with the contribution of revolutions to human rights. Although rights have a long intellectual, legal, and political history in the West, going back to the Greeks, rights did not turn into human rights through a straightforward, continuous development. This story is rather one of jumps and discontinuities, largely marked by revolutionary episodes in seventeenth- and eighteenth-century Europe. Many scholars agree that an important first step was taken in the seventeenth century by the Dutch philosopher Hugo Grotius when he defined "natural rights" as something self-possessed and conceivable separately from God's will. He suggested that people could use their rights—unaided by religion—to establish the contractual foundations for social life.[8] Grotius published his book in 1625 in the midst of the Dutch revolution for independence from the Spanish.

The next important stage in development of the notion of human rights came during the English Civil War of the 1640s. The English Levellers took Grotius's theory and gave it a practical, political sting. In "The Agreement of the People" of 1647, for instance, the Levellers insisted on their "common" or "native" rights, implying that the government must guarantee them: "for, as it cannot be imagined that so many of our countrymen would have opposed us in this quarrel if they had understood their own good, so may we safely promise to ourselves that, when our common rights and liberties shall be cleared, their endeavors will be disappointed that seek to make themselves our masters." After listing their demands, they concluded, "These things we declare to be our native rights, and therefore are agreed and resolved to maintain them with our utmost possibilities against all opposition whatsoever."[9] The Levellers did not carry the day but they nonetheless showed the radical implications lurking in natural rights and showed, moreover, how a revolutionary upheaval could bring these implications into the light of day.

In these early days—indeed right down to 1789—the actual composition of natural rights was vague. For Grotius, they were life, body, freedom and honor (a list that seemed to call slavery, in particular, into question). John Locke equated natural rights with "Life, Liberty and Estate," in other words, with property of various sorts (and so he did not call slavery into question).[10] Most English discussion about rights swirled around their existence or nonexistence rather than their precise makeup. Thomas Hobbes inaugurated an enduring counter-tradition that argued that the idea of rights was meaningless, either because such rights had to be given up in order to establish an orderly civil society (Hobbes's own position), or because they counted for nothing compared to positive law (Jeremy Bentham's position) or (in the case of Robert Filmer, for example) compared to divine right. In one of the strongest statements of one version of this position Bentham insisted that "Natural rights is simple nonsense; natural and imprescriptible rights (an American phrase), rhetorical nonsense, nonsense upon stilts."[11]

Both the pro- and anti-rights positions had their origins in political crisis. The same would hold for the eighteenth-century Americans and French who turned to rights arguments in the midst of their own political upheavals. At the moment that rights were perceived to be violated, they could be defined as either traditional or universal. The English tended to define them as the traditional rights of freeborn English men (though Locke did not), but the Americans and especially the French defined them in universal terms at the end of the eighteenth century. By dispensing with historical traditions, the Americans and especially the French (since Americans still clung to traditional arguments to some extent) made rights potentially accessible to everyone. In other words, rights had to shed their historical garments in order to become human rights, rights potentially applicable to everyone.

How did this happen? The Americans and the French universalized rights in the course of their eighteenth-century struggles for national self-definition. Although the English Whigs had defended the notion of natural rights in the Revolution of 1688, they had not attempted to found the legitimacy of all government upon their guarantee. The Bill of Rights of 1689 referred to the "ancient rights and liberties" established by English law, deriving from English history. It did not declare the *equality, universality, or naturalness* of rights, all essential requirements for a true concept of "human rights." In contrast, the American Declaration of Independence of 1776 and the French Declaration of the Rights of Man and Citizen of 1789 both claimed a right of revolution to establish or re-establish the natural, equal, and universal rights of individuals, and both linked legitimacy to the guarantee of individual, natural rights.[12]

Until 1774 at least, Americans drew on a mish-mash of philosophical, legal, and historical arguments about *British* rights. When British authority collapsed in 1774, Americans came to consider themselves in something like a state of nature; they called conventions to represent popular will and drafted constitutions that often included bills of rights. Rights had to be "declared" as part of this transition from a state of nature back into civil government. Thus the Declaration of Independence maintained: "We hold these truths to be self-evident, that all men are created equal, that they are endowed by their Creator with certain unalienable rights, that among these are life, liberty and the pursuit of happiness." Rights would never have been declared to be inalienable and self-imposed without the revolutionary moment created by the collapse of traditional authority.[13] Everyone did not agree on the importance of declaring rights or on the content of the rights to be declared. Nevertheless, the revolutionary moment opened the door to the declaration of rights. Rights would not have taken the form they did as inalienable and self-imposed, that is, as human rights, without a revolutionary break with the past.

The revolutionary origins of human rights in France are even more striking. Before 1789, French legal and philosophical commentary on rights did not enjoy the depth and vibrancy characteristic of the British rights tradition. In France under the Old Regime monarchy, rights were a form of privilege; they were the consequence of a particular type of society, not a foundation for it. As the

Parlement of Paris argued in 1776: "The first rule of justice is to preserve for every man what belongs to him . . . , a rule that consists not only in maintaining the rights of property, but also in preserving rights attached to the person and those which derive from the prerogatives of birth and estate."[14] Rights were attached to individuals only insofar as they were members of social networks or institutions (the nobility, a guild, a city, a monastery, etc.) that had legal standing. Despite, or perhaps because of, this lack of an elaborated tradition, the French revolutionaries developed the most self-consciously universalistic conception of rights ever seen in the world at that time. During the discussion of a declaration of rights in the opening days of the French Revolution, one deputy exclaimed, "[The Americans] have set a great example in the new hemisphere; let us give one to the universe."[15] In August 1789 the deputies to the National Assembly declared, "Considering that ignorance, neglect or contempt of the rights of man are the sole causes of public misfortunes and governmental corruption, [we] have resolved to set forth in a solemn declaration the natural, inalienable and sacred rights of man." They declared the rights of all men, that is, human rights. Before 1789 such a declaration was inconceivable.

The impact of the declarations of rights in the new United States and in France was immediate. It can even be traced in Great Britain, where no revolution occurred. According to the ESTC—English Short Title Catalogue—the number of titles that included some mention of rights steadily declined from the early 1700s to the 1750s and then steadily rose until the 1790s, when the number literally exploded, quadrupling in the 1790s as compared to the 1780s or any other decade in the eighteenth century.[16] Human rights had entered the discourse.

THE ENLIGHTENMENT ORIGINS OF HUMAN RIGHTS

The history of the revolutionary spurts forward in rights shows that something happened to the conception of rights between 1689 and 1776–1789 to transform them from the rights of a particular people—freeborn English men—into universal natural rights, the French *droits de l'homme* or "rights of man." Men—especially men and only later women—began to talk fervently about universal rights in ways that at least implied their equality for all "men," remembering that "men" could mean either males or humankind. Yet as historians have repeatedly emphasized, these men excluded whole categories of people—slaves, servants, the propertyless, women, and at first, religious minorities—from this supposed equality. How could people hold such seemingly contradictory views?

Such contradictions were sustainable in the eighteenth century because the conception of "rights of man" was originally very vague (many would argue that human rights are still too vague). By the end of the eighteenth century many if not most French political commentators, even supporters of the monarchy, considered the existence of natural rights to be self-evident. Nevertheless, they were hard-pressed to say just what those rights entailed. With the help of the ARTFL Project, the American Resource, Treasury of the French Language, online at the University of Chicago and developed over the years in collaboration with the National Center for Scientific Research in France, it is possible now to trace the emergence of the language of the "rights of man."[17]

The earliest use of "rights of man" that I have found in ARTFL is in Rousseau's *Social Contract* in 1762. "Rights" had been used as a term before, but not "rights of man." "Rights" appeared relatively rarely in any form in the seventeenth century. There were about as many mentions of rights just in the decade of the 1750s (or 1760s or 1770s) as there were in the entire seventeenth century. Rights appeared in all kinds of contexts: the rights of the church, the rights of the tomb, the rights of the father, and, indeed, the rights of the church were dominant between 1600 and 1620. The most important precedessor to "rights of man" was "natural right" or "natural law" (*droit naturel* has both meanings in French). However, *droit naturel* did not always mean natural law or right in the sense of Grotius or Locke; it sometimes meant simply making sense within the traditional order. Thus, for example, Bishop Bossuet, a spokesman for Louis XIV's absolute monarchy, used "natural right" to discuss under which conditions someone went to heaven. Throughout the eighteenth century "natural right" continued to be used in this context (as what was fitting for a particular individual or group), but such usage paled next to increasing use of the term to mean a right given by nature and hence applicable to all men.

Denis Diderot's article on *droit naturel* in the *Encyclopedia* (1755) called attention to the self-evidence of natural law or right: "NATURAL LAW (RIGHT). The use of this term is so familiar, that there is almost no one who would not be convinced inside himself that the thing is obviously known to him. This interior feeling is common both to the philosopher and to the man who has not reflected at all."[18] This brief quote goes to the heart of the paradox of human rights: belief in them rests on their self-evidence, which can only be proved by belief in them. The belief is nonetheless powerful for its tautological foundation: "There is almost no one who would not be convinced inside himself that the thing is obviously known to him." The self-evidence of natural rights also explains why they depend on revolutions rather than continuous development. They had to be discovered, but they had to be already present. Their existence is not proved or disproved by their actual presence in the legal tradition, but by their resonance with each individual's "interior feeling." In short, I suggest, the credibility of natural rights flows from new conceptions and practices of what it means to be a self as much as from previous intellectual or legal influences.

The self-evidence of the "rights of man" did not preclude vagueness about their actual legal and political content. In 1787 a Calvinist pastor, Rabaut Saint

Etienne, wrote to the French government to protest the government's language in the recently released and long sought Edict of Toleration for Calvinists:

> They have moved into the preamble of the edict the thinking expressed by the Keeper of the Seals in his speech on the subject: that non-Catholics *only get from the law what natural rights cannot refuse them, that is, the legal expression of their natural rights*. But we know today what natural rights are, and they certainly give to men much more than the edict accords to Protestants: it seems to me that it would have been better to suppress this thought. The time has come when it is no longer acceptable for a law to overtly overrule the rights of humanity that are very well known all over the world.[19]

Rabaut did not go on to specify those rights, and he explicitly agreed in his letter that the king could not authorize public worship by non-Catholics. In other words, by 1787 the concept of natural rights seemed self-evident, at least to the intellectual elite, but its content was uncertain. As late as 1787 Rabaut thought it meant some kind of religious toleration, but even he, a Protestant minister, did not think it necessarily meant full civil and political rights for religious minorities.

So sometime around the middle of the eighteenth century, perhaps particularly in the decade of the 1760s, the "rights of man" came to make sense where they had not before. The term enters into the discourse. Some clues about its provenance can be found in its earliest usages in the 1760s and 1770s. The *Mémoires secrets* of Bachaumont have this entry for June 13, 1763:

> the actors of the *comédie française* today played, for the first time, *Manco*, of which we previously spoke [a play about the Incas in Peru]. It is one of the most badly constructed tragedies. There is a role in it for a savage which could be very beautiful; he recites in verse everything that we have read scattered about on kings, liberty, the rights of man, in *The Inequality of Conditions*, in *Emile*, in *The Social Contract*.[20]

This brief entry suggests that rights of man had already entered into ordinary discourse thanks to the influence of Rousseau (though Rousseau himself only used it one year before), and most interestingly, it suggests that it came up in particular in reference to colonial peoples. It is the savage who recites verses on liberty and the rights of man.

Although much remains to be done in pinning down the appearance and use of the concept of "rights of man," it does appear that the notion of the rights of man—as opposed to rights—appeared rather suddenly and with little definition of their actual content. Most of those using the phrase in the 1770s and 1780s, such as d'Holbach or Mirabeau, referred to the rights of man as if they were obvious and needed no justification or definition. D'Holbach argued, for instance, that if men feared death less, "the rights of man would be more boldly defended."

Mirabeau denounced his persecutors who had "neither character nor soul, because they have no idea at all of the rights of men."[21] No one came up with lists of inalienable rights before the revolution of 1789.

THE FRENCH REVOLUTION AND RIGHTS

Before 1789 Enlightenment authors and state officials argued over the status of rights in general. During 1789 and afterwards both supporters and opponents of the revolution had to take a stand not only on whether rights existed and what weight they should have in constitutional affairs but also on the precise content and purview of those rights. So even though the notion of rights of man had begun to take shape before 1789, the revolution gave it an immense push forward. The Declaration of the Rights of Man and Citizen aimed to define "the natural and imprescriptible rights of man": liberty, property, security, and resistance to oppression. It also outlined several other rights: equality before the law, admissibility to all public offices, protection from arbitrary orders or imprisonment, freedom of religion, and freedom of the press.

The passing of the Declaration of the Rights of Man and Citizen in August 1789 did not resolve the issue of rights; it only began to open them up. In December 1789 the deputies began to debate the unresolved status of non-Catholics; the Declaration said nothing explicit about religious minorities. Immediately the new National Assembly agreed to extend all civil and political rights to Protestants, and after much reluctance, it voted full civil and political rights to Jews in September 1791. The rights of free blacks and slaves were bound to come up for discussion, too, but as the experience of the new United States showed most dramatically, rights could be declared even as slavery was maintained. In March 1790 the Assembly voted to exempt the colonies from the constitution and to prosecute anyone who attempted to prompt uprisings against the slave system. Agitation on the question did not end, and in May 1791 the Assembly granted political rights to a limited number of free blacks and mulattos. Then in August 1791 the slaves of Saint Domingue began what was to become over the next several years the first successful slave revolt in history. A month later, the Assembly rescinded the rights of free blacks, only to reinstate them a few months later. In August and September 1793 French agents officially suppressed slavery in St. Domingue. Although their actions were initially denounced in the National Convention as part of a plot with England, the Convention voted to abolish slavery in all the French colonies in February 1794.

The Declaration of the Rights of Man and Citizen had pushed the deputies to recognize rights in ways that were unimaginable before 1789. Yet in one major area of rights, there was very little official movement. The rights of women did not excite the same kind of interest in prerevolutionary France as the rights of Protestants, Jews, or blacks. Nevertheless, women's rights, too, came up in the wake of the Declaration, most notably in the writings of Condorcet (July 1790) and Olympe de Gouges (especially September 1791). Women organized their own political clubs and participated in a variety of new ways in political life but never got political rights like those of Protestant, Jewish, or black men. But the issue of women's rights did make it onto the table and could only have made it onto the agenda of political discussion because "human rights" were under discussion. As Constance Pipelet, later de Salm, argued, "it is especially during the revolution . . . that women, following the example of men, have most reasoned about their true essence and have acted in consequence."[22] Like many others, she saw that the notion of human rights had an implacable logic, even if it had not yet worked itself out in the case of women, that other half of humanity.

THE AUTONOMOUS SELF AND
THE ORIGINS OF HUMAN RIGHTS

As the philosopher Charles Taylor has argued, rights are fundamentally about autonomy: "To talk of universal, natural, or human rights is to connect respect for human life and integrity with the notion of autonomy. It is to conceive people as active cooperators in establishing and ensuring the respect which is due them."[23] In the eighteenth century, all "people" were not imagined as equally autonomous, but the consequences of these implicit differentiations did not become clear until after 1789. How did this notion of autonomy take root and become so general that French revolutionaries found it impossible, for example, to deny the rights of Jews or slaves, even though many found it difficult to imagine them as fellow Frenchmen? And how did it allow them to continue to exclude women when they could not exclude Protestant, Jewish, or slave men, not to mention actors and executioners, who also got their full rights?

The belief in the self-evidence of the human rights of autonomous individuals depended not only on alterations in the intellectual climate but also on subtle changes in the perception of bodies and selves. A notion of individual moral autonomy depends on two related developments: 1) an increasing sense of the separation of bodies from each other (your body is yours and my body is mine by self-possession and we should both respect the space of each other's bodies), and 2) an increasing sense of empathy between psyches across space (we are alike in some fundamental fashion). To be autonomous a person has to be legitimately separate, but to have rights go along with that autonomy a person's selfhood must be appreciated in some more affective or emotional fashion. Human rights depend both on self-possession and on the recognition that all others are equally self-possessed; it is the incomplete development of the latter, of course, that gives rise to all the inequalities of rights that we now know so well.

Some of the developments that make for separateness and empathy are long-term. The separation of the individual from the webs of community belonging so as to become an autonomous agent of his and even her own destiny; the development of notions of interiority and depth of psyche from the Christian soul to the Protestant conscience to eighteenth-century notions of *sensibilité*; the rising threshold of shame about bodily functions and the growing sense of bodily decorum (sleeping alone or only with a spouse in bed, using utensils, not throwing food on the floor or wiping body excretions on your clothing)—all these take place over a very long term of several centuries.

But certain things do happen quite quickly in the eighteenth century. Audiences begin to watch theatrical performances or listen to music in silence; portraiture and genre painting begin to displace the great mythological and historical canvases of academic painting; torture as part of the judicial process and the most extreme forms of corporal punishment come to seem unacceptable; the absolute authority of fathers over their children comes under intense scrutiny; novels and newspapers proliferate. All of these contribute in one form or another to a sense of the separation and self-possession of individual bodies and the possibility of empathy between separate psyches imagined to be in some fundamental way alike. Benedict Anderson explored the ways in which newspapers and novels created new forms of "imagined community" such as nationalism.[24] I do not contest this linkage; I want to argue for a parallel development of "imagined empathy": new forms of empathetic identification with individuals who are now imagined to be in some fundamental way like you. This is the psychological foundation of democracy and human rights.

A few examples from French history will have to suffice to underline the magnitude of change in the experiences of bodies and selves in the eighteenth century. The *question préparatoire* (torture to extract confession of guilt), though not used much in the eighteenth century, remained part of the criminal code until 1780; the *question préalable* (torture just prior to execution to extract the names of accomplices) was used more frequently and only abolished in 1788.[25] Under Old Regime law, the death penalty could be inflicted in five different ways: drawing and quartering, burning at the stake, breaking on the wheel, hanging, and decapitation. Drawing and quartering and burning at the stake fell into disuse in the eighteenth century, except for certain notorious cases, but what reformers called cruel forms of punishment remained until the revolutionaries replaced them all with one form of death penalty, the guillotine.[26] Torture and cruel punishment came to seem incompatible with self-possessed, rights-bearing individuals.

If the question of torture went directly to the status of bodies, then the question of paternal authority went to the status of the autonomy of selves as decision makers. Revolutionary laws on paternity demonstrate the depth of concern felt about infringements on autonomy. The revolutionaries abolished both primogeniture and the infamous *lettres de cachet* in March 1790. Primogeniture relegated all the children except the oldest male to secondary status, and *lettres de cachet* had been used by parents to incarcerate children who would not obey their dictates. In August of the same year, the National Assembly established family councils to hear disputes between parents and children up to age twenty rather than allowing fathers exclusive control. In April 1791 the Assembly decreed that all children, both male and female, must inherit equally. In August 1792, to cite just one more example, the deputies lowered the age of majority to twenty-one and declared that adults could no longer be subject to paternal authority.[27] In short, the revolutionaries considered excessive paternal authority one of the most important issues before them; they felt it necessary to carefully define and defend the boundaries of autonomy, which had become a subject of contention in the late eighteenth century.

While bodies and selves were both the subject of new legal dispositions, new forms of print culture such as novels and newspapers created new types of psychological identification. Reading a novel (in the eighteenth century and not before) a reader identified with an ordinary person unknown to him or her personally but with whom the reader empathized thanks to the narrative form itself. The novel disseminated a new psychology and a new social and political order all at once; by its forms of narration it made servants like Pamela, the heroine of Richardson's novel by that name of 1740, the equal and even the better of rich men such as Mr. B, her employer and would-be seducer. The novel made the point that all selves are fundamentally similar because of their inner psychic processes; reading the novel drew the reader into those psychic processes and created a sense of equality through passionate involvement in the narrative. Can it be coincidental that the three greatest novels of psychological identification of the eighteenth century—Richardson's *Pamela* and *Clarissa* (1748) and Rousseau's *Julie* (1761)—were all published in the two decades that preceded the appearance of the concept of "the rights of man"?

There is an important paradox in these novels. In them, the eighteenth-century obsession with freedom and constraint—with autonomy as a new feature of social life—revolved around female characters created by male authors. There were important male characters such as Robinson Crusoe and Tom Jones and there were many prolific female authors. But the iconic figures of intense psychological identification were these three female characters. Men as well as women identified with their fates. From letters to the authors we know that upper-class men, even military officers, intensely identified with these women. Apparently, the antinomies of autonomy and dependence, of freedom and constraint, could be most intensely experienced via characters who could only aspire to autonomy and never really fully attain it, that is, women. A problem lurked in this paradox: If women could be shown to be so noble, so intensely human, so longing for freedom, then how could they be deprived of their rights? Men, and women, too, would expend great effort in providing an answer.

Wherever we turn, the origins of human rights point to paradoxes: paradoxes about history (how can a self-evident notion that claims to depend only on human nature have a history?), paradoxes about revolution (how can revolution be the origin both of rights and the denial of rights?), paradoxes about universalism (how can equal, natural, and universal rights be denied to some?), and paradoxes about psychological origins (why are women the focus of psychological identification if they are to be denied full participation as humans?). The paradoxes of human rights do not in any way diminish their historical importance or their relevance today. They simply measure the depth of the challenge that human rights posed to hierarchical societies based on privilege and birth and the continuing challenge they offer to inequality, injustice, and despotic authority of all kinds. As long as inequality, injustice, and despotic authority endure, the self-evidence of "the inherent dignity and of the equal and inalienable rights of all members of the human family" will seem paradoxical.

NOTES

1. The text of the Declaration was approved on December 10, 1948, by the General Assembly of the United Nations. *Yearbook on Human Rights for 1948* (Lake Success, N.Y.: United Nations, 1950), p. 466.

2. Max Horkheimer and Theodor W. Adorno, *Dialectic of Enlightenment*, tr. John Cumming (New York: Continuum Publishing, 1975), pp. xi, 6, 117–118. Horkheimer and Adorno repeated many of the charges of Martin Heidegger against the Enlightenment (and the entire modern world) without criticizing Heidegger's own adherence to the Nazi Party.

3. Dorinda Outram, *The Body and the French Revolution: Sex, Class, and Political Culture* (New Haven: Yale University Press, 1989), p. 164.

4. Lawrence Birken, *Hitler as Philosophe: Remnants of the Enlightenment in National Socialism* (Westport, Conn.: Praeger, 1995), p. 14.

5. I leave to the side the ludicrous argument by Geoffrey Galt Harpham, "So . . . What *Is* Enlightenment? An Inquisition into Modernity," *Critical Inquiry* 20 (1994): 524–556. His thesis, that the Catholic Inquisitions are Enlightenment institutions, does not warrant discussion, and I only cite it to show how Enlightenment can be distorted to mean just about anything by those with no scholarly scruples.

6. Patrick Girard, *La Révolution Française et les juifs* (Paris: Robert Laffont, 1989), p. 81. All translations from the French are mine unless otherwise noted.

7. Stanley F. Chyet, "The Political Rights of Jews in the United States: 1776–1840," *American Jewish Archives* 10 (April 1958): 14–75.

8. For self-possession, see Richard Tuck, *Natural Rights Theories: Their Origin and Development* (Cambridge: Cambridge University Press, 1979); for an especially clear discussion of the secularization of natural law, see Knud Haakonssen, *Natural Law and Moral Philosophy: From Grotius to the Scottish Enlightenment* (New York: Cambridge University Press, 1996), p. 29. See also Léon Ingber, "La tradition de Grotius. Les droits de l'homme et le droit naturel à l'époque contemporaine," *Cahiers de philosophie politique et juridique*, no. 11: "Des théories du droit naturel" (Caen, 1988): 43–73.

9. Samuel Rawson Gardiner, *The Constitutional Documents of the Puritan Revolution, 1625–1660* (1906), pp. 333–335.

10. John Locke, *Two Treatises of Government* (Cambridge: Cambridge University Press, 1963), pp. 366–367.

11. As quoted in Maurice Cranston, "Are There Any Human Rights?" *Daedalus* 112 (Fall 1983): 4.

12. On the difference between the American Declaration of Independence and the English Declaration of Rights of 1689 see Michael P. Zuckert, *Natural Rights and the New Republicanism* (Princeton: Princeton University Press, 1994), esp. pp. 3–25.

13. For a brief but highly pertinent discussion, see Jack N. Rakove, *Declaring Rights: A Brief History with Documents* (Boston: Bedford Books, 1998), esp. pp. 32–38.

14. As quoted in Keith Michael Baker, *Inventing the French Revolution: Essays on French Political Culture in the Eighteenth Century* (Cambridge: Cambridge University Press, 1990), p. 114.

15. Mathieu de Montmorency, August 1, 1789, *Archives parlementaires* 8 (Paris, 1875): 320.

16. I am grateful to Jennifer Popiel for research on this point. I have made no distinction in the use of the terms "rights" and have not excluded the considerable number of reprints over the years. The number of uses of "rights" in titles increased twofold from the 1760s to the 1770s (from 51 in the 1760s to 109 in the 1770s), stayed about the same in the 1780s (95) and then quadrupled to 418 in the 1790s.

17. <http://humanities.uchicago.edu/ARTFL/ARTFL.html>. ARTFL includes a selection of largely canonical texts from the Middle Ages to the present; it does not have every French language text. Nevertheless, because it includes whole texts, it is a wonderful resource for tracing changes in language.

18. Denis Diderot and Jean Le Rond d'Alembert, eds., *Encyclopédie ou Dictionnaire raisonné des sciences, arts, et des métiers*, 17 vols. (1751–1780), vol. 5 (Paris, 1755): 115–116.

19. *Bulletin de la Société de l'histoire du protestantisme français* 33 (1884): 360–361. Emphasis his.

20. *Mémoires secrets pour servir à l'histoire de la République des lettres en France, depuis MDCCLXII jusqu'à nos jours*, vol. 1 (London, 1780: reprint 1970), p. 230.

21. P. H. d'Holbach, *Système de la Nature* (1770: London, 1771), p. 336, and H. Comte de Mirabeau, *Lettres écrites du donjon* (1780: Paris, 1792), p. 41.

22. Constance D. T. Pipelet, "Rapport sur un ouvrage du cit. Théremin, intitulé: De la condition des femmes dans une république." *Le Mois* 5, no. 14, year VIII (apparently prairial), p. 232.

23. Charles Taylor, *Sources of the Self: The Making of Modern Identity*, (Cambridge: Harvard University Press, 1989), p. 12.

24. Benedict Anderson, *Imagined Communities: Reflections on the Origin and Spread of Nationalism* (London: Verso, 1983), esp. pp. 25–36. Anderson sees novels and newspapers as creating a sense of simultaneity of time in which ordinary life is validated, thus giving rise to a new sense of community (which facilitates nationalism). I am more interested in how they generated a new sense of self and empathy between separate selves across space (thanks to this simultaneity in homogenous, empty time).

25. John H. Langbein has contested the "fairy tale" that attributes the abolition of torture to the influence of Enlightenment writings against it. Although his account has

much to recommend it, it ignores the fact that torture was still used, in particular in the cases that most seized the French and European imagination. It is significant, then, that his book includes no reference to the cases which made Voltaire famous, those of Calas and the chevalier de la Barre. John H. Langbein, *Torture and the Law of Proof: Europe and England in the* Ancien Régime (Chicago: University of Chicago Press, 1976).

26. Useful information on the actual use of torture and forms of the death penalty can be found in Julius R. Ruff, *Crime, Justice and Public Order in Old Regime France: The Sénéchaussées of Libourne and Bazas, 1696–1789* (London: Croon, Helm Limited, 1984).

27. Lynn Hunt, *The Family Romance of the French Revolution* (Berkeley: University of California Press, 1992), pp. 40–41.

2

The Chinese Revolution and Contemporary Paradoxes

Jeffrey N. Wasserstrom

It may be tempting for readers to assume, after confronting the various conundrums introduced in the preceding chapter, that they are now familiar with all of the main paradoxes they need to keep in mind while reading this book. They may also be tempted to assume that the key human rights documents of later epochs have become freer of internal tensions and contradictions than the eighteenth-century ones that are Lynn Hunt's main focus in her essay on origins in chapter 1. In fact, however, neither of these assumptions is true, as I try to show in this chapter by looking closely at one major twentieth-century upheaval (the Chinese Revolution) and one unusually important recent text (the "Universal Declaration of Human Rights" adopted by the United Nations in 1948). My main argument is that to engage with contemporary revolutions and present-day debates and documents not only requires making the acquaintance of new conundrums but also re-encountering several of those identified by Hunt.[1]

To suggest that one has to face familiar paradoxes as well as novel ones today is not to imply that human rights discourse has gone essentially unaltered since 1789—a period during which new revolutionary ideologies have appeared and many features of political life have undergone complex transformations. Many things about the way that the idea of human rights is thought about, discussed, and acted upon have certainly changed a great deal as we have moved from the era of the Atlantic Revolutions to what some refer to (though I think problematically) as the contemporary postrevolutionary one. To begin with, human rights discourse has developed from being a narrowly Western to a decidedly global affair. Today, it is something that has both influenced and been influenced by many different cultural traditions. And, reflecting this, the key texts that now define the discourse tend to be the work of international bodies as opposed to the kinds of national ones that produced the declaration of 1789 (examined in chapter 1 by Hunt) and its American counterpart of 1776 (analyzed in chapter 4 by Michael Zuckert).

There are, nevertheless, certain fundamental patterns that have *not* changed, and this is why familiar paradoxes remain important. One continuity is the tendency for defenders of human rights discourse to present it as a simple and straightforward set of ideas, when in reality it has always been and still is something that is complex and often internally contradictory. Take, for example, the enduring notion that the term "human rights" refers to a small cluster of tightly interconnected basic protections. This persists even though the number of activities qualifying as human rights abuses in the eyes of the UN has expanded dramatically in recent decades, as a series of special conventions have been ratified to supplement the already extremely wide-ranging Universal Declaration of 1948.[2] Another illustration of this phenomenon is that, though debates continue to rage as they have for centuries over just what human rights are and who is entitled to them, commentators often present the discourse as something that should be readily understandable to anyone of good faith.

More specifically, what are the contradictory pulls identified by Hunt as embedded within human rights discourse that have never gone away? One cluster of issues that we continue to grapple with today, just as Parisians did in 1789, is those that arise from the unresolved (and often unacknowledged) tension between visions of rights as based in common membership in a species and those rooted in common membership in a nation. Do we gain rights (and if so, which ones) by virtue of our humanity, which makes us worthy of the "imagined empathy" to which Hunt refers? Or do we gain them through our status as national citizens—that is, as members in good standing of what Benedict Anderson describes as a special sort of "imagined community"? Questions of this sort cannot be answered through appeal to UN documents, as tempting as that route is to take. This is because framers of these texts typically simply pretend that the tension between the rights of people and the rights of citizens does not exist. For example, Article 21 of the Universal Declaration states that "everyone" should have the ability to take part in governmental activities, either "directly or through freely chosen representatives," but surely those who created and approved this document really meant that law-abiding adults should enjoy this right. Otherwise, the implication would be that all democratic regimes that deny electoral privileges to children and felons are committing a "human rights" abuse.

Other competing pulls and paradoxes embedded within UN documents are distinctive products of the current period, which result from problems that were not confronted by the Jacobins who concern Hunt or the drafters of the American Declaration of Independence discussed in chapter 4 by Zuckert. Most notably, we now have to deal with conundrums of cross-cultural understanding and misunderstanding that were largely irrelevant to participants in eighteenth-century debates, as well as in the seventeenth-century ones analyzed in chapter 3 by David Zaret. These novel conundrums arise from the paradoxical status of human rights discourse as something that is ideally supposed to provide a "common language" for international debate that stands above culture and beyond history, yet in practice can never fully escape the distorting effects of particularistic understandings. This is because, whenever people of flesh-and-blood actually discuss human rights, they bring to the table their own senses of the connotations of the terms and concepts involved. They also come with their own distinctive historical experiences and their own senses of which aspects of the past should be treated as relevant parts of contemporary debates.

A curious specific paradox within this general one is that the Universal Declaration was crafted and later ratified by groups composed of individuals from many different kinds of societies and yet it continues to be criticized by some as reflective only of "Western" individualistic influences and "bourgeois" concerns. Critics of the Declaration often gloss over the fact that a Confucian scholar helped write the document. Nor do they acknowledge that it contains certain phrases—references to the world as family writ large, comments about all people having "duties to the community" as well as rights—that were intended to acknowledge the importance of what are now sometimes called, albeit problematically, "Asian values." These same critics also frequently fail to note that several of the document's thirty articles refer to rights that can only be considered "individualistic" and "bourgeois" if those terms are used in an extremely elastic fashion. Article 22, for example, speaks of a right to "social security" and Article 25 of protecting laborers from having to work excessively long hours.

In the contemporary era, we need to deal with two other distinctively post-1789 paradoxes, each of which is linked to nationalism as opposed to acknowledged or glossed over varieties of internationalism. There is, first of all, the peculiar fact—analyzed well in several later chapters such as Florence Bernault's on Africa, Alexander Woodside's on Vietnam, and Alice Bullard's on New Caledonia—that the Western discourse of human rights and Euro-American colonialist practices frequently made their impact on non-Western lands virtually simultaneously. Thus, ironically, many people were introduced to Enlightenment ideas associated with liberty at the same moment that they were encountering foreigners from Europe or North America determined to deprive them of various freedoms.

The second paradox of nationalism concerns the tension between visions of human rights that stress only the need to protect individuals from the state and those that also emphasize the importance of defending the sovereignty of nations. The implications of this paradox have become very clear in 1999 (the year in which I am writing) because of the ongoing crisis in Kosovo—a topic Robin Blackburn and David Rieff treat in contrasting, though by no means diametrically opposed, ways in chapters 11 and 12. One reason debates associated with Kosovo and the air strikes that NATO launched against Serbia in the spring of 1999 have been so muddied is that "human rights" can be invoked in so many ways by both critics and defenders of bombing. This is because many international accords both refer to the necessity of protecting individuals from government violence and raise to the status of a "human right" the ability of nations to function as autonomous units, states to be sovereign entities free from outside interference. This means that, in discussions of the policies of Slobodan Milosevic's regime toward ethnic Albanians in Kosovo and the steps taken by NATO to force a change in them, human rights could be and have been invoked in varied ways by those arguing for opposing viewpoints.

For example, throughout the spring of 1999, both of the main groups that concern me here—spokespeople for the American and Chinese governments—continually framed their very different positions on Kosovo in terms of human rights issues. In the United States, the Clinton administration defended the air strikes against Belgrade by insisting that these were needed to put an end to grotesque violations of the human rights of ethnic Albanians. Spokespeople for the Chinese Communist Party (CCP) in Beijing, meanwhile, insisted throughout late March and April that these same NATO bombing raids should be condemned by the international community because they transgressed the sovereignty of a regime that had come to power through legitimate means in Yugoslavia. An added cause for concern in the People's Republic of China (PRC) is the precise way that NATO went about its mission. Namely, NATO did not seek and then wait for UN support for intervention, allowing that international body to serve as an arbiter of the human rights issue, but went it alone. This meant that China, a permanent member of the UN Security Council, was excluded from participation in debates on intervention, as was Russia—a country whose treatment by NATO Blackburn examines in more detail in his contribution to this volume.

When NATO missiles hit the Chinese embassy in Belgrade in early May, killing three journalists from the PRC—at a time when I happened to be in China—protesters in Beijing and other cities added a new "human rights" angle to their critique of NATO. A banner I saw carried through the streets of the capital read, "When Americans speak of 'human rights' [*renquan*], does this include the destruction of embassies?" Ironically, the protests triggered by the bombing also led the Western media Clinton administration commentators to incorporate additional "human rights" concerns into their statements. When Chinese demonstrators threw paving stones and paint balls at the U.S. embassy in Beijing, this was decried as a "human rights" violation. More generally, the crisis in Sino-American relations that came in the wake of the Belgrade bombing was described as unfortunate in part because it derailed ongoing attempts by Washington to get Beijing to take steps to improve its domestic human rights record.[3]

These prefatory remarks about the nature of contemporary conundrums and the ease with which Washington and Beijing can end up coming at issues from totally different directions having been made, my goal in the rest of this chapter is to accomplish four things. First, to further analyze the Universal Declaration providing a clearer sense of the nature of the paradoxes and tensions that bedevil contemporary international debates. Second, use critiques and defenses of the human rights record of the CCP to show how efforts to work through these conundrums often lead to unproductive stalemates, in which two or more parties speak past rather than engage with each other. Third, I suggest that a useful way to break through this kind of impasse, especially when attempting to assess the behavior of regimes that are inheritors of revolutionary legacies, is to shift from focusing on competing understandings of "rights" to looking at how the category of "human" is defined and acted upon in different settings. Fourth, I demonstrate that too much energy has been spent lately dividing countries up into particular sorts of unproductive binary categories—categories whose employment ends up leading into analytical blind alleys. What I have in mind more specifically is the tendency in much recent writing on human rights to posit a sharp distinction between lands influenced by "Western" ideas as opposed to "Asian" values and between countries with "liberal" or "free-market capitalist" versus "Socialist" or "Marxist" political and economic traditions. There is no question that differences can be identified in the approaches to rights of Mencius as opposed to Mill, Lenin as opposed to Locke, and so forth. Nevertheless, in the end, discussions in which countries are divided up along East-West or Liberal-Socialist binaries generally end up generating more heat than light.

The main problem with these binaries, at least when used to explain why some regimes tend to place more emphasis than others on individual civil liberties or collective social and economic rights, is that most national histories are too complex to reduce to a single category. How, for example, do we square an American liberal and capitalist tradition that emphasizes individualism and bourgeois rights, as opposed to collective social guarantees, with Franklin Roosevelt's "Economic Bill of Rights" speech?[4] The status of China as a "Confucian" nation that lacks a cultural tradition of valuing things such as individual freedom of expression can be questioned in a similar fashion. As Marina Svensson has shown, in the period lasting from the 1890s through the 1940s one finds many Chinese intellectuals of varying political orientations, ranging from iconoclastic founding members of the CCP to liberals with great respect for some Confucian ideals, defending the rights of individuals.[5] Clearly, in cases such as these and those of many other contemporary countries, we are dealing with complex and continually shifting multistranded *traditions* to be drawn on and reworked, not an unchanging and enduring univocal *tradition* that limits people to just a single option where human rights are concerned.

How then can we move beyond conventional binaries when trying to make sense of the current Beijing regime? My argument is that, while something can certainly be gained by acknowledging that the CCP of today is an organization shaped by both Confucian and Marxist traditions, other things about it are more useful to stress. The most significant thing to pay attention to when assessing it is the continuing, though thankfully somewhat abated recently, obsession of CCP leaders with presenting themselves as defenders of a sacred *Geming* (Revolution), imagined as a fragile entity that outsiders and traitors are determined to destroy. This is to place the CCP in a category that is not defined by its location in Asia or its attachment to any particular ideology but to put it instead in a category defined by conformity to a pattern followed by many different regimes. This category includes all organizations whose leaders have attempted to legitimate their power by promoting heroic visions of themselves as embattled protectors of a popular and democratic revolutionary effort to save and protect the nation.

In mobilizing a language of patriotism and conspiracy, which divides people into supporters and enemies of a grand nationalistic revolutionary project and periodically portrays the latter as somehow less than fully human, recent Chinese political leaders have often fallen into a familiar trap, with disturbing consequences for human rights. In falling into this trap, they have followed in the footsteps of many earlier regimes, ranging from that of the French Jacobins at the time of the Terror to that created in China by Chiang Kai-shek and his associates in the late 1920s.

One conclusion of this line of argument is that no account of the CCP's current human rights record can be complete unless it takes into account the continuing hold of this paranoid strain in Beijing political rhetoric. We must come to terms with the dynamics by which the CCP has, at various moments and in various ways, reduced opponents to the status of *fei renmin* (nonpeople).

A second conclusion, however, is that the harshest critics of China's present rulers, by overlooking the significant moves that have been made in recent decades toward lessening the hold and effect of this sort of dehumanizing language, distort our understanding of the current situation. There is still much to despair about where China's human rights record is concerned. There are also, however, some important aspects of it that should inspire us to be at least cautiously optimistic. Perhaps the most important of these is that it is becoming less and less common for whole categories of people to be stigmatized as *fei renmin*.

Any effort to move along these lines and gain a better understanding of bases for hope and outrage when viewing the contemporary Chinese political scene leads us back inevitably to the theme of this book. This is because, to a great extent, making better sense of the CCP's human rights record requires us to look very carefully at the complex interplay between ideas about human rights and the influence of revolutionary mythologies and revolutionary legacies in the contemporary world.

1998: A SNAPSHOT

With my goals stated, before examining the Chinese case in more detail, I want to pause to reflect on the way international human rights debates were framed in 1998, the year when I first outlined this chapter. After all, 1998 was a year of considerable significance in the history of human rights discourse, and it is worth noting what the debates central to it looked like just before they were reshaped by the crisis in Kosovo and subsequent 1999 events such as the upheavals in East Timor. What made 1998 so significant for the history of human rights discourse was that it marked the fiftieth anniversary of the ratification of the Universal Declaration, the UN's first and still most important document devoted to the subject.

This anniversary was, not surprisingly, commemorated in a variety of ways throughout much of the world. For example, universities in many countries held symposia on the topic. In addition, special sections of academic and general journals devoted to international affairs were set aside for consideration of what had been accomplished in the last half-century and what still needed to be done to make the ideals of the Universal Declaration a reality. These commemorative activities provide an illuminating window on contemporary assessments of the human rights situation on the eve of the crises of 1999.

One of the most intriguing of the events, which I learned about through a published "invitation" in the *London Review of Books* (*LRB*), was a three-day "Festival of Human Rights" sponsored by Amnesty International and other organizations that took place in Britain. According to the advance publicity for the gathering, the festival's aim, like that of many of the symposia, was to draw attention to the importance and global reach of the human rights project broadly conceived and also to the abuses of human dignity that continue to occur. The *LRB* invitation called on everyone to come and "show that human rights belong to us all," and told participants that they would have opportunities to get involved in ongoing struggles for change. It claimed that there would be "over 100 debates and workshops" as well as street theater performances and that Internet access would be provided to all interested parties. The eclectic international roster of speakers would, according to the advertisement, include dissident and former *laogai* (gulag) resident Wei Jingsheng, Indian environmental activist Vandanna Shiva, and American pop singer Suzanne Vega.

There are good reasons why the fiftieth anniversary of the Universal Declaration inspired varied and impassioned activity of the sort suggested by the invitation to the London festival. The document remains one of the boldest general manifestos on human rights ever written. It is also a work that has been lauded for its effort to provide participants in international debates with a basic fluency in a shared language of rights that can rise above—or at least aspires to rise above—historical and cultural particularities. The list it contains of protections to which "everyone" is entitled, simply by virtue of their common humanity, has been praised, with good reason, for providing us with intelligible universal standards by which to judge the behavior of individual leaders and governments. Subsequently clarified and supplemented by a series of additional UN documents focusing on particular types of rights, such as the right to religious freedom, it quickly became and today remains the central definitional text for most international debates.

The Universal Declaration is also important because it has been accepted as legitimate by an unusually large number of contemporary regimes—those allied with radical Islam, which Timothy McDaniel discusses in chapter 13, being among the rare remaining exceptions. Delegates from many countries initially approved the document, meeting with fewer objections than would be the case with many supplementary texts, such as the 1986 "Declaration on the Right to Development" that some UN member states, including the United States, still refuse to acknowledge as binding. In addition, the Universal Declaration has now been accepted as legitimate by various nations that did not exist or lacked UN representation in 1948 or that once had leaders who rejected the Universal Declaration on the grounds that they viewed it as a "bourgeois" and "imperialist" document. Both the breathtaking scope of the document and its steady movement toward genuinely universal acceptance were cited as causes for celebration by many participants in 1998 commemorative events.

At the same time, many of those looking back over the half-century that had passed since the Universal Declaration's ratification were quick to note that the human rights project continued to be plagued by deeply rooted problems. It was not just, many claimed, that gross violations of human rights continued to occur in many countries, though this was certainly the case. It was also that, fifty years on, it was still an open question whether UN documents could ever truly serve as providers of a "common language" and "universal standards" for the international community. Many insisted that there was even reason to wonder, on this score, whether things had been moving in the right or wrong direction in the second half of the 1990s.

The problem, at least according to a variety of American commentators who weighed in on the topic in 1998, was that too many political leaders outside of the West still failed to understand properly the meaning of the Universal Declaration. These non-Western actors, the argument went, tended in subtle and not so subtle ways to undermine this text and the UN human rights mission in general. The most basic sorts of misunderstandings, according to this line, were those that typically prevailed in countries influenced by Asian values or not yet fully developed economically, and the worry was that distorted visions of the human rights project seemed to be getting more, not less, widespread.

As a result of all this, the most pessimistic commentators maintained, fifty years after the optimistic moment when the Universal Declaration was ratified the human rights project faced two seemingly intractable problems. The first was quite straightforward: There were still far too many abusive regimes in power. The second was more complex and had to do with a paradoxical recent development: While year by year fewer and fewer countries refused to accept the Declaration out of hand, there seemed to be more and more leaders ready to claim that certain kinds of rights did not fit in with their lands' distinctive traditions. There were also increasing numbers of regimes ready to argue that certain kinds of rights could not be protected effectively until a particular nation became richer.

ASSESSING THE CCP

Not surprisingly, references to the PRC often figured prominently in both the most optimistic and most pessimistic of commentaries inspired by the Universal Declaration's fiftieth anniversary. This is only natural, since Chinese developments can be used quite easily to augment both the celebratory and cautionary strains outlined above. On the optimistic side, the PRC stands out as an important example of a recent addition to the list of nations whose officials accept the validity of the Universal Declaration. Its latecomer status is due in part to the fact that the PRC was not founded until the Communist Party took power in 1949 and was not granted a seat at the UN until the 1970s. In addition, CCP leaders were initially prone to dismiss the text as a "bourgeois" document, a work designed to bolster capitalism. They also viewed human rights discourse as part of a new Western form of cultural imperialism—a subtle yet invidious successor to the more nakedly aggressive forms of foreign encroachment that had transformed pre-1949 China into a "semicolonial" as well as "semifeudal" state.

To speak positively of *renquan* (human rights) in China between the 1950s and 1970s was thus to lay oneself open to the charge of being soft on the twin menaces of capitalism and imperialism. To do so was to become vulnerable to the accusation of being insufficiently critical of the forces that had once deprived the Chinese of all semblance of national autonomy and could do the same thing again. To accept human rights discourse could be interpreted as tantamount to a desire to reduce the Chinese homeland once more to the status it had when Japan and various Western capitalist powers had carved out spheres of influence inside China's borders. In spite of its focus on equality, the Universal Declaration was equated, in a sense, to the "unequal treaties" of the nineteenth century, imposed on China by outside force, that had transformed cities such as Shanghai into quasi-colonial multinational treaty ports containing self-governing foreign-run enclaves.

By 1998, however, the situation had become very different indeed in China, since one could publish works promoting human rights without being accused of toadying to imperialism or abandoning the principles of Marxism-Leninism-Mao Zedong thought. More than that, the major centers of learning in the PRC, such as academies of social sciences, were now producing massive reference works which detailed the history of human rights struggles and discourses, with entries extolling everything from the writings of Rousseau to the musings of Deng

Xiaoping. Ironically, the shift had been so dramatic that one could even find, in this era of "Socialism with Chinese Characteristics," official publications that presented documents such as the Universal Declaration as promoting precisely the sorts of values that China needed to embrace in its move to modernize.[6] Paradoxically, the same human rights discourse that had once been dismissed as intimately related to imperialism was now even harnessed at times to the cause of denigrating the system of enclaves and spheres of influence alluded to above. General polemics against imperialism had begun by the mid-1990s to stress, for example, that one of the things that made the treaty-port system of old so intolerable was that it allowed Westerners and Japanese free rein in abusing the human rights of native residents.[7]

Turning from works on imperialism to speeches and publications on human rights by officials and scholars with close ties to the CCP, one also found by 1998 this new kind of linkage to imperialism being developed in interesting, albeit sometimes initially bewildering, ways. For instance, in works comparing China's human rights record with that of Western countries, passing reference was often being made to an infamous treaty-port icon: a notice banning "dogs and Chinese" that was said to have stood for decades by the entrance to Old Shanghai's best-known park.[8]

Recent archival research has shown that the standard and widely believed story of such a sign's existence, or at least its placement, is more properly treated as an urban legend than a narrative of historical fact. Even though all Chinese other than servants were indeed banned from entering the Public Garden in Shanghai's foreign-run International Settlement for most of the period lasting from the early 1880s until 1928, regulations dealing with animals and people were always listed separately. There was, at least, no prominently placed notice with the much-quoted explicitly dehumanizing wording. Like urban legends, moreover, this one has a tendency to travel: Some claim that the sign once stood by the International Settlement's racetrack, others that it stood outside a Tianjin, as opposed to a Shanghai, park.

In spite of all this, the tale has long served and continues to function as an emotionally potent shorthand for a discriminatory set of exclusionary practices that most definitely did exist. These practices not only kept many Chinese ratepayers from using certain parks that their taxes helped maintain, but also until 1928 prohibited all Chinese living in the International Settlement from voting in local elections. In a sense, references to the sign have long operated in Chinese Communist writings much as photographs of "whites only" drinking fountains do in critical studies of the American South during the era of Jim Crow laws.[9] Some Chinese authors have gone further and said that the exclusionary rules imperialists enacted in treaty-port enclaves such as the International Settlement were morally equivalent to South Africa's apartheid system. This is important in part because the South African system had come, by 1998, to be seen by many people in China as elsewhere as one of the quintessential examples of a recent human rights abuse.

There are a variety of intriguing aspects of this sign and its use as a symbol. Two main things are worth noting here. The first is that the way the sign was being treated by 1998 and continues to be treated today in the PRC—as a symbol for a particular sort of abuse—demonstrates the extent to which the CCP's earlier tendency to dismiss human rights discourse out of hand has dissipated. Were human rights still treated as a bourgeois concept, the punch of the elevation of the legendary "No Dogs or Chinese" notice to the status of the ultimate abuse would not exist.

The second is that apologists for the Beijing regime were by this time routinely starting to integrate comments on the sign into comparative assessments of the human rights records of various countries. In particular, some were taking the United States and other Western countries to task for failing to apologize for the human rights abuses committed by imperialists on Chinese soil before 1949—abuses for which this sign functioned as a useful metonym. The unwillingness to admit to any culpability for past wrongdoings of this sort, according to Yü Quanyu, one such apologist, made Western criticisms of the CCP's current human rights record despicably hypocritical.

The comments by Yü I am referring to come from a fascinating speech comparing U.S. and PRC human rights records that he gave at a Sino-American conference on the subject held in Beijing in 1994. It should be stressed that at no point in this speech, during which he had a great deal to say about the American government's failure to protect the social and economic rights of its own citizens, did Yü question the moral validity of human rights discourse per se. He did, however, present this discourse as applying to a wider set of issues (including homeless rates in the two countries, on which score he claimed China did much better than the United States) and a broader temporal span (back to the post–Opium War enactment of unequal treaties) than did the American participants in the symposium. As a result, he ended up with an assessment of each country as having serious human rights issues to address, and hence recommended that each side focus less on criticizing the other and more on getting its own house in order. He also argued that each side should be judged in part on its own stated vision of which rights were most important to protect.

It is worth noting that, as even a cursory comparison of Yü's speech with official reference books shows, his approach to the topic of human rights is not all that different from a variety of recent PRC works in its handling of many issues. There is nothing peculiar, for example, about his insistence on a broad definition of the category of human rights and a long-term view of historical relevance. Many works produced in the PRC likewise give close attention to social and economic rights and treat imperialist activities of the recent and not so recent past as things that must be kept in mind when comparing the records of different nation-states. Nor is his matter-of-fact acceptance of the validity of human rights discourse as providing standards by which all regime should be judged, peculiar. Nor finally is there anything anomalous about his choice of the Shanghai sign as a symbol for the many imperialist transgressions against the human rights of Chinese nationals.[10]

Texts such as Yü's, peculiar as they may seem to many Americans, could be cited to give support to celebratory assessments of the world scene circa 1998, if for no other reason than that he took for granted the need to combat human rights abuses. Nevertheless, the words and deeds of the Beijing regime and its supporters also provided a good deal of ammunition for pessimistic commentators in 1998—again for understandable reasons. This is because, as many analysts then and since have noted, whatever CCP officials and apologists have to say about *renquan*, the Beijing regime continues to commit flagrant human rights abuses on many fronts. Critics of the PRC continue to be quick to point out, for example, that the *laogai* (Chinese gulag) system remains in full operation—some even go so far as to equate this with not just Stalin's gulags but also Hitler's concentration camps. In addition, these commentators have stressed, freedom of religion has remained one right—and there are others—that most Chinese are unable to enjoy.

Beyond this, the harshest critics of CCP behavior also emphasize that a willingness to endorse the human rights project as a noble enterprise has not prevented the Communists from insisting that the PRC be judged by special standards. Beijing's leaders and apologists—and once again Yü Quanyu is a typical case in point—have routinely argued that, due to China's status as a "developing" country with "Confucian" and "Socialist" traditions, the CCP's record on protecting individual rights needs to be treated differently from that of Western capitalist countries. They have often claimed that the real heart of the major UN human rights documents lies in their defense of national sovereignty and promotion of social well-being. Thus, they stress, it is a distinctively Western peculiarity to insist that individual civil liberties should be given the most weight in all assessments of the human rights records of specific regimes.

It was easy, in light of all this, for Western analysts to place the PRC of 1998 in the category of countries with problematic understandings of the Universal Declaration. This is precisely the kind of nation, they would note, whose leaders have hindered the development of human rights discourse into a common language for international debate. This is because, the argument continues, even when the Beijing regime came to accept the validity of human rights discourse in the abstract, whenever concrete issues were up for discussion it brought to the table an overly particularistic understanding of "rights" and an odd sense of historical proportion.

It is easy to see why critics of the CCP continue to see a problem in the regime's willingness, on the one hand, to accept the validity of the Universal

Declaration, but then to proceed, on the other, to frame discussion of human rights issues in a particularistic fashion. Beijing's assertions that China is a "special case" and needs to be treated as such can be cited to support this vision of the PRC as a problematic case; so, too, can the occasional residual references, which continue to creep into CCP discourse, to international efforts to pressure China to improve its human rights record as abuses of the basic right of nations to be autonomous and states to be sovereign.

Conversely, however, harsh Western and particularly American criticisms of the CCP's human rights record often seem strange and particularistic to citizens of the PRC—again with justification. Here I am not thinking only of officials and apologists, but also of some Chinese I know who are neither self-proclaimed dissidents nor uncritical defenders of the current regime. They are mystified to discover that, even though much has changed for the better in China during the past decades, there are still prominent American commentators ready to insist that the CCP of today is as evil as any regime of modern times. When so much has gotten better, they wonder, how can people such as liberal former *New York Times* columnist Abe Rosenthal and the widely syndicated conservative pundit George Will present Beijing's current rulers as morally equivalent to the villains who ran Nazi Germany? Why, they ask, do Americans find it so natural to focus on some parts of the Universal Declaration as opposed to others? And why, when the current CCP regime has tried to distance itself from policies pursued before the late 1970s, do some Western commentators insist that the famine of the late 1950s and political persecution campaigns of the 1960s are directly relevant to discussion of China's contemporary human rights situation?

In short, during the debates over human rights that took place as the passage of fifty years since the Universal Declaration was signed was being marked, we found both sides in Sino-Western debates on human rights agreeing on some things but still talking past rather than to each other. All participants in the Sino-American debates took for granted the basic validity of human rights discourse and assumed the UN documents on the subject were important. Nevertheless, each often saw the other as bringing to bear overly particularistic, indeed distorted, understandings of the major texts, as well as parochial senses of what is and is not a relevant historical point of reference. In such a situation, a discourse of rights that was supposed to serve as a "common language" ended up doing little to facilitate meaningful exchanges of views. And the passage of another year, which has seen new layers of tension and misunderstanding associated with Kosovo and related events added to the mix, has seen an increasing range of sources for miscommunication.

The troubled state of affairs summarized above becomes less surprising and mystifying if we remember an often overlooked point: As noted earlier, the Universal Declaration and related documents are themselves paradoxical works riddled with internal tensions. Recognizing that this is true does not require that we abandon all efforts at universalistic assessment and embrace a form of extreme moral relativism, in which human rights can mean whatever a given party wants the term to mean. It does suggest, however, that we need to find a better way to work through the sort of stalemate sketched out above relating to Sino-American debates than that of simply allowing each side to castigate the other for having the "wrong" understanding of human rights.

It is here that shifting attention from the "rights" to the "human" side of the phrase "human rights"—a moved suggested earlier in this chapter—can be so useful. In calling for such a shift, I want to stress that, while it goes against the grain of most formal debates on human rights, it is not something that violates the basic tenor of UN documents on the subject. The Universal Declaration begins, after all, with a "recognition of the inherent dignity" as well as the "inalienable rights" of "all members of the human family." This language suggests that it is always worth asking questions such as the following when human rights disagreements break out: How exactly has a particular regime defined the "human family" over the course of time and how has it acted upon these definitions? And how have its definitions of the "human family" compared, in terms of degrees of inclusiveness and exclusiveness, to those of other ruling groups? These are the main questions I ask of the CCP below. In doing so, I want to emphasize that I am shifting the debate in a direction that not only fits in well with the language of UN documents but also falls into line with the rhetoric of many Chinese revolutionaries, Communist and non-Communist alike. From the first years of the twentieth century onward, after all, Chinese radicals of all political stripes have been claiming that one of the most horrific things that both foreign and domestic oppressors have done has been to treat people as less than fully human. A common trope that appears over and over again in the literature produced by Chinese revolutionaries is that imperialists and rulers of one or another native ancien régime treated the common people of China as animals or slaves. This is one reason that the legendary "No Dogs or Chinese" sign has had such staying power as a symbol of humiliation and outrage, being used in this fashion by everyone from Sun Yat-sen to Yü Quanyu.

EMPHASIZING THE "HUMAN" IN HUMAN RIGHTS

How exactly does a shift toward focusing on visions of what it means to be "human" as opposed to how "rights" are defined place into a different perspective debates about UN documents and revolutionary regimes? Let us begin with the former and with the Universal Declaration. The crucial thing to keep in mind about the term "human" as it appears in this key text is its two-sided nature, something that has already been mentioned above but deserves closer scrutiny. Words like "everybody" sometimes mean literally "all Homo sapiens," but they often really connote "certain kinds of people in certain types of circumstances."

This is not just the case when the issue is things we ordinarily think of as rights that go along with citizenship, such as the ability to participate in elections. These are certainly relevant illustrations, but I doubt very much that any of those involved in creating and ratifying the Universal Declaration seriously believed that each of the other kinds of rights enumerated could, would, or even should be possessed by every person in every imaginable circumstance. For example, the signers would have taken it for granted that there would always be exceptional types of people—again, as with voting, the very young children and convicted felons among them—who could reasonably be denied the supposedly universal "freedom of movement" guaranteed by Article 13. They would also have assumed that, in the midst of certain kinds of dire national emergencies, many people would need to have some of their rights of due process, such as those spelled out in Article 10, temporarily suspended. They would probably have agreed as well that, though Article 3 guarantees "everyone" the "right to life," it would not be considered a human rights violation each time one soldier killed another during a war.

One way to make sense of what is actually going on in this document and others like it is to envision two types of imagined continuums operating behind the scenes in human rights discourse—one having to do with types of people, the other with circumstances. The exact compositions of each of these will vary from political context to political context, but the function of each is always to limit in some way the universal reach of supposedly universal rights.

What do I mean by a continuum associated with types of people? This is one that has, at the high end, all those individuals defined by a state as valued citizens who deserve to be granted the broadest possible spectrum of rights. At the other end are people defined as less deserving of rights because they are too young, because of other putative biological characteristics that make them seem less than fully human, or because they have committed transgressive acts that set them beyond the pale of society. The second continuum, which has to do with circumstances, also has a distinctive high and low end. Here we find at one extreme prosperous and stable times of normalcy, in which rights can be spread fairly widely and at the other extreme moments of potentially apocalyptic crisis, in which it is viewed as understandable that constraints are placed on the exercise of certain kinds of rights.

Keeping this in mind and turning back to revolutions carried out in the name of democracy or popular rule, the first thing to note is that these upheavals typically destabilize or completely transform the preexisting spectrum running from citizens down to the dehumanized. They tend to do so in ways that have mostly positive implications, at least in theory, for those of us who think that, ideally, as many people as possible should be given as broad an array as possible of basic freedoms and protections. Most important, revolutionaries of the sort I have in mind tend to espouse a concern with expanding the concept of citizen to include groups that, under the ancien régime, were disenfranchised. They often stop far short of granting full citizenship to all those denied it under the old order, of course, but some of those formerly excluded from the category of citizen do end up getting included. In addition, even when they remain excluded, such people often gain something from the emergence of debates that raise the possibility of their inclusion in the future, as Hunt stresses in the preceding chapter.

On the negative side, these same revolutionaries often move to dehumanize new groups—usually all those deemed to be insufficiently sympathetic to the new order. In addition, and perhaps most significantly, they often show a fondness for declaring that dire emergencies exist, of a sort that justify the use of extraordinary repressive measure to silence and disarm real and imaginary enemies of the sacralized entity known as the Revolution. The new order tends to be presented, at least at first, as a fragile one that is threatened, in myriad and secret ways, by the overturned ruling classes, hostile foreign regimes, and fifth column traitors. It is no mere coincidence that texts portraying enemies as beasts often proliferate, just as campaigns of terror are launched to "save" the revolution and, not accidentally, the nation itself from protean categories of enemies.

Keeping these things in mind and returning at last to the Chinese case, we see both the Nationalist Revolution of the 1920s and the Communist one that followed conforming to a familiar basic pattern. Both can be called popular or democratic revolutions, if goals as opposed to effects are stressed. That is, the leaders of each claimed to be acting in the name of *minzhu*, a Chinese term that is often translated as "democracy" but can also be rendered "popular sovereignty," since *min* means people and *zhu* means rule. Both Chiang Kai-shek and Mao Zedong argued that to democratize China it was necessary to extend citizenship to previously disenfranchised groups. Both insisted, however, that threats to the revolutionary project made it vital, in the short run, to take repressive actions against certain groups. They also shared the view that at such times it was necessary to limit some freedoms (such as open dissent) even for those deemed citizens. In addition to all this, both launched terrors in which certain categories of enemies were dehumanized.

The anti-Communist purges of the late 1920s and the CCP campaigns against "capitalist roaders" that preceded and accompanied the Cultural Revolution are the kinds of terrors I have in mind. In 1927, the Nationalists portrayed Chinese "reds" as demonic and bestial traitors. Real and suspected Communists, in addition to being rounded up and killed, were denounced as the *zougou* or "running dogs" of the Russians. They were said to act like immoral animals, not civilized people, a charge reinforced by a popular phrase that said the term for Communism, *gongchanzhuyi* (sharing production) was a code word for *gongchangongqi* (sharing wives).

The Anti-Rightist Campaign of the 1950s and then the purges that came with the Cultural Revolution saw similar things happen on a much larger scale. There was also the important added twist, especially in the latter case, that inheritance as well as action could be used as grounds for denigration and violence. From the 1940s on, the Communists gave clear signals that, in the Party's eyes, not all Homo sapiens were politically *min* or people; bad elements and counterrevolutionaries became *fei renmin* in CCP texts; in the worst of times, merely being related by blood to someone in a suspect category could earn an individual this denigrating label.[11]

Literacy primers used in Communist base areas before 1949 hinted at this coming trend: They defined the *min* in *minzhu* (democracy or popular rule) as referring exclusively to workers, peasants, soldiers, and revolutionaries, not landlords and capitalists. This definitional approach made "democracy" and "dictatorship of the proletariat" completely compatible—indeed made a dictatorship of the proletariat seem a more fully realized form of *minzhu* than the political system created during the bourgeois democratic stage of the Revolution. Reinforcing formal definitions were visual cues, not only in illustrated primers of the 1940s and 1950s, but also in the omnipresent political posters of the 1960s and 1970s, which combined slogans referring to "the people" with representations of workers, peasants, and soldiers.[12]

Nonpeople suffered ritual dehumanization and physical abuse throughout the first years of Communist rule, but things reached a peak in the late 1960s. Then, everyone with a direct blood tie or an imagined ideological one to a foreign power or ancien régime class was in danger of being denigrated as an ox-demon or dubbed a criminal (a dehumanizing term that contains part of the Chinese character for dog). This escalation in the language of abuse was matched by an increase in physical violence and various forms of public humiliation, since *fei renmin* were not individuals whose dignity or persons were seen as deserving of protection.

BASIC ISSUES REVISITED

Where does all this get us in terms of the paradoxes discussed at the beginning of this essay and the question of assessing the current human rights record of the CCP? First, focusing on shifting categorization and patterns of dehumanization gives us a way to conceptualize the very real improvements in Chinese human rights practices that are ignored by too many of the most unrelenting critics of the CCP. There are certainly still far too many abuses occurring in the PRC, but there is no longer as great a tendency to place large groups of people in the nonhuman category simply because of their parentage and class background. If, as sociologist Daniel Chirot argues convincingly, a key element of modern tyrannies is the tendency for regimes to vilify people on the basis of inherited traits, then China may be said to have become decidedly less tyrannical.[13] The good news is simply that the category of counterrevolutionary now tends to be reserved for those whom the states claims have done certain things—joined a particular type of organization, participated in a particular type of protest—not just sees as belonging to the wrong lineage.[14] One thing that makes the *laogai* radically different from Nazi concentration camps is that those incarcerated in it today tend to be people that the state claims at least broke a law, not just were born into the wrong group.

The bad news, of course, is that far too many people are still treated inhumanely in China, in part because of the regime's insistence that the Revolution has remained a fragile entity under threat. The paranoid tendency to treat all critics as traitors, to treat every movement as a conspiracy, and to see nefarious plots between outsiders and domestic dissidents where these do not exist is certainly not as pronounced as it once was. On the other hand, it has also not disappeared completely by any means. This was illustrated in 1989 by the justifications the government offered for the brutal crackdown of that year; CCP spokesmen and Deng Xiaoping himself alluded to conspiracies with international backing that sought to destroy the Revolution. It was illustrated again in 1996 by the reasons given by the state for the handing down of harsh new sentences to the dissidents Wang Dan and Liu Xiaobo, two noteworthy figures in the Tiananmen protests who had remained politically active in the years following the massacre. Each was accused, unfairly, of being part of an international anti-CCP conspiracy. And it was illustrated yet again in 1999, both in the steps taken against those who have tried to form political parties to compete for power with the CCP and in the ones taken against members of the Falun Gong sect. In each case, the authorities have defended their decisions to use harsh measures to put an end to the activities of these individuals with references to nefarious conspiracies of not just national but also international proportions.

How, though, the reader may ask, does any of this help us make better sense of the often bewildering aspects of CCP apologist texts, which refer to treaty-port era abuses and other imperialist transgressions as though they were directly relevant to contemporary debates? After the preceding analysis, I would hope that such a reader would find it easier to place this kind of rhetoric in a somewhat more illuminating perspective. Take, for example, the concern Yü Quanyu and other defenders of the Beijing regime evince in detailing pre-1949 offenses committed by the West. This should now seem less bizarre, if for no other reason than that, to a revolutionary defending a new order, it is always relevant to recount the sins of the ancien régime. In Chinese Communist terms this old order has long been defined as one that involved an alliance of foreign imperialists and domestic despots. Polemicists like Yü, therefore, have a view of human rights and indeed of history that cannot be disentangled from images of imperialism, at least until they are willing to say that the revolutionary crisis has passed and ordinary times have begun. Until then, they will insist that there is a basic continuity between colonial aggression and the capitalist West's current concern with bringing more open political forms to China.[15]

I think there is a disturbing implication to the preceding discussion of the human side of the human rights equation that may be worth pondering, which takes us back to Old Shanghai's famous park sign. Even if the use apologists for the current regime make of the Public Garden can be dismissed as a diversionary tactic, and even if the stories of a sign explicitly dehumanizing Chinese by comparing them to dogs are urban myths, morally troubling aspects of the situation still remain. Most notably, we cannot ignore the fact that exclusionary policies based on race *did* exist and were a basic part of life in one of the places, Western-run treaty-port enclaves, where people from China first came into contact with the language of rights associated with the European Enlightenment. And, for that matter, "taxation without representation" was a basic reality to some Chinese living in the International Settlement for many decades, since they were banned from voting in elections for the powerful Municipal Council in charge of local affairs. Only in 1928, the same year the Public Garden was opened to all those willing to pay a newly introduced entrance fee—designed to keep out not only the "less respectable" classes of Chinese but also similarly denigrated groups such as White Russian refugees—were rate-paying Chinese given the franchise.[16]

This suggests that there are very real problems with presenting America (or the West in general) as a teacher of humanistic values whose Asian students have been and continue to be slow to understand and accept the lessons being offered—a common theme in U.S. discussions of human rights issues. Even if all that counts is the contemporary scene, taking such a position is both presumptuous and patronizing. When history is brought into the picture, there are even bigger drawbacks. After all, would not the most obvious lesson for Chinese residents of Shanghai to learn from treaty-port park rules be that, in Western eyes, not all people were entitled to the same rights and perhaps were not even equally human?[17]

CONCLUSION

To end on this note, however, would be to give a bit too much ground to apologists such as Yü Quanyu. The treatment above of the sins of the treaty-port era also fits in too easily with the arguments of those who would romanticize the situation that existed in China before the West came along. In terms of letting Yü off too easily, it is crucial to remember that, when all is said and done, the CCP's record on human rights remains an abysmal one. Even when it comes to imperialism, at least as strong a case can be made for condemning Chinese incursions into Tibet as for denouncing earlier Western ones into China or NATO actions in Yugoslavia. In addition, in spite of the improvements that have been made in some spheres, the current regime's record on many fronts leaves much to be desired. This is especially true if attention is paid not just to issues such as religious toleration and freedom of expression typically discussed in American critiques of the CCP, but also to issues that have tended not to interest U.S. commentators much. Paradoxically, it is in the realm of the very sorts of social and economic rights that are supposed to be prized so highly by those influenced by Marxist and Confucian traditions that China seems to be moving in a particularly worrisome direction just now. The disintegration of the social welfare safety net for workers who have lost their jobs as state industries have privatized, increases in violence against women—these are just some of the danger signals that have appeared or taken on new importance in the post-Mao and post-Deng eras.[18]

How then does ending with a reference to treaty-port abuses of human rights give too much ground to those who would romanticize the time before the Opium War? The people I have in mind are those who would paint too rosy a picture of China's Confucian tradition—that is, those who would judge Western imperialists by their failure to be benevolent and judge Confucianism by its promise of humane treatment for all. Western imperialists, for all their faults, did not teach the Chinese how to symbolically dehumanize "others," after all. Long before Shanghai's exclusive public parks were built, Han Chinese were incorporating the symbol for dog into the characters for neighboring ethnic groups. Westerners were also not the first to exert power in oppressive ways on Chinese soil and set themselves at the top of social hierarchies. Such exertions and such hierarchies were part and parcel of an imperial state system and patriarchal family order that was associated with Confucianism and condoned by those who espoused its ideal of benevolent rule.

All this suggests that, as we continue the struggle to define and defend an ever broadening vision of human rights, we need to come to terms with a particularly troubling phenomenon that may well be the closest thing to a true cultural universal relating to the matter at hand. This is the tendency for people with radically different agendas and belief systems to fall into the common trap of agreeing that, at least for some purposes or at some moments, not all human beings are equally human. We need to be vigilant not only about making sure that regimes accept the notion that individuals are entitled to a spectrum of rights, but also that they treat *all people* as deserving of those rights.

One of the glorious things about revolutions is that they temporarily create breathtaking visions of a social tabula rasa, a blank slate from which all old patterns of dehumanization have been magically erased. Tragically, however, all revolutionaries to date have gone on to inscribe on the pristine surface that lies before them novel patterns of dehumanization. One of the virtues of focusing on the links between revolutions and human rights, as we do throughout this book, is precisely that it places in such harsh relief both the promise and the heartbreak of so many struggles for total transformation. Those that have taken place in China are no exception.

NOTES

1. I am grateful to audiences at the University of Northern Colorado, the University of Lund, and Indiana University for comments on earlier versions of the arguments presented here. I also want to thank Marina Svensson and Lin Chun (who generously shared with me copies of their unpublished works on related topics), Lynn Hunt and Marilyn Young (who gave me very useful critical assessments of the first draft of this piece), Robert Bickers and Marcia Ristaino (who brought key documents to my attention), Richard Wasserstrom (who pushed me to clarify my general approach to human rights), and the Spencer Foundation and the National Endowment for the Humanities (who funded my research on related topics).

2. For the full text of the Universal Declaration and the other main UN texts on human rights, see Walter Laqueur and Barry Rubin, eds., *The Human Rights Reader*, rev. ed. (New York: Meridian, 1989), pp. 196–204, 215–238, 263–271, 278–286, and 290–295.

3. It was possible in the spring of 1999, I should stress, to claim that NATO air strikes were wrong but not because they violated the national sovereignty of Yugoslavia. For more on this, see chapters 11 and 12 by Blackburn and Rieff. The former leaves open the possibility that it is justified for foreign forces to intervene in the domestic affairs of states to prevent particularly egregious human rights abuses, but his focus is on showing why this specific intervention was ill conceived and self-serving. Rieff, while also critical of NATO's handling of the Kosovo crisis, explicitly states that an enlightened form of imperialism, which presumably will periodically involve violations of national sovereignty claims, is the best defense we now have against a slide into global barbarism.

4. Roosevelt's 1944 speech is reproduced in Laqueur and Rubin, *Human Rights*, pp. 313–314.

5. Marina Svensson, "The Chinese Conception of Human Rights: The Debate on Human Rights in China, 1898–1949," (doctoral thesis, Lund University, 1996).

6. See, for example, Wang Jiafu and Liu Hainian, eds., *Zhongguo renquan baike quanshu* [Human Rights Encyclopedia of China] (Beijing: Zhongguo baike quanshu chubanshe, 1998).

7. Song Qiong et al., *Zhongguo keyi shuo bu* [China Can Say No] (Beijing: Zhonghua gongshang lianhe chubanshe, 1996).

8. A case in point is Zhang Xinmin et al., *Zhongguo renquan cixu* [Chinese Dictionary of Human Rights] (Bejing: Nanhai chubanshe, 1993), p. 1151. For evidence to back up the discussion of this notice below, see Robert Bickers and Jeffrey N. Wasserstrom, "Shanghai's 'Dogs and Chinese Not Admitted' Sign: Legend, History and Contemporary Symbol," *China Quarterly* 142 (June 1995): 444–466.

9. One difference is that the only visual evidence here takes the form of a pair of dubious phototographs: one of a blurry notice board often said to show, though it actually does not, a regulation pairing the words "dogs" and "Chinese"; the other a forgery created by an overeager post-1949 propagandist. For a fascinating discussion of photographs of segregationist signs in the American South, see Elizabeth Abel, "Bathroom Doors and Drinking Fountains: Jim Crow's Racial Symbolic," *Critical Inquiry* 25, no. 3 (Spring 1999): 435–481; my thanks to Susan Gubar for bringing this work to my attention.

10. The speech, delivered on August 12, 1994, was printed in the September 11, 1994, issue of *Guangming ribao* [Guangming Daily], p. 3; an English translation appears in Foreign Broadcast and Information Service, *China Daily Report,* September 27, 1994, pp. 42–46. Parallels to Yü's speech can be found in many works, including Liu Shulin et al., *Dangdai Zhongguo renquan zhuangkuang baogao* [A Report on the Contemporary Human Rights Situation in China] (Liaoning: Liaoning renmin chubanshe, 1994), see especially pp. 6 and 14; and Zhang, *Zhongguo renquan cixu.* See also the comments on imperialism and human rights, by Yü Quanyu among others, in Song et al., *Zhongguo keyi shuo bu.*

11. Here and elsewhere, my discussion of *fei renmin* builds on that in Michael Schoenhals, "'Non-People' in the People's Republic of China: A Chronicle of Terminological Ambiguity," *Indiana East Asian Working Papers on Language and Politics in Modern China,* # 4 (1994).

12. On these posters, see Harriet Evans and Stephanie Donald, eds., *Picturing Power in the People's Republic of China: Posters of the Cultural Revolution* (Lanham, Md.: Rowman & Littlefield, 1999), and the website <http:www.indiana.edu/~easc/>.

13. Daniel Chirot, *Modern Tyrants* (Princeton: Princeton University Press, 1994).

14. A related positive sign is that references to "counterrevolutionary" crimes were struck from the legal code in 1997; those convicted of such crimes before that point have not, however, been released or had their sentences altered.

15. Recent historical events outside of the PRC have, unfortunately, sometimes served to keep just this sort of thinking alive. The year of 1999 was not only one when dissidents and Falun Gong members were attacked for being in league with foreign enemies. It was also one when journalists killed by NATO bombs were presented by Beijing, with considerably more justification, as but the latest in a long line of "revolutionary martyrs" to die at the hands of weapons wielded by a foreign power with too little respect for Chinese lives.

16. For one of several 1920s uses, by a Chinese writer, of the argument that "taxation without representation" is unjust, see C. Y. W. Meng, "Chinese on the Municipal Council," *The China Weekly Review,* April 21, 1928, pp. 218–219.

17. Here, again, there is a 1999 analogy. In the midst of the anti-NATO protests of last May, much was made in the official Chinese press and student posters of the fact that the Western media seemed to place a disproportionately high value on the lives of the three American servicemen held briefly by Serbian forces just before the Belgrade embassy was hit. It seemed, some claimed, that the humanity of these three soldiers was prized more highly in the West than that of the three "revolutionary martyrs" from the PRC.

18. For a stimulating discussion of these human rights issues, see Michael Dutton, *Streetlife China* (Cambridge: Cambridge University Press, 1998); see also various contributions to Timothy B. Weston and Lionel M Jensen, eds., *China beyond the Headlines* (Lanham, Md.: Rowman & Littlefield, 2000).

Part II

Anglo-American Events and Traditions

3

Tradition, Human Rights, and the English Revolution

David Zaret

Discourses on human rights emerged in the context of modern revolutions even though revolutionary politics and regimes afforded little more support—far less, in some cases—for such rights than their prerevolutionary antecedents. This paradox confronts any serious attempt to uncover the uneven connections between human rights and revolutionary traditions. Using the mid-seventeenth-century English Revolution (1640–1660) as a case study, I describe one of the earliest examples of this paradox and offer several reasons for its occurrence in England. Of course, this development was not unique to England; it appears in many other societies whose path to the modern world was marked by revolutionary insurrections against an unpopular ancien régime. But nascent conceptions of human rights—these invoke inherent rights of individuals against gross abuses of power that violate baseline standards of decency and equity—appear earlier in England than elsewhere. Precociousness marked this development: it occurred in a revolutionary context framed by millennial expectations, long before formal doctrines of human rights appeared in the Enlightenment. Assertions of inherent rights of individuals in opposition to despotism flowed, not from theoretical principles enunciated by philosophers of Enlightenment, but from popular politics among a minority within a minority, a small part of the activist core that supported the Long Parliament in its struggle with Charles I. We shall see how a creative reworking of extant traditions led groups such as the Levellers to their commitment to a nascent doctrine of human rights.

REVOLUTION VERSUS HUMAN RIGHTS

Human rights are the basis for claims by individuals that impose limits on other claims arising from legislation, policy or advocacy. Against laws, administrative rulings, or political agendas, human rights are trump cards[1] that override gross threats to the rule of law, rights to life and property, and freedom of association, communication, and conscience.[2] Though this list is neither exhaustive nor definitive, it does fairly represent basic protections in many formulations of human rights. Disagreement exists over whether these rights are tied to constitutional rights specifically associated with democratic citizenship and the extent to which they extend to and rely on specific social and economic rights. All formulations of human rights treat them, ideally, at least, as universal and unconditional—for example, as birthrights claimed for freeborn English subjects, in the Bill of Rights appended to the U.S. Constitution, as "the natural, inalienable, and sacred rights of man" in France's Declaration of the Rights of Man and Citizen, and, more recently, in Articles 3–18 of the Universal Declaration of Human Rights in 1948.

Thus defined, human rights exhibit several points of conflict, not only with the absolutist politics of premodern monarchies, but also with revolutionary politics. For example, many commentators point out that, for the tasks of seizing power and, more crucially, consolidating control by a revolutionary regime, calling attention to inherent ethical limitations on the exercise of power is a distraction if not impediment. Also important are implications of a principal goal of revolutionary politics: restructuring social life in order to implement an emancipatory morality. It is not simply more social equality that distinguishes revolutionary from other political agendas but the intent to populate society with more perfect moral beings. Of course, considerable variation exists across different revolutionary movements in the metaphysical underpinnings of this goal: divine providence in the English Revolution, nature in the French Revolution, and the laws of history invoked by Marxist revolutionaries in the twentieth century. Yet in all varieties of revolutionary political thought, the gulf perceived to exist between the existing and desired social order is enormous. Its consequence is demolition of a broad range of extant traditions—political, intellectual, cultural, and social—as a primary objective of revolutionary policy. This warfare with tradition puts revolutionary politics on a collision course with precepts of decency, dignity and equity that lie at the core of human rights. Revolutionary politics rely on a mode of social criticism that, as Michael Walzer observes, issues from critics whose stance toward their society is that of alien observers. Unlike critics-from-within whose critique of corruption and inequity proceeds immanently (that is, derives from creative reinterpretation of extant traditions of a society), revolutionary politics appeals to standards that have little or no connection to tradition. "The problem with disconnected criticism, and thus with criticism that derives from newly discovered or invented moral standards, is that it presses its practitioners toward manipulation and compulsion."[3] Nothing better illustrates this insight than the shrewd discussion by Steven Lukes of "the moral disasters of Marxism in practice." Like Walzer, Lukes links the failure of Marxist politics, from a human rights standpoint, to disconnected criticism. Marxist critiques, writes Lukes, were dedicated to "pursuit of socialist ends, and indeed to the justification of these ends in terms of a 'liberating morality'; and . . . to the dismissal of all moral talk as dangerous ideological illusion, rendered anachronistic by the discovery of scientific laws of economic development."[4]

But if it is wrong to treat human rights as an immediate consequence of the revolutionary impulse in modern history, it would be equally mistaken to dismiss the relevance of revolutionary epochs of the past few centuries for modern discourses on such rights. Totalitarian developments notwithstanding, human societies often emerged from years or even decades wracked by revolutionary politics with sharper, more expanded doctrines on human rights. This would be puzzling if it were merely a consequence of a collective learning process, prompted by totalitarian excesses in toppling old regimes and securing new ones from the threat of counterrevolution. Despotic politics in old regimes afforded just as many opportunities for drawing the conclusion that power should be limited by conceptions of basic rights. The difference between old regimes and revolutionary eras for advances in thinking about human rights was the cultural innovation that typically flourished in revolutionary epochs. A contingent but nonetheless important connection between revolution and human rights thus existed because of the intellectual ferment and experimentation facilitated, inadvertently or otherwise, by several common occurrences in revolutionary eras. These included the often temporary disabling of agencies of social control that limited oral and written discourse, turnover in the ranks of clerics, educators and other officeholders who controlled the levers of cultural production, and growing opportunities for popular participation in political discussion and debate as contending elites issued appeals to public opinion in competitive efforts to mobilize fiscal and human resources for sustained, violent conflict.

One additional point completes this sketch of the paradoxical relationship between revolution and human rights in modern times. So far I have suggested that a positive relationship exists between revolutions and discourses on human rights because the former removes obstacles to bold initiatives in thought, to new perspectives in what today we call normative political philosophy. From whence do these initiatives and perspectives come? The case of the English Revolution suggests that they originate in well-established social and political traditions that unevenly anticipate key themes in modern discourses on human rights, such as rights to life, property, due process under law, and the right to express grievance. Revolutionary upheavals open up opportunities for creative reworking of extant traditions that supply leads for thinking about these human rights and wholly new ones, such as freedom of speech and conscience. The paradox, then, is that such upheavals allow for and may even actively encourage innovations in extant traditions; but revolutionary ideologies are dismissive of the critical potential in traditions, and traditional insights into and strictures on dignity, decency, and equity are the seed bed of modern conceptions of human rights. "A little to the side, but not outside: critical distance is measured in inches."[5] If Walzer's appraisal of immanent criticism fairly describes the critical stance of proponents of human rights, we can resolve the paradoxical relationship between the creation of this commitment and revolutionary upheavals in modern history. What enables the latter to establish conditions favorable to the former is the revolutionary impulse to sweep aside all tradition, which dissolves obstacles to progressive appropriation of a society's traditions even as it suggests that traditions per se are morally and politically bad things.

THE DEVELOPMENT OF THE IDEA OF HUMAN RIGHTS

Human rights in Western societies, like other, lesser types of right, *recht* and *droit*, attach to individuals and advance the moral precedence of the individual over society. This is a distinctively modern perspective. But discourses that invoke these rights in the modern world were not invented out of thin air. Long before the toppling of ancien régimes by the English and, later, the French Revolutions, the rhetoric of liberty and freedom was well established in the Middle Ages. Unlike modern doctrines, however, invocation of liberty and freedom in medieval theory and practice associated rights with corporate groups (with municipalities, guilds, Cathedral clergy, and so on) and treated them as privileges that exempted members of those groups from exactions or regulations that applied to everyone else. Social and political life in medieval society was mapped onto a complex web spun by rulers who granted, modified, reissued, and revoked privileges and immunities in the ordinary exercise of sovereign authority. Invocation of freedom or liberty did not, then, refer to universal rights of individuals but to their social location, their place in a welter of overlapping, often conflicting, corporate affiliations. Though the nature of these affiliations and conditions under which they obtained juridical expression varied from one society to another, this medieval background was a common inheritance of England and many other Western nations.

During the seventeenth-century English Revolution this medieval inheritance was transformed in the direction of modern ideas on human rights. To be sure, that which was transformed in the 1640s and 1650s was not identical to doctrines and practices in the Middle Ages. In the early seventeenth century, the corporate structure of English society and its political and juridical underpinnings differed greatly in many respects from England under the reign of Edward III. When Parliaments assembled under the reign of the last Tudor monarch, Elizabeth I, and first two Stuart kings, James I and Charles I, their members routinely invoked a broad range of privileges to defend proceedings that increasingly departed from medieval practice. Yet, members of both houses of Parliament regarded the freedom of Parliament, as they called it, to be medieval in origin, if not older. Moreover, the rights this freedom bestowed on individual members were distinctly medieval: They provided individuals with immunities from otherwise general rules—for example, prohibition against popular discussion of public issues because this was a privilege attached to sovereign authority. By the early seventeenth century, the opening of Parliament began with a well-established ritual in which the Speaker petitioned the monarch to grant the Commons its putatively ancient liberties, which bestowed on its members freedom of speech, freedom for access to the ruler, and freedom from arrest. Here it is important to avoid anachronism. In Elizabethan and early Stuart England, references to liberties of English subjects, commonplaces in political discourse, did not refer to rights of individuals but to corporate privileges enjoyed by their representatives in the Commons. When those representatives spoke out in support of the liberties and rights of English subjects, which they did with increasing frequency and urgency in the early-seventeenth century, they were resisting what they perceived as encroachment on privileges and immunities of the Commons. In this discourse, the prevailing corporate perspective on society subsumed references to individual rights. Subsequently, several principal rights commonly found in enumerations of human rights—e.g., individual rights to rule under law, security of life, and property—grew out of these traditional privileges and immunities, when under the pressure of political events framed by conflict between the Crown and Parliament contemporaries ceased to defend individual rights indirectly, by invoking corporate privileges and immunities, and did so directly during the English Revolution.

Evidence for a second link between tradition and modern doctrines on human rights exists in the petitioning ritual for the liberties of the Commons that occurred at the opening of a Parliament. Like other medieval societies, England had well-established procedures for expressing grievance by petition. The parliamentary ritual was merely a formalized expression of an extremely widespread practice by which contemporaries advanced requests, of a public and private nature, to every conceivable seat of authority. As we shall see, when the request was linked to expressions of grievance, that is, when contemporaries requested redress of an inequity or oppression, a petition was expected to be presented by local authorities on behalf of a corporate structure—a municipality, parish, guild, and so on. During the English Revolution, a transformation in this medieval practice led to several modern ideas, some of which are central to any conception of human rights (e.g., the right to assemble and petition for redress of grievances) and some to conceptions that link such rights specifically to democratic modes of governance (e.g., the right to form political associations, to freedom of speech and the right to appeal to public opinion as a means to influence a legislative agenda).

In the following two sections, I describe these two parallel developments in the rise of modern ideas on human rights. Beginning with medieval antecedents, I trace two sets of rights—rule of law and security of life and property; freedom of speech and petitioning for redress of grievance—to a creative reworking of traditions of liberty and freedom that replaced corporate privileges and immunities with individual rights. These developments occurred under the pressure of events as sporadic conflict between James I and his Parliaments hardened into political gridlock under Charles I, which, after eleven years of personal rule, was resolved by the summoning of the Long Parliament (1640), a civil war between it and Charles (1642–1646), a period of factional politics and abortive counter-revolution, the Regicide and creation of a republic (1649), Cromwell's Protectorate (1653–1658), and the Restoration of the Stuart monarchy in 1660. Political exigency in these events facilitated a decoupling of corporate privileges and individual rights in English rhetoric of liberty and freedom. For example, when the Long Parliament seized the reins of power from Charles I, it established a tyrannical regime that was at least as oppressive of the fundamental rights of English subjects as policies pursued by Charles I during his eleven years of personal rule. Opposition to this development came from several quarters. All invoked the same doctrines of traditional liberties advanced earlier by Parliament in defense of its privileges, but now such liberties were interpreted as rights of individuals who were oppressed by parliamentary ordinances and edicts of tyrannical County Committees. This opposition uniformly invoked the birthrights of English subjects and extended well beyond the ranks of radicals, such as the Levellers, who supported the Long Parliament in its conflict with Charles. For it came also from Royalists and Neutralists, known as Clubmen, in the provinces.

TAXES, PRIVILEGES, AND RIGHTS

Fiscal issues are the unobvious point of departure for thinking about the relevance of traditional doctrines of parliamentary privileges and immunities for modern views on human rights. The evolution of Parliament—from a principally juridical institution, a high court, to one that originated legislation—is intertwined with fiscal requirements of the Crown. English monarchs had two sources of revenue. One flowed from the "fisc," the complex of demesne lands and prerogative revenues (e.g., wardships) attached to the Crown, whose disposition was not subject to direct control by Parliament. In theory, the government was expected to fund ordinary expenses from this source. The other increasingly important source flowed from taxes imposed on the wealth of subjects for "necessary" expenses intended to preserve the commonwealth.

In the century prior to the outbreak of the English Revolution, successive regimes confronted a fiscal dilemma posed by growing costs of government, which were principally military in nature, and the declining value of the royal demesne. From the beginning of the reign of Elizabeth I in 1558 until 1640, Crown income as a percentage of overall government revenue declined from nearly 30 percent to 12 percent.[6] Confronted by this dilemma, early Stuart kings had to tap alternative streams of revenue as royal prodigality at home and a policy of subventions for military allies on the continent drained the treasury. The monarchs could expand prerogative taxes or rely on parliamentary consent to larger subsidies. Experiments with the former were politically unpopular; many contemporaries saw this as an infusion of continental absolutism that threatened the balance of power established by England's "ancient constitution." But the latter course required a consent that successive Stuart Parliaments were increasing unwilling to yield. A pro-Spanish and pro-French tilt in early Stuart foreign policy limited England's participation in continental wars of religion to a policy of fiscal subventions for Protestant forces. Not only was this unpopular with Puritan members of Parliament, it also undercut the Crown's justification of parliamentary taxation as a necessity to preserve the commonwealth. "The 'case of necessity' had to be laid before subjects in parliament and accepted by them as genuine . . . Parliament's grant of taxation to meet such a designated and acknowledged necessity of the realm was (along with legislation) the foremost of those acts of shared government that characterized a mixed monarchy." In this context, "necessity" meant imminent peril and had been invoked in times of war or revolt. Necessity, of course, is a highly elastic concept, and "the less urgent and evident the danger the greater was the scope for excuses by subjects, for pleas of goodwill and promises of redress of grievances by the king." To condition supply on redress of grievances was not a novel development, but such bargaining, which dates back to the Hundred Years War, "was subtle and pragmatic, and did not represent a free interplay of interests."[7]

Yet, by the early seventeenth century, protestations to the contrary indicate that Parliament was indeed using the power of its purse to bargain with the king over redress of popular grievances. A prolific London letter writer, John Chamberlain, observed in 1614 that after James spoke to Parliament about his fiscal needs, he promised to consider requests for redressing grievance, but "not in the way of exchange or merchandising (which course he will not allow nor cannot abide to hear of)." A member of the 1621 Parliament, Sir Thomas Wentworth, informed his constituents about a grant of a new subsidy to James and his promise "to ease his loving subjects of all their just grievance" as a token of his appreciation for "our no merchant-like dealing with him."[8] The precise nature of these grievances—religious objections to pro-Catholic alignments in foreign policy and anti-Puritan policies in the state church, abuse of prerogative powers to raise revenues—is less important than the consequence of being coupled to issues of "supply" in parliamentary debates. After failure of negotiations over a "great contract" in the 1610 Parliament—this would have abolished many prerogative taxes in exchange for a regular subsidy—the Crown resorted to unpopular fiscal expedients, such as "voluntary" benevolences, the forced loan, ship money, and more.

In this context, countermeasures by the Crown sought to decouple issues of supply and grievances by circumventing parliamentary control over the former. But this only provoked more strident political discussion in the Lords and Commons. General issues pertaining to the nature and scope of sovereign authority and the liberties of English subjects assumed greater importance in recurrent debates in increasingly factious Parliaments over the relative priority of supply and grievances. What spurred discussion of these general issues were royal efforts to acquire by exercise of the Crown's prerogative powers that Parliament was increasingly unwilling to give. Referring to a host of unpopular prerogative taxes (such as purveyance, impositions on imports and exports, and alehouse taxes) members argued on the floor of the Commons in 1610 that resolution of these grievances should precede any vote for new subsidies for the king. Distasteful though this bargaining may have been to King James, it provoked him less than the willingness of some members to discuss the nature and scope of his prerogative power, which he expressly forbade in messages that ordered them "to give over all such arguments . . . as may any way tend to the examination of his power and prerogative in general."[9] The consequence of this abridgement of the parliamentary privilege of free speech, noted several members, was dire: "If we may not say this is our right . . . then we must bear any wrong, if a commandment come to us not to dispute it." Thus, members critical of prerogative taxes found themselves between a rock and hard place, being equally unwilling "to argue the prerogative of my sovereign" or "to lose the liberty of a subject." Nevertheless, the author of this last point concludes, "The prerogative is great yet it is not endless nor boundless, but justice and equity are the bounds of it." As limits to the king's prerogative powers, justice and equity are part of "the liberty of the subject." This liberty, another member remarks, distinguishes England "from many other commonwealths" and has three branches: "One is that we are masters of our own and can have nothing taken from us without our consents; another that laws cannot be made without our consents . . . the third is that the Parliament is the storehouse of our liberties."[10] Widespread agreement existed that these liberties, which set limits to prerogative powers of kings, were a birthright of English subjects. Referring to James's order not to discuss his power "in general," the London letter writer cited above worried "that if practice should follow the positions, we are not like to leave to our successors that freedom we received from our forefathers."[11]

On many other occasions early Stuart Parliaments invoked the ancient liberties of the subject to defend their corporate privileges. For example, the narrow issue in 1604 over whether the Commons or Chancery had jurisdiction in certifying elections (ultimately decided in favor of the Commons) gave rise to debate over claims by James that parliamentary privileges derived from royal grace and not from inherited or ancient rights of his subjects. If this were so, then, like other privileges, Parliament's liberties could be modified or revoked unilaterally by the king. A committee convened by the Commons issued *The Form of Apology and Satisfaction*, which declared that James's position tended "to the utter overthrow of the very fundamental privileges of our House and therein of the rights and liberties of the whole commons . . . which they and their ancestors from time immemorial have undoubtably enjoyed." These "are our right and due inheritance no less than our very lands and goods."[12] It appears, then, that the rhetoric of liberty, which evolved in tandem with the representative function of Parliament for granting the consent of the Commons to taxes, was applied to nonfiscal matters under the general rubric of parliamentary privilege as the storehouse of the liberties of the subject. Because contemporary perspectives on these liberties did not focus on individual rights but on corporate privileges, a restricted franchise was not perceived to undermine the liberty of the subject. No contradiction existed between upholding this liberty and defending the right of the Commons to certify elections from which most adult males, and all women, were excluded. All the same, it is remarkable to observe the extent to which, in application, these corporate rights subsumed protections for individuals similar to those in modern conceptions of human rights, namely, rights to the rule of law and to security of life and property. Admittedly, considerable uncertainty and disagreement existed over the precise source of these liberties. Were they to be derived from maxims about equity and justice or from hazy traditions alleged to have flourished before the Norman Conquest? Or should they be limited to explicit laws and statutes? Even under this latter, limiting stricture, Parliament framed its Petition of Right in 1628, which responded to prerogative taxes and quartering of soldiers by invoking the fundamental liberties of English subjects. These included protections against arbitrary imprisonment, forced quartering, substitution of martial for common law, and taxation without parliamentary consent.

In view of these developments in early Stuart England, many features of political discourse in revolutionary England are wholly unsurprising. References to birthrights and inherited liberties pervade sermons, speeches, and pamphlets that cultivated popular support for the Parliament (the Long Parliament) that assembled in November 1640. This was facilitated by the collapse of controls on printing and pulpit oratory that had been vested in prerogative courts, such as the Star Chamber and Court of High Commission. Abolition of these courts was among the earliest acts of reform by the Long Parliament. In London and in the provinces, political rhetoric relied on a theme advanced earlier in the century by opponents of prerogative taxation: Parliament was the storehouse of the ancient liberties of the subject. In this view, King Charles threatened not only the privileges of Parliament but also the birthrights of freeborn English people in his abortive effort to arrest five parliamentary leaders in January 1642 and six months later in raising a Royalist Army. Traditional rhetoric on liberty and freedom was, then, the primary source for doctrines of native birthrights that we most often associate with radical political groups in the English Revolution, such as the Levellers and their allies the Agitators in Cromwell's New Model Army. One Agitator, Edward Sexby, advanced a commonplace idea when, in the famous Putney debates in 1647 over the army's stance on constitutional issues, he argued that English soldiers were not mercenaries; they had enlisted in that army "to recover our birthrights and privileges as Englishmen."[13] If we acknowledge that traditional rhetoric on liberty was the point of departure for its invocation in radical politics, then we can readily see why many radical ideas, such as Leveller proposals for widening the franchise and reforming the universities and the legal system, were "frequently expressed in a phantasmagoric historicism like the Levellers' dreams of the halcyon days of Edward the Confessor."[14] Moreover, we can just as readily understand why radical political rhetoric was not unique in its appeal to inalienable rights of English subjects. Across the political spectrum, many opponents of free quartering, force loans, and other dictatorial edicts by the Long Parliament and its County Committees invoked these claims against parliamentary tyranny. Against the inevitable excesses and illegalities of a revolutionary regime, Royalist pamphlets and petitions refer no less consistently or stridently than Leveller writings to native birthrights and fundamental liberties of English subjects. In several notable instances, Royalist and Leveller leaders adopted an allied stance in opposition to a parliamentary tyranny that trampled liberties which guaranteed to English subjects rights to life, property, and the rule of law.[15]

However, one crucial point separates radical use of traditional ideas on the liberties of the English subject from its invocation by other opponents of the Long Parliament and by Parliaments both before and during the 1640s. When corporate privileges and not individual rights were the principal issue, doctrines of liberty offered weak or inconsistent opposition to despotic politics. Thus, successive Parliaments in the 1620s saw no contradiction between acting as the storehouse of the people's liberties and repressing any who dared to dispute this point. In 1628, after Roger Maynwaring preached sermons that upheld the prerogative power of the Crown to levy taxes, Parliament ordered his imprisonment and disabled him from holding public office. Even its members were not exempt from this treatment by a Parliament that would not tolerate censorship of its discussions by anyone other than itself. But after 1640, among some radical groups a creative reworking of traditional doctrines led to innovative claims on behalf of inalienable rights that protected individuals from abuses of power. That which was fused in traditional doctrines of liberty—namely, its corporate and individual denotations—became separated in Leveller political thought, in countless arguments that delineated inherent limitations to the exercise of legal and political authority. The result was unprecedented political claims on behalf of inalienable rights of individuals. For example, after the Long Parliament imprisoned a Leveller leader, Richard Overton, for violating parliamentary privileges, he issued an "Appeal to the People." Overton conceded the lack of any legal precedent for such an appeal. Instead, he invoked reason—the "fountain of all just precedents"—to justify appeals to public opinion against "all betrusted powers" when their "tyranny" betrays trust because "by natural birth," says Overton, "all men are equal, and alike born to like propriety and freedom." Referring to "all and every particular and individual man and woman," the Leveller leader John Lilburne argues that human beings are

> by nature all equal and alike in power and dignity, authority and majesty, none of them having by nature any authority, dominion, or magisterial power one over or above another; neither have they or can they exercise any, but . . . by mutual consent and agreement, for the good benefit and comfort each of other, and not for the mischief, hurt, or damage of any; it being unnatural, irrational . . . for any man or men to part with so much of their power as shall enable any of their Parliamentmen, commissioners, trustees, deputies . . . or servants, to destroy and undo them therewith.[16]

At the core of these arguments is a distinctively modern theme: that individuals own their freedom just as much as they do their property and on the same terms, as inalienable rights. Two remarkable features of Leveller ideology require a comment. First, because it accorded priority to reason over precedent, Leveller thinking moves doctrines of specifically English birthrights in the direction of human rights. The latter derives not from the mists of English history but, instead, from an appeal to reason. The appeal to substantive reason (equity, justice) in Leveller political thought was the wedge that split apart individualist and corporate referents in the doctrine of liberty. Second, Leveller doctrines of inalienable rights go beyond minimalist definitions of human rights (e.g., security of life and property, rule of law) that prohibit "negative" actions by government and encompass fundamental rights of democratic citizenship and other positive rights.

THE RIGHT TO PETITION

The right to express grievance and other communicative rights are central to modern conceptions of human rights. Like rights to life, property, and the rule of law, these communicative rights also have roots embedded in traditions that extend far back in history and that were not unique to England. And like the doctrines of liberty that we just surveyed, their appearance in a recognizably modern form can be traced to a process of reworking extant traditions during the English Revolution. Petitions are an ancient and widespread form of communication. Ancestors of electronic petitions on the Internet are preserved in papyri records of antiquity, in civil pleadings, and in requests for favors and exemptions from taxes. This broad range of application also appears in Merovingian and Carolingian petitionary formulas in the early Middle Ages. The evolution of medieval governance routinized procedures for sending petitions to monarchs and parliaments, much of whose daily work in England involved receiving and responding to petitions. In Tokugawa Japan and Old Regime Russia, traditions provided for petitions as a vehicle for expressing grievances from peasants. Petitioning was, then, a venerable tradition when it became embroiled in early modern revolutions, most notably in the English and French Revolutions.

In prerevolutionary England, contemporaries regarded procedures for petitioning as venerable traditions. These traditions did not distinguish between individual requests for favors and collective expressions of grievance. Deference, humility, and supplication were the principal features of petitionary formula. Medieval England had traditions for petitioning that made receipt of pleas from petitioning subjects a visible, time-consuming part of kingship; Henry IV received about 3,000 petitions each year. The same holds for the business of parliaments, which met as high courts that received and tried petitions. More than 16,000 petitions went to parliaments from the thirteenth to fifteenth century. Predominantly juridical in nature, they conveyed complaints, decried miscarriage of justice, or requested relief from taxes, forest laws, and other regulations. The history of petitions to parliament reflects growing complexity in medieval institutions. In the early fourteenth century, parliaments added legislative to their original juridical functions; distinctions were drawn between private petitions and parliamentary or commons petitions that raise collective grievances. By the early sixteenth century, however, a subsequent innovation superseded petitions. Legislation proceeded by "bill," which delineated the substance of a legislative act, and not by petition. Private bills are still called petitions and parliaments continue to "petition" monarchs, most notably in cases of conflict between them. In early seventeenth-century England, not only were petitions used for many different purpose, they were also objects of popular knowledge, well-suited to a hierarchical world in which deference and patronage functioned like money. The word "petition" was a common figure of speech, used literally and metaphorically to signify deferential request for favor or redress of a grievance. For grievances, petitions over every conceivable affront or inequity went to every seat of authority. Contemporaries held strong views on the right of individuals and corporate groups to petition over grievances, which, before and after 1640, was widely regarded as "the indisputable right of the meanest subject."[17]

At first, it seems odd that the right to express grievance by petition was so strongly entrenched in a society whose politics rested on deference and patronage. But like other medieval rights, the right to petition was far from absolute. By tradition, petitioning was a privilege (in the medieval sense) that exempted petitioners from general norms that prohibited popular discussion of public matters. Severe limits existed for expressions of grievance in petitions. The rhetoric of petitions portrayed grievance as an apolitical conveyance of information, principally by emphasizing deferential, juridical, and spontaneous attributes of the grievance. Other restrictions further stipulated that grievance should be local, directly experienced, not critical of laws or indicative of discontent with authority, and not made public. Typically, a petition came forward from "humble" suitors who submitted information on local conditions to a petitioned authority. A traditional petition referred local grievances to central authority; it did not load its message with normative claims about the "will of the people" and it had little in common with modern ideas about appeals to public opinion. To petition was to enter a privileged communicative space in which petitioners enjoyed limited immunity against general norms of secrecy in political communication. Because it conformed to a corporate perspective on society in which political conflict and factions could only be perceived as deviant behavior, the tradition of petitioning was well suited to a world in which patronage and deference were the common coin of the political realm.

In the 1640s, the traditional petition underwent a transformation that recast it as a political device for ideological conflict. The impetus for this development was revolutionary necessity. Pym and other Parliamentarian leaders initiated the practice of using petitions to whip up popular support for proposals or policies that faced substantial opposition in one or both houses of Parliament. Coordination of petition campaigns and tactical maneuvers in Parliament was a political art practiced to perfection by Pym as he and his allies promoted a purge of anti-Puritan incumbents from parishes, a bill of attainder for treason against the king's principal advisor, the earl of Strafford, a purge of bishops and other "malignants" from Parliament itself, and seizure of control over the militia, which precipitated the outbreak of civil war in the summer of 1642. By this time, hundreds of petitions had poured into the Long Parliament, drawn up by parishes, municipalities, and counties, often at the instigation of political elites in Westminster. Though Pym and his supporters initiated the practice of political petitioning, it was not limited to Parliamentarians as the other side quickly became adept at this in order to marshal support for Charles's position on religious and political issues. For political petitioning, considerable planning and organization was necessary. For example, the "Root & Branch" petition from London citizens, which requested sweeping religious reforms, such as abolishing the office of bishop, had about 15,000 signatures and was presented to Parliament by 1,500 petitioners on December 11, 1640. When the printing of petitions became routine after 1641, especially for larger ones on contentious issues, the transformation of traditional petitioning into competitive appeals to public opinion was essentially complete. Political use of printed petitions violated petitioning traditions and more general norms of secrecy and privilege in political communication because it constituted and invoked the authority of public opinion in order to lobby Parliament on pending business.

Political petitioning originated in mass petitions orchestrated by political elites in the early 1640s. But popular developments quickly led in directions neither anticipated nor welcomed by parliamentary leaders, when Levellers, army Agitators, and Royalists presented their petitions to Parliament in 1647. This process exhibits a cumulative quality, in which prior practice supplies a legitimating precedent for ever more radical initiatives. In the winter of 1642–1643, rival petitions commended peace and war policies to the Long Parliament and delineated hardening positions of Royalists and Parliamentarians. Petitions in the spring and summer of 1643 mark emergence of the Independents, who opposed moderate Presbyterian policies that pursued religious reform via an accommodation with Charles I. Competitive petition campaigns between these two factions in 1645 and 1646 were followed in 1647 and 1648 by petitions from the army and Levellers after Parliament pursued abortive plans to consolidate power by disbanding the army and then resisted proposals to put the king on trial for treason. At the same time, Royalists in the provinces organized petitions that called for the disbanding of the army and a treaty with the king.

In this development, all sides invoked traditional arguments on the right to petition against ever more strident efforts by Parliament to suppress opposition. Yet, once again, it is important to draw distinctions between radical and conservative use of tradition. The principal issue in Leveller petitions quickly became parliamentary tyranny when Leveller leaders were jailed. Thus, in addition to requests for an expanded franchise, an end to imprisonment for debt, and other legal reforms, Leveller petitions upheld the right of private persons to assemble for the purpose of framing petitions, to present them to Parliament, and publish them to the nation. By tradition petitions—especially those dealing with public grievances—were supposed to be initiated by local elites in the name of corporate entities, e.g., counties, guilds, and municipalities; thus one consequence of innovation in the practice of petitioning is the birth of the "party." Moreover, among Levellers partisan use of petitions as a political device to lobby Parliament led to a principled stance that defended general communicative rights as part of the inalienable liberty of individuals. Levellers demanded of the Long Parliament "that you will precisely hold yourselves to the supreme end, the freedom of the people; as in other things, so in that necessary and essential part of speaking, writing, printing, and publishing their minds freely." Central to this point is an insight gained from practical experience with use of petitions to lobby Parliament: government must "hear all voices and judgments, which they can never do but by giving freedom to the press."[18]

Here, indeed, we witness the point at which a distinctively modern view of human rights has emerged from traditional rhetoric on liberty and freedom. What facilitated this reworking of tradition was the practical experience of innovative uses of petitions in the factional politics of the English Revolution, one of whose consequences, oddly enough, was growing confidence in the rationality of individual reason. Confronted by the problem of competition between rival petitions that advanced contrary opinions, some contemporaries upheld consent, reason, and representation as criteria of the validity of opinions invoked in public debate. Innovation in petitioning was, then, a practical precedent for "people's public use of their reason,"[19] a development that Jürgen Habermas and many other commentators describe as a theoretical development, an intellectual discovery during the eighteenth-century Enlightenment. In the seventeenth-century English Revolution, this practical precedent led to a host of novel ideas that expanded contemporary thinking on the scope of liberty and freedom. Some petitioners came to see the need for formal constitutional arrangements that would enforce the authority of public opinion; accordingly, they advanced liberal-democratic models of government. Others justified their petitioning, though they were women, by appealing to reason in explaining why both sexes ought to enjoy equal liberty in this regard.

To be sure, this movement toward modern doctrines of human rights had many inconsistencies and little immediate political success. It was intertwined with a vision of godly politics—best exemplified by Oliver Cromwell—that did not extend to atheists and Catholics many fundamental freedoms associated with native birthrights. Moreover, proponents of radical politics who advanced the most novel ideas on liberty and freedom were defeated, first by Cromwell and later by the Restoration of the Stuart monarchy in 1660. Perhaps this was inevitable, given the gross discrepancies between radical invocation of individual rights and prevailing assumptions about the irrationality of human nature, the corporate structure of society and the centrality of deference and patronage in politics. But Leveller ideas did not disappear. A long list of examples shows their survival from Whigs and freethinkers in the late seventeenth and eighteenth centuries to the rise of the Chartist Movement.[20] Thus, in the genesis of human rights—individual rights to security of life and property, rule of law, freedom of communication, and the right to express grievance—the English Revolution was a transition point in which modern thinking on inalienable and universal rights of individuals issues from traditional rhetoric on liberty and freedom. Though this was neither anticipated nor desired by nearly all principal participants in events of the English Revolution—certainly not by political and military elites who interrupted the reign of the Stuart dynasty—it does fairly represent the paradoxical relationship between revolutions and human rights in the modern world.

NOTES

1. See Ronald Dworkin, *Taking Rights Seriously* (Cambridge: Harvard University Press, 1977).

2. This broadly follows John Rawls, "The Law of Peoples," in *On Human Rights*, ed. S. Shute and S. Hurley (New York: Basic Books, 1993), p. 68.

3. Michael Walzer, *Interpretation and Social Criticism* (Cambridge: Harvard University Press, 1987), p. 64.

4. Steven Lukes, *Marxism and Morality* (Oxford: Oxford University Press, 1985), pp. xi, 24–25.

5. Walzer, *Interpretation and Social Criticism*, p. 61.

6. Michael Braddick, *The Nerves of State: Taxation and the Financing of the English State, 1558–1714* (Manchester: Manchester University Press, 1996), p. 10.

7. G. L. Harris, "Medieval Doctrines in the Debates on Supply, 1610–1629," in *Faction and Parliament: Essays on Early Stuart History*, ed. Kevin Sharpe (London: Methuen, 1985), pp. 76, 77, 88.

8. Norman McClure, ed., *The Letters of John Chamberlain* (Philadelphia: The American Philosophic Society, 1939), I. 525; J. P. Cooper, ed., *Wentworth Papers 1597–1628* (London: Camden Society, 1973), p. 152.

9. McClure, *Letters of John Chamberlain*, II. 86.

10. McClure, *Letters of John Chamberlain*, II. 92, 94, 109.

11. McClure, *Letters of John Chamberlain*, I. 301.

12. J. R. Tanner, ed., *Constitutional Documents of the Reign of James I* (Cambridge: Cambridge University Press, 1930), p. 221.

13. A. S. P. Woodhouse, ed., *Puritanism and Liberty: Being the Army Debates* (London: Dent, 1938), p. 69.

14. Mark Kishlansky, "Ideology and Politics in the Parliamentary Armies," in *Reactions to the English Civil War*, ed. John Morrill (London: Macmillan, 1982), pp. 164–165.

15. Robert Ashton, *Counter-Revolution. The Second Civil War and its Origins, 1646–1648* (New Haven: Yale University Press, 1994).

16. Woodhouse, *Puritanism and Liberty*, pp. 317, 327.

17. David Zaret, "Petitions and the 'Invention' of Public Opinion in the English Revolution," *American Journal of Sociology* 101, no. 6 (1996): 1511. My subsequent discussion of petitions draws on this article.

18. D. M. Wolfe, ed., *Leveller Manifestoes of the Puritan Revolution* (New York: Humanities Press, 1967), pp. 328–329.

19. Jürgen Habermas, *The Structural Transformation of the Public Sphere: An Inquiry into a Category of Bourgeois Society*, trans. from the German by Thomas Burger, with the assistance of Frederick Lawrence (Cambridge: MIT Press, 1989), p. 27.

20. Christopher Hill, *Collected Essays*, vol. 2 (Amherst: University of Massachusetts Press, 1986), pp. 108–109.

4

Natural Rights in the American Revolution: The American Amalgam

Michael Zuckert

THE RIGHTS OF MAN AND 1776

Thomas Jefferson, as it turned out, was to die on July 4, 1826, the fiftieth anniversary of the Declaration of Independence, but of course nobody knew that in advance. So it happened that the mayor of Washington, D.C., invited Jefferson to help the capital city celebrate that capital event. Ill health prevented Jefferson's attendance. He sent instead what proved to be his last letter, a letter in which he attempted to state what he took the Declaration and the revolution it announced to mean to the world: "May it be . . . what I believe it will be, the signal of arousing men to burst the chains under which monkish ignorance and superstition had persuaded them to bind themselves . . . All eyes are opened, or opening to the rights of man."[1] The American Revolution, according to Thomas Jefferson, was about the "rights of man."

Except for the fact that the exact phrase "the rights of man" was not much in use in the America of the 1770s, evidence more contemporaneous with the Revolution supports Jefferson's judgment. Leaving aside pamphlets, newspapers, sermons, and other unofficial expressions of opinion (where appeal to natural rights was profuse and consistent) and concentrating only on official or semiofficial documents, we can see how pervasive the appeal to natural rights was.[2] Jefferson's own Declaration of Independence is surely the most famous example, for it has plausibly been called "the paper which is probably the best known that ever came from the pen of an individual."[3] Among the "truths" there held "to be self-evident" were these: "that all men . . . are endowed by their Creator with certain unalienable rights; that among these are life, liberty and the pursuit of happiness; [and] that to secure these rights governments are instituted among men."

As Jefferson always said, his Declaration was not in the least unique in its appeal to natural rights. The 1772 Boston declaration of "The Rights of the Colonists" (drafted by Samuel Adams) began with a long list of "the natural rights of the colonists as men," among which were the familiar rights to life, liberty, and property together with "the Right to support and defend [those rights] in the best manner they can."[4] Prior to the Declaration of Independence the most significant statement by an America-wide body was the Declaration and Resolves of the First Continental Congress, issued in 1774; that document declared in its first resolution the familiar triad of rights: "life, liberty, and property," rights held under "the immutable laws of nature."[5]

When independence came in 1776 and the new states moved to form constitutions most included a statement about natural rights either as part of the justification for independence or as part of the statement of fundamental principles meant to underlie the constitution. George Mason's important draft of the Virginia Declaration of Rights of June 1776, for example, began by stating those rights "which . . . do pertain to them and their posterity, as the basis and foundation of government." The rights so declared are close if not quite identical to those listed in Jefferson's Declaration: "that all men . . . have certain inherent natural rights . . . among which are the enjoyment of life and liberty, with the means of acquiring and possessing property, and pursuing and obtaining happiness and safety."[6] The Virginia statement on rights was copied almost verbatim into the revolutionary Pennsylvania Declaration of Rights of August 1776.[7] The Delaware Declaration of Rights, adopted in September of 1776, also appealed to "natural and inalienable rights" and included the usual "right to be protected in the enjoyment of life, liberty, and property," as well as a "right to worship Almighty God according to the dictates of their own consciences and understandings."[8] The Georgia Constitution of 1777 did not speak of natural rights but of acts of the British government "repugnant to the common rights of mankind," which in the context of the whole document appear to be much the same as the rights affirmed in the other documents.[9] The New York Constitution of 1777 based itself on the right of the people of New York "to institute and establish such a government as they shall deem best calculated to secure the rights, liberties, and happiness of the good people of this colony."[10] Vermont more or less followed Virginia in affirming the "natural, inherent, and unalienable rights" of men, and in insisting that "all government ought to be instituted and supported . . . to enable the individuals who compose it, to enjoy their natural rights." Like the Continental Congress that issued the Declaration of Independence, the Vermonters recognized that "whenever those great ends of government are not obtained, the people have a right . . . to change it, and take such measures as to them may appear necessary to promote their safety and happiness."[11]

Finally, the last two of the revolutionary constitutions also gave prominent place to natural rights. The opening words of the 1780 Massachusetts document could hardly have highlighted the theme of rights more: "The end of the institution . . . of government is to secure the existence of the body-politic; to protect it; and to furnish the individuals who compose it, with the power of enjoying, in safety and tranquility, their natural rights and the blessings of life."[12] Its first article declared the "natural, essential and unalienable rights" which "all men" possess. The list is familiar: "the right of enjoying and defending their lives and liberties; that of acquiring, possessing, and protecting property; in fine, that of seeking their safety and happiness."[13] The New Hampshire State Constitution spoke almost identically of natural rights as its neighbor Massachusetts.[14] The Americans were neither ignorant of nor shy about appealing to natural rights. Jefferson was correct: The American Revolution was indeed about "the rights of man."

Despite this plentitude of apparently incontrovertible evidence many competent historians and other students of the Revolution deny the importance of natural rights. One of the best-known legal historians of our time, John Philip Reid, titled one of his essays, "The Irrelevance of the Declaration," by which he meant the irrelevance of the Declaration read as a document of natural rights and natural law; he also pronounced "the irrelevance of natural law,"[15] not only to the Declaration of Independence rightly understood, but also to the revolutionary cause as a whole. Natural rights is a topic that has received much "emphasis" from historians, but it "was of little concern to people during the pre-revolutionary era."[16] Reid also insisted, in one of his books, that the "British Constitution, not Locke [and his natural rights philosophy] supplied American Whigs with their theoretical motivation."[17] He claimed as well that "(e)very right for which the Americans contended was located in British constitutional theory."[18]

An equally prominent political historian, Jack Greene, has argued that the American position in the Anglo-American dispute was principally informed not by a notion of natural rights but by traditional notions of the rights of Englishmen, the royal charters of the separate colonies, and especially by "long standing constitutional custom" and historical precedent. For Greene, the Anglo-American dispute "is essentially a constitutional one pitting opposing interpretations of the colonial position in the imperial order."[19]

The Americans of the revolutionary era indeed supply important testimony on behalf of those who emphasize the constitutional rights of Englishmen: Those who opposed the British and eventually led the Revolution called themselves Whigs, a title pointing back to those who made the Glorious Revolution of 1688–1689 in Britain, a revolution usually taken (and so taken by colonial Americans) to be a quintessesential expression of British constitutionalism.

We cannot dismiss the tendency to ignore or deny or depreciate natural rights as a mere error, but must see instead a genuine paradox: How can it be that natural rights, prominent on the very surface of the Revolution, can yet plausibly be denied by eminent scholars and politicians? How did the Americans of the revolutionary moment understand natural rights and what role did those rights play in the revolution they made?

TWO THEORIES OF RIGHTS

Reid, Greene, and the others insist the American Revolution was not about natural rights but about constitutional rights, or rights of Englishmen. Those latter rights found their most authoritative expression in the Declaration and Bill of Rights issued at the time of the Glorious Revolution of the late seventeenth century. We can only begin to clarify the role and meaning of natural rights in the American Revolution by beginning with a comparison of the two revolutions and their respective theories. Contrary to what many scholars say, the two revolutions were really quite different, but it is easy to be deceived because each revolution produced a document that purported to "declare" the causes of, and thus explain and in some sense justify, its revolution. The very names of the two documents suggest similarity between them: The Glorious Revolution produced a Declaration of Rights which sounds like very much the same sort of a statement of a philosophy of rights that the American Declaration of Independence is.

To understand what natural rights theory is and the differences between it and the notion of rights in the English document it is helpful to lay out a series of variables that together go to make up what we might call a "regime of rights." The key variables are: 1) the source and 2) the possessors of rights; 3) the bearers of corresponding duties; and 4) the substance and 5) the function of rights. When compared along these dimensions we will see that the English and American theories of rights differ nearly altogether. (Although it is beyond the scope of this essay, a similar comparison between the American and French declarations of rights would display how close if not quite identical these two are.)

Source of Rights

According to the Declaration of Independence the source of rights is "the Creator." The creator as understood in the Declaration appears to be not so much the God of Christianity or revealed religion but the God of nature, for the document speaks of "the laws of nature and of nature's God." "Nature's God" is the God who stands behind nature, is visible in nature, and is accessible to the natural human faculties. The creator is thus "nature" understood as the product of a divinity, whose existence is inferable from nature itself. In principle the God of nature is knowable by all human beings according to public standards of truth; the God of nature is emphatically not the God known only to one or another specific religious tradition.[20]

In the English Declaration of Rights, on the other hand, "the rights and liberties asserted and claimed . . . are the true, ancient and indubitable rights of the people of this kingdom." These are "ancient rights and liberties." The English document is nowhere near so explicit as the American document, but it pointedly does not find the source of rights in nature or nature's God. If anything, they derive their authority, their very being perhaps, from their antiquity: not nature or a divinity but history and prescription.

Possessors of Rights

Perfectly in accord with tracing the source of rights back to nature or nature's God, the American Declaration asserts these rights to be the endowment of all men. Not deriving from a sectarian God, the rights most certainly are not limited to members of any sect, or even to Christians. Contrary to what is often said, the rights belong to men of other races as well, at least according to those who drafted the American document. The drafting committee's version includes as one of the most serious charges against the king the accusation that he had "waged cruel war against human nature itself, violating its most sacred rights of life and liberty in the person of a distant people . . . [by] carrying them into slavery." There can be no doubt that Jefferson and his fellow drafters considered the slaves to be men and rights possessors. True, this clause was dropped from the final version of the Declaration, but not because it was doubted that the slaves possessed natural rights.[21]

Equally in accord with tracing the source of rights to antiquity and prescription, the English document declares rights that belong only to "the people of this kingdom," not to "all men." Most of the rights proclaimed are not even rights of the English people taken individually. For instance, the first "right of the people" announced is "that the pretended power of suspending laws, or the execution of laws, by regal authority, without consent of parliament, is illegal." This and most of the other rights are not possessions or endowments of the English people, but are powers of Parliament, or perhaps better yet, nonpowers of the monarch acting without Parliament. It is as though America would proclaim it a right that the Senate give its advice and consent to treaties. This is clearly a very different matter from the kind of individual rights asserted in the natural rights philosophy, or even in the Constitution's Bill of Rights.

The rights-bearing entities in the English Declaration are for the most part political bodies. It is the "right of the people" that political bodies exercise their own powers, an important feature of constitutional government but not at all the same as natural rights. The commitment to constitutionalism in the Declaration of Rights means, in the first place, a commitment to nonabsolutism: The king does not possess powers to make laws (or ignore laws), to tax, to jail people, to deploy the armed forces of the community all by himself. The core is the sharing of power—those major powers of the community can be exercised only by joint action of king and Parliament.

According to the theory of the constitution as embedded in the Declaration of 1688 the sharing of power between these political bodies bespeaks a deeper kind of sharing—the joint possession of authority by the different estates or classes of the realm. The Declaration is promulgated in the names of "lords spiritual and temporal, and commons." The two first comprise the House of Lords, the last is represented in the House of Commons. Together, they make up the kingdom. The Declaration's constitutionalism at bottom is this sharing or participation in rule among these elements of the community and the monarch. This notion of constitutionalism harkens back at least to Aristotle and Polybius and their theory of the mixed regime, or, as it was often called in England in the seventeenth century, the Mixed Monarchy.

Finally, and perhaps most definitively, English constitutionalism is meant to procure rule of law, rather than the mere rule or will of the monarch, which is best guaranteed by maintaining the integrity and centrality of Parliament as the embodiment of the community whose active and shared consent is needed for laws to exist.

Little of this is contrary to the implications of the natural rights philosophy (especially not the emphasis on rule of law and nonabsolutism), but there are significant differences. According to the Declaration of Independence (and Locke, whom the Americans are following here) human beings possess their rights not as members of an organized community, not as a member of one of the "estates" of the kingdom, but in a far more primitive way. First, as already noted, these are rights of individuals, equally possessed by each and every, whatever their place in society. Second, they are an endowment from their "creator"; that is to say, not only not the gift of history or society, however understood, but inherent in each (as the Virginia Declaration of Rights and other of the state formulations had it). They are also in an important sense primitive and original; human beings according to the Declaration of Independence possess these rights prior to the formation of government (conceptually and perhaps historically), for it is for the sake of these rights that "governments are instituted among men." Jefferson's text indicates this by identifying the rights as belonging to human beings in the situation of equality (no government, no authority) in which they were created. The natural rights belong to human beings in what political philosophers of the age often spoke of as a "state of nature," a notion that does not necessarily imply human beings ever existed in a state of solitariness. The real point of the doctrine of the state of nature is to deny the position taken in the Declaration of Rights. Human rights are not a result of the way society is organized or authority within it arranged; rights are not in any sense a social gift or product—although the security of rights, a rather different matter, is.

Duty Bearers

Every right in the full sense implies a corresponding duty in someone. These duties may vary a good deal in character, ranging at one end from a simple duty of forbearance in (some) others to a duty to supply that to which the rights bearer possesses a right. Thus the right to free speech imposes duties on the government in particular: the duty to forbear from interfering with the exercise of the right. At the other end, the rights accruing to Peter from his contract for lawn care service by Paul imply a duty in Paul to supply the services contracted for.

In the case of the American Declaration the rights belong to "all men" in a condition prior to and independent of political life. The corresponding duty bearers would thus seem to be "all comers"—all other human beings and collectivities (e.g., government) when such are in place. The duties in the first instance appear to be merely of forbearance—Peter's right to life implies only Paul's duty not to interfere with Peter's life, not the duty to give Peter life! Since government is "established" to secure rights according to a kind of contract, government becomes the duty bearer corresponding not only to the primary natural rights but also to a derivative right to security in one's rights. This is more than a duty to forbear; it is the duty to supply the protection. If government fails to do this, then it has not lived up to its obligation and the people have the right to "alter or abolish" the malevolent or incompetent government that fails to perform its duties. This is the so-called right of revolution, which the Declaration of Independence is especially keen to announce and justify.

The duty bearers corresponding to the rights in the English Declaration are not so easy to identify, largely because the rights listed are so various. So far as they are mostly affirmations of limitations on the power of the king, or, conversely, affirmations of parliamentary powers, the duty bearer seems mostly to be the king. Thus, it is the king who is explicitly identified as the one who is not to "suspend the laws . . . without consent of parliament." Likewise, the right of "raising or keeping a standing army within the kingdom in time of peace, unless it be with the consent of parliament" seems to impose a duty of forbearance on the king.

Substance of Rights

The American Declaration lists a series of "unalienable rights" but it specifies that these are only some "among" those with which "all men" are "endowed." There is nonetheless a kind of coherence to the list supplied, as there is to the more common list of "life, liberty, and property." The other documents of the revolutionary era should make clear that the substitution in the Declaration of Independence of a right to the "pursuit of happiness" for a right to property certainly does not necessarily signify a rejection of the latter right.[22] Many of the state constitutions contained both, so obviously the "pursuit of happiness" does not in any sense cancel the right to property. John Adams's formulation in the Massachusetts document is suggestive, for he lists the standard life, liberty, and property, and then says "in fine, that of seeking and obtaining their safety and happiness." The "in fine" suggests that Adams sees the happiness right as a summative right, the resultant and ultimate product of the other rights.

The rights affirmed in the Declaration, or in the parallel documents of the age, have an intellectually satisfying coherence. The first right, the right to life, is a right to what is most one's own, one's life. Given the nature of a human life, it is difficult to see how it could be anything other than one's own, how it could in any sense belong to others. Given the dependence (or base) of life in or on the body, the right to life must contain a right to bodily immunity, the right not to have one's body seized, invaded, controlled by others.

The right to liberty extends the right to life: Not only does one possess a rightful immunity against the depredations of others on one's body, but one has a right to the use of one's body. Human beings are such that we can take control of our bodies and invest our bodies' movements with our intentions and purposes; we can act. The natural right to liberty proclaims the prima facie rightfulness of active use of the body. The right to liberty, like the right to life, carries along with it a corresponding duty in others of forbearance, but in itself it is more active than the right to life.

The right to property involves an extension of rights from the spheres of one's own life, body, and actions to the external world. It proclaims the rightful power of human beings to make the external their own in the same way they can make their bodies their own. Philosophers within the liberal tradition, most memorably Locke and Hegel, took great effort to justify this seemingly problematic extension of right from what is most clearly one's own, one's body and actions, to what is not evidently so, external things. We cannot here follow out that effort, but much of the subsequent history of political thought and practice has consisted in an effort to come to terms with that extension and its justifications, where coming to terms often means, as in the case of Rousseau and Marx, challenging the legitimacy of the extension.

The three basic rights together amount to the affirmation of a kind of personal sovereignty, a rightful control over one's person, actions, and possessions in the service of one's intents and purposes. When seen as an integrated system of immunities and controls the specific rights add up to a comprehensive right to pursuit of happiness, i.e., the right to pursue a shape and way of life self-chosen. Of course this right, as well as the other more specific rights, is not absolute. The rights of specific others, as well as the public good, i.e., the genuine common needs of the community, serve as valid limitations on one's rights.

The rights affirmed in the American Declaration thus do form a kind of system, coherent, complementary, intelligibly related to each other. This quality differentiates the rights in the American Declaration from those in the English

Declaration. The latter lists thirteen rights, ranging from the rights that the king not suspend or dispense with laws, not levy taxes, not keep a standing army without the consent of Parliament, to the rights of subjects "to petition the king" and not to be subjected to excessive bail. The rights, as stated earlier, are part of the English commitment to constitutional government, but they hardly form a system of inherently interrelated parts. Although obviously important, the rights in the Declaration of Rights do not reach the level of fundamentality or universality visible in the Declaration of Independence's rights.

Function of Rights

Natural rights hold an obvious place of high honor in the scheme of political thought put forth in the American Declaration: "in order to secure these rights governments are instituted among men." The securing of natural rights is altogether the end or purpose of legitimate government. Government operates via laws and the use of legitimate coercive authority to control and limit what people may do. The very fact of legitimate government proves that the various rights cannot be "absolutes." As Jefferson said in 1802, "Man . . . has no natural right in opposition to his social duties."[23] The law can properly limit rights and can intrude into the basic sphere of immunities of the individual. But this may be done only when justified; as a provision of the American Constitution later stated, "no person may be deprived of life, liberty, or property without due process of law." Law correctly limits rights not only on behalf of the specific rights of others but also in pursuit of "the public good." Rights securing requires a community and an effective government, and these in turn have many requisites not translatable directly into rights of specific individuals. The most obvious case is defense. Equally important, if less obvious, is what we might call a society's "rights infrastructure"—the pattern of social institutions and characterological types that makes rights securing possible. Although rights securing requires government (coercive authority) it cannot rely solely on government: we do not and cannot have a policeman on every corner. Also, we must have policemen on whom we can rely to secure rather than oppress rights.

Just what the rights infrastructure requires has turned out to be a very controversial matter within liberal political communities. Some, like John Stuart Mill and contemporary libertarians, limit legitimate governing action to more or less direct rights-securing behavior.[24] All else would be rejected as unjustifiable paternalism. Others say that society may legitimately foreclose such options to individuals as the right to use drugs or to view pornography, because widespread practices such as those derogate from the rights infrastructure, for instance, by eroding the necessary personal responsibility of citizens or by diminishing the necessary respect for others as full-blown and autonomous rights bearers. Concern for the rights infrastructure may also require that governments provide services beyond direct protection to rights; for example, Thomas Jefferson was of the view that public education was a requisite to the rights infrastructure.[25] Some level of social support may also be requisite.[26] The natural rights philosophy of the American Revolution does not necessarily mean what some take it to mean—the sole legitimacy of the so-called night watchman state. On the other hand, it does not necessarily imply (or foreclose) what others take it to mean—the modern welfare state.[27] The natural rights theory is quite certain in affirming the ends of political life ("to secure these rights"), but there is nonetheless a great range of possibilities as to what this requires in practice. The coming of liberal politics cannot mean the end of politics, for there remain many difficult political questions to be addressed—and readdressed—within a natural rights polity.[28]

Rights not only function as standards for the conduct of good and legitimate government, but they serve also, as the Declaration makes clear, as standards for the invocation of one of the important rights, the right to alter or abolish governments which are "destructive of these ends," that is, the security of the primary rights. The "present King of Britain" evinces by his "long chain of abuses and usurpations . . . a design to reduce [the Americans] under absolute despotism," a form of government that does not recognize or secure their rights.

Most striking, by contrast, about the English Declaration of Rights is how silent it is on the ends of government. It contains nothing corresponding to the Americans' firm announcement of the ends of political life. The rights do not function as a justification or triggering condition for the invocation of the right of revolution, either, for the document nowhere invokes or affirms such a right or describes the action being taken in 1688 as a revolution. The king is said to have "abdicated," not been deposed or overthrown.

The rights announced, having far more the character of constitutional powers and arrangements than of rights in the ordinary sense, seem to be means rather than ends. One would not say, for example, that the right of Americans to have the Senate advise and consent to treaties is an end of the polity. The Declaration of Rights sets out intently silent about the ends these means serve. The Americans, it is clear, are far more theoretical; they state a position, briefly and concisely to be sure, that has all the earmarks of a theory—rationalist, systematic, comprehensive. The English document has little discernable theory to it.

NATURAL RIGHTS AND
THE AMERICAN REVOLUTION REVISITED

This brief survey of the two rights regimes helpfully clarifies the American natural rights theory by holding it up beside such a starkly contrasting alternative position. The differences are so clear, indeed, that one wonders how competent observers can disagree over which of them was the driving presence in the American Revolution. The resolution of this conundrum lies in the peculiar dynamics of the American Revolution: the Revolution was, in some sense, about both kinds of rights. The Americans, especially at first, merely agitated for the "rights of Englishmen," rights they claimed they had securely enjoyed before British policy began to shift at the end of the French and Indian War a decade or so before the Declaration of Independence. The Americans asserted that these were rights they possessed under their colonial charters or under the general principles of the constitution as specified in the 1688 Declaration of Rights.

By 1776 (well before that, actually) the Americans were also appealing to their natural rights under the social contract theory of politics that they wrote into their revolutionary-era statements. In fact, the copresence of appeals to both constitutional rights (as in the Declaration of Rights) and natural rights (as in the Declaration of Independence) has posed a problem of interpretation for generations of students of the Revolution. The two most prominent explanations for this phenomenon are the Succession Thesis and the Irrelevancy Thesis. According to the first, the Americans began with appeals to positive right—constitutional and charter rights—and, unsuccessful with this appeal, radicalized their position over time, ending up with the appeal to natural rights (including the right of revolution) by the time of the Declaration of Independence.[29] Proponents of the Irrelevancy Thesis, on the other hand, deny that the two kinds of appeals succeeded each other in such a neat temporal order. Indeed, although natural principles of right were aired more frequently as the controversy moved the Americans closer to independence, the Americans never gave up on the appeal to constitutional rights and these latter were always the important ones. The invocation of natural rights lent some rhetorical cachet to the movement but signified little more.

Neither the Succession or the Irrelevancy Thesis captures the place of natural rights in the American Revolution as well as a third position, the Amalgam Thesis. As both the other theories agree, the Americans began with an appeal to their rights as Englishmen, their rights under the constitutional settlement that concluded the Glorious Revolution. The controversy between America and Britain was indeed a legal/constitutional one above all. The single most striking fact about that constitutional battle, however, is that both parties appealed to the same constitutional principles (those in the 1688 Declaration of Rights) and derived their own versions of the normative imperial constitution from that appeal.

The constitutional issues raised in the more than decade-long controversy were far more complex than a brief essay like this can compass, however. To simplify in a way that does not falsify overly much, it is sufficient to note that the British expressed their notion of the constitution in the series of acts of legislation, taxation, and administration that became the center of controversy in the 1760s and 1770s. The most revealing of these was the Declaratory Act of 1766, passed at the same time that Parliament repealed the hated stamp tax. The operative part of the law was drafted to put the Americans on notice that, even though giving in to American wishes and protests about the Stamp Act, Parliament was not conceding an inch on the constitutional principle at stake: "[B]e it declared by the King's most excellent majesty, by and with the advice and consent of the lords spiritual and temporal, and commons, in this present parliament assembled, and by the authority of the same, that the said colonies and plantations in America have been, are, and of right ought to be subordinate unto and dependent upon the imperial crown and parliament of Great Britain, [which], had, hath, and of right ought to have full power and authority to make laws and statutes of sufficient force and validity to bind the colonies and people of America, subjects of the crown in Great Britain, in all cases whatsoever." Strong stuff, but it was a most plausible interpretation of the British constitution as that received authoritative exposition in the Declaration of Rights. The mandate there was rule by joint authority of king and Parliament. The Declaratory Act says no less: The colonies are presumed bound and subject to all relevant acts of king and Parliament. Conceding that the Americans possessed "the rights of Englishmen," their right was fulfilled when the king acted in and through Parliament.

The Americans protested that this could not be the true and proper interpretation of the constitution. On the one hand, it was not the interpretation they were used to; for the most part king and Parliament had refrained from legislating and taxing the colonies and instead had left such matters to the colonial assemblies. On the other hand, the colonists read the constitution through the lens of the natural rights theory of legitimate government. This second kind of argument was attractive for two reasons. First, the argument from precedent was not perfectly valid; there were occasions when Parliament had exercised powers beyond those the theory validated. In such cases the colonists were forced to pick and choose among precedents, a practice that opened them to legitimate criticism so far as precedent per se was the ground of their position.

Moreover, precedent was not a very strong argument in itself, especially when precedent lacked the great antiquity the English Whigs claimed for the constitutional practices they defended. Colonial history ran nowhere as far back as Magna Charta. The argument from precedent per se ran into the related difficulty that the established practices could be explained merely to be policies pursued by king or Parliament, resting on their authority and thus reversible by the same authority.[30]

The colonists saw in the natural rights theory a much stronger base for their position, for they were able to use it to show the superiority of their version of the constitution over that of the British. The British version could not be correct, they thought, once one interpreted or understood the constitution in terms of the rationale for constitutional practices as those came to light in the natural rights theory. To take only the most famous example, why did the constitution, as reiterated in the Declaration of Rights, require the consent of Parliament to tax measures? If the king had the power and right to tax without the consent of Parliament, i.e., of the taxpayers or their representatives, then the right to property was not recognized; if property could be taken at the mere will of the king, then it was not really property, goods to which the owners had an exclusive right, the recognition and protection of which was the business of government. Under such a regime the subjects would not be recognized as free rights bearers. In the language of the day, they were "slaves," neither self-owning nor genuinely owners of pieces of the external world.

Parliament could vote taxes for Englishmen and yet recognize the rights of men because Parliament represented and thus could speak and give consent for the right bearers. But the colonists were not (and they came to see, could not be) represented in Parliament. Parliamentary action vis-à-vis them, under the circumstances, derogated from their status as free and rights-bearing persons just as much as if the king acted alone. The resulting amalgam of constitutional and natural right gave the colonists a perspective on the meaning of the constitution that was by no means necessary or evident from every point of view. The amalgam in effect replaced the older notion of shared power which is found in the Declaration of Rights, with the quite different natural rights commitments.[31]

The important point is that the natural rights philosophy gave the Americans a way to interpret the constitution that was at work even when they were apparently talking only about the constitution and appealing to constitutional rather than natural rights. It was thus not a major shift for the Americans to give more weight to the purely natural rights aspects of their position when the British authorities resisted the American theory of the constitution; it was also not inconsistent with this shift for the Americans to continue to insist on their rights as Englishmen, as their amalgam led them to understand these rights. Both the Succession and Irrelevancy Theses see something of this position, but neither captures how both rights regimes intertwined in this unique amalgam.

The Declaration of Independence gives further insight into the way appeals to constitutional and natural rights interacted. As partisans of the Irrelevancy Thesis insist, that part of the Declaration which lists the misdeeds of the king identifies, for the most part, violations of the constitution, indeed in some cases violations of the very constitutional rights earlier invoked in the Declaration of Rights. Yet these abuses and grievances are introduced in an entirely different way than in the English document. They are "facts to be submitted to a candid world," facts meant to show the king's intent to establish "a tyranny over these states." Showing that is important, in turn, because "when a long train of abuses and usurpations . . . evinces a design to reduce them under absolute despotism, it is their Right, it is their Duty, to throw off such government." The list of abuses is introduced as the center of the effort to show that the conditions the natural rights philosophy says justify "altering or abolishing" the established regime do in fact exist. The Americans take constitutional violations to have such high probative value because they show that the king is unwilling to abide by the moderate, power-sharing, and rule-of-law oriented arrangement captured in the constitution. Violations of the constitution, even if they mean nothing more, imply a dangerous disposition to natural-rights-denying-absolutism.

The constitutional rights do signify more, however. Some of them, e.g., trial by jury (which the king has compromised), are readily seen as devices to help secure natural rights.[32] Perhaps not everything in the Declaration of Rights can be so understood, but much can. To the eighteenth-century mind (not only English and American, but even French, as in Montesquieu) it was one of the marvelous facts of political history that England had evolved, perhaps quite unknowingly, a set of practices very suited to the task of providing for the security of natural rights (especially when these practices were interpreted with a natural rights hermeneutic). Thus, again, the appeal to constitutional rights stands as a kind of surrogate for the appeal to natural rights.

This widely perceived congruence between established practice and the natural standards of right is one factor that made the American Revolution so much more successful than the French Revolution. In the latter case, the new order to be brought in differed so radically from the old order that a massive demolition job had to be performed before anything new could be built. In America this was not the case; although the Americans innovated in many and important ways, they were also free to maintain deep continuities with the precedent order at the level of both political structures and the legal system.

Although continuity with the political and legal past was indeed a prominent part of the story of the American Revolution, one must not overstate that point either. The Revolution saw a significant movement for widespread legal, political and social reform, the most well-known example of which probably is Thomas Jefferson's sponsorship of a "revisal" of the Virginia legal code in the wake of the Revolution.[33] As Jefferson and his fellow legislators saw it, the natural rights philosophy required major changes in the laws of the state, changes ranging from the law of land tenure to the disestablishment of the Anglican church; Jefferson could not achieve all that he sought, such as a major initiative in public education and provision for the gradual abolition of slavery. Nonetheless even his failures—and the failures of the revolutionary generation as a whole—indicate the issues that would find themselves on the agenda of nations making the commitment to natural rights.

Political innovation of great significance also occurred, as the Americans indicated when they adopted as the motto of the new nation the slogan, *novus ordo saeclorum*, a new order for the ages. That very commitment to innovation revealed in summary form the great distance the commitment to "the rights of man" had led the Americans from the political implications the Britons of 1688 drew from their rights regime.

The English Declaration of Rights presented itself as aiming at nothing more than the reaffirmation and reestablishment of old rights, i.e., of the traditional constitutional order, and at "settling the succession of the crown." The latter was necessary because of the alleged "abdication" by James II; the former because of that same king's repeated violation of rights. Careful scholars like Lois Schwoerer insist that the post-1688 regime contained far more innovation than the document announcing it let on;[34] granting that, and granting that the assertion of an unequivocal right to control the succession was also innovative, nonetheless it signifies greatly that the document had no theoretical resources to contain or justify any innovations. Moreover, the innovations it promoted were less those making for a new order and more a filling in and perfecting of the old order. The Declaration, as already suggested, aimed to reaffirm and perfect the existing regime of shared authority among the estates.

The political innovativeness of the Americans found expression above all in a principled commitment to republicanism, that is, to government drawn from the great body of the people and operating according to the principle of majority rule. This commitment to republicanism meant that the political order underwritten in and supported by the English Declaration of Rights was definitively rejected as illegitimate: no king, no nobles, no politically empowered clergy. The Americans concluded that the "rights of man" required a republican government for at least two reasons. Since the rights of man implied also the primal equality of all human beings in a hypothetical state of nature, all political power had to be conceived as deriving from the consent of the governed and to be solely for the sake of securing the rights of the governed and the public good. No one could lay claim to even a particle of political power merely on the basis of birth or nature. Furthermore, political society rests in universal human qualities independent of religious or theological commitment. Hierarchies within churches thus have no more of a claim to political authority than do hereditary nobles or monarchs. The embrace of natural equality does not require a rigidly egalitarian society or polity, but it does require that all political power ultimately be traceable to the people. As James Madison put it in *Federalist 39*: "[I]t is essential . . . that [government] be derived from the great body of the society, not from an inconsiderable proportion or a favored class of it . . . It is sufficient . . . that the persons administering the government be appointed, either directly or indirectly, by the people."[35]

The need for dependence on the people was reinforced by reflection on the purposes of government under the natural rights philosophy. Since government exists to "secure" the rights of the people rather than for some purposes of the rulers, government can be best kept "on task" if it is thoroughly responsible to and dependent on the people. The Americans were convinced that king and Parliament, precisely because of their lack of responsibility to the ruled in America, acted without due regard for the rights and interests of the colonials.

With the commitment to republicanism (in our terms, democracy), revolutionary-era America introduced a new standard into political life, a standard which had an astounding impact on the world. Although that commitment was an inference from natural rights, it also contributed to the American paradox of rights: The Americans spoke so much of republicanism that this came to appear to many to be their primary commitment, perhaps even a commitment conflicting with rights. That was not so, however, since republicanism for them, like the appeal to their rights under the English constitution, was an appeal permeated with natural rights. The paradox within the paradox of natural rights in the American Revolution is that very often even when (or especially when) the Americans were not speaking explicitly of rights, their discourse and actions were driven by their attachment to "the rights of man."

NOTES

1. Jefferson to Roger Weightman, June 24, 1826, in *Thomas Jefferson: Writings*, Literary Classics of the U.S., ed. Merrill Peterson (New York: Viking Press, 1984), p. 1517.

2. John Phillip Reid, "The Irrelevance of the Declaration," in *Law in the American Revolution and the Revolution in Law: A Collection of Review Essays in American Legal History*, ed. Hendrik Hartog (New York: New York University Press, 1981), pp. 49–50.

3. Moses Coit Tyler, "The Declaration of Independence in Light of Modern Criticism," in *A Casebook on the Declaration of Independence*, ed. Robert Ginsberg (New York: Crowell, 1966), p. 94; Joseph Ellis, *American Sphinx: The Character of Thomas Jefferson* (New York: Alfred A. Knopf, 1997), pp. 10, 63–64.

4. [Samuel Adams], "The Rights of the Colonists and a List of Infringements and Violations of Rights," 1772, in *The Roots of the Bill of Rights*, 2 Vols., ed. Bernard Schwartz (New York: Chelsea House, distributed by Scribner, 1980), 1, p. 200.

5. Declaration and Resolves of the First Continental Congress, 1774, in Schwartz, *Roots*, 1, p. 216.

6. Virginia Declaration of Rights, 1776 (Mason Draft), in Schwartz, *Roots*, 2, pp. 241, 242. For the final, very similar version as adopted, see Schwartz, *Roots*, 2, p. 234.

7. Pennsylvania Declaration of Rights, in Schwartz, *Roots*, 2, p. 264.

8. Delaware Declaration of Rights, 1776, in Schwartz, *Roots*, 2, p. 277.

9. Georgia Constitution, 1777, in Schwartz, *Roots*, 2, p. 291.

10. New York Constitution, 1777, in Schwartz, *Roots*, 2, p. 302; cf. 2, p. 303.

11. Vermont Declaration of Rights, 1777, in Schwartz, *Roots*, 2, pp. 319–322.

12. Massachusetts Declaration of Rights, 1780, in Schwartz, *Roots*, 2, p.339.

13. Schwartz, *Roots*, 2, p. 340.

14. Schwartz, *Roots*, 2, pp. 375–376.

15. Reid, "Irrelevance," p. 47.

16. Reid, "Irrelevance," p. 49.

17. John Phillip Reid, *Constitutional History of the American Revolution: The Authority to Legislate* (Madison: University of Wisconsin Press, 1991), p. 5.

18. Reid, *The Authority to Legislate*, pp. 5, 15.

19. Jack Greene, "Origins of the American Revolution: A Constitutional Interpretation" in *The Framing and Ratification of the Constitution* ed. Leonard Levy and Dennis Mahoney (New York: Macmillan, 1987), pp. 36, 38. For similar positions, see, inter alia, John Phillip Reid, *Constitutional History of the American Revolution: The Authority of Rights* (Madison: University of Wisconsin Press, 1986); Stephen Conrad, "Putting Rights Talk in its Place," in *Jeffersonian Legacies*, ed. Peter Onuf (Charlottesville: Univesity Press of Virginia, 1993); Daniel Boorstin, *The Genius of American Politics* (Chicago: University of Chicago Press, 1953), pp. 66–98; Barry A. Shain, *The Myth of American Individualism* (Princeton: Princeton University Press, 1994), p. 246 ff; Pauline Maier, *American Scripture* (New York: Knopf, Distributed by Randon House, 1997), p. 245 and context; Wilmoore Kendall and George Carey, *The Basic Symbols of the American Political Tradition* (Baton Rouge: Louisiana State University Press, 1970).

20. For a more complete exposition, see Michael P. Zuckert, *The Natural Rights Republic* (Notre Dame: University of Notre Dame Press, 1996), pp. 25–26, 59–62; see also Allen Jayne, *Jefferson's Declaration of Independence* (Lexington: University Press of Kentucky, 1998), pp. 38–40, 173–174.

21. On dropping the grievance on slavery, see Maier, *American Scripture*, p. 146; Thomas West, *Vindicating the Founders: Race, Sex, Class and the Origins of America* (Lanham, Md.: Rowman & Littlefield Publishers, 1997), pp. 2–5. Jefferson and slavery has become in the last several decades one of the most widely discussed topics in American history. It is too large to take up here, but the most important point is the following: Whatever Jefferson's practice as a slaveholder, and whatever his views of racial differences, and whatever his opposition to a multiracial society, he never once retreated from the position contained in the excised grievance on slavery—that slavery is a crime against human nature, that the slaves are human beings with natural rights, and that the slave trade was an abomination. The most recent reconsiderations of Jefferson and slavery are Conor Cruise O'Brien, *The Long Affair* (Chicago: University of Chicago Press, 1996); and Paul Finkelman, *Slavery and the Founders: Race and Liberty in the Age of Jefferson* (Armonk, N.Y.: M. E. Sharpe, 1996).

22. For an argument that it does, see Richard Matthews, *The Radical Politics of Thomas Jefferson: A Revisionist View* (Lawrence, Kans.: University Press of Kansas, 1984), p. 27.

23. Jefferson to the Danbury Baptist Association, January 1, 1802, in Peterson, ed., *Jefferson*, p. 510.

24. John Stuart Mill, *On Liberty* (New York: Cambridge University Press, 1989).

25. Jefferson, "A Bill for the more General Diffusion of Knowledge," in Peterson, ed., *Jefferson*, p. 365.

26. See Michael P. Zuckert, *Natural Rights and the New Republicanism* (Princeton: Princeton University Press, 1994), p. 271.

27. For example, Robert Nozick, *Anarchy, State and Utopia* (New York: Basic Books, 1974).

28. Cf. Francis Fukuyama, *The End of History and the Last Man* (New York: Free Press, 1992).

29. A classic version of the Succession Thesis is Carl L. Becker, *The Declaration of Independence* (New York: A. A. Knopf, 1942).

30. See James Wilson, Considerations on the Nature and Extent of the Legislative Authority of the British Parliament, Philadelphia, 1774.

31. For a more comprehensive exposition of the Amalgam Thesis, see Zuckert, *The Natural Rights Republic*, pp. 92–117, 240–243.

32. On the rights-securing character of juries, consider Montesquieu, *The Spirit of the Laws*, tr. Anne M. Cohler, Basia C. Miller, and Harold Stone (New York: Cambridge University Press, 1989), pp. xi, 6.

33. More generally, on the transformative power of this revolution, see Bernard Bailyn, *The Ideological Origins of the American Revolution* (Cambridge, Mass.: Belknap Press of Harvard University Press, 1967), ch. 6; Gordon Wood, *The Radicalism of the American Revolution* (New York: A. A. Knopf, 1991).

34. Lois Schwoerer, *The Declaration of Rights, 1689* (Baltimore: Johns Hopkins University Press, 1981), p. 22.

35. James A. Madison, Alexander Hamilton, and John Jay. *The Federalist Papers*, ed. Clinton Rossiter (New York: Mentor, 1961), p. 241.

Part III

Variations on European Themes,
1871–1917

5

Paris 1871/New Caledonia 1878: Human Rights and the Managerial State

Alice Bullard

During the French colonization of the Melanesian islands of New Caledonia a profound "affective disjuncture" between the French and the Kanak led in French circles to widespread allegations of Kanak affective perversity. Charges of affective perversity—such as male homosexuality, lack of domestic sentiments, and a love of despotism—quickly formed the basis for broader charges of Kanak immorality. These charges, in turn, formed the foundation in French arguments that Kanak society was incapable of properly possessing land. Kanak rights to property ownership—we should note that the Kanak had occupied and produced on this land for some 3,000 years—dissolved in the face of French colonization.[1]

However, despite the overriding importance of affective relationships between the French and the Kanak in the historical circumstances that led to the expropriation of Kanak land and the near extinction of their race, it is a mistake to argue that *granting* human rights depends on affective affinity between peoples. The emphatic identification between individuals, presented by Lynn Hunt in her contribution to this volume as a vital basis for human rights, is treated here as a significant dimension of political relations. However, the ideal of human rights is most essentially grounded in a sense of the universal sanctity of individual human life; it is an ideal of justice. No theory of human rights can be judged adequate if it prioritizes affect or empathy over justice; such a theory degrades the very ideal of justice. Moreover, such a theory impedes a vision in which individuals or downtrodden groups can fight for rights they justly deserve. Rather, an affective theory of rights encourages a view that those who possess rights and power at some magical historical conjuncture develop a laudable ability to empathize with those previously considered inhuman or otherwise inherently undeserving of rights. Any infraction of human rights prior to this magical blossoming of the heart can then be dismissed as simply a product of the historical

79

period rather than the human evil it was. Moreover, historians who point out the violation of rights and the vilification of peoples can be dismissed as hopelessly anachronistic.

An ideal of rights based in justice allows the identification of rights and their violation in widely diverse historical settings. It may well be the case that injustice was humanly unavoidable in certain periods or conditions, or that a defender of one kind of rights was a violator of another. History is full of examples of human imperfection and the less-than-perfect pursuit of ideals; indeed, no individual or culture has a completely privileged access to understanding justice (although that does not remove an injunction to strive for justice). Historians can identify the successes and failures in the development of movements for human rights through analyzing cultural conflicts and struggles for terrain and power. The standard employed in this essay for evaluating the pursuit of human rights is a standard based in justice rather than affect; indeed, affect is seen to just as easily impede rights as to foster their recognition.

FRENCH IMPERIALISM IN NEW CALEDONIA

International power relations drove the French to seize this small group of islands in the southwest Pacific in 1853 to provide a strategic counterbalance to British Australia. Intent on making these islands part of the French Empire, the national government designed colonial policies to encourage settler colonization. Inspired by the example of Australia, the French decided that the most expeditious means of peopling these islands with their own nationals was to transport thousands of prisoners and force them to colonize. Some 4,500 revolutionaries from the Paris Commune of 1871 constituted the most significant group of prisoners shipped off to New Caledonia. Denounced as "savage destroyers of civilization," these revolutionaries suffered deportation to islands inhabited by the redoubted Kanak "savages."

The French metropole and colonial authorities viewed both the "savage" Kanak and the "savage" Communards as deeply immoral beings who were cut off from universal social laws and values. The characters, or personhood, of the Kanak and Communards reflected this "immorality." A proper person, according to the conservative standards of the day, was a "self-possessed" individual; this term reflects both the idea of the possessive individual and the affective dimension that Jean-Jacques Rousseau called self-love (*amour de soi-même*), a natural love of oneself and the instinct of self-preservation, that—guided by reason and modified by compassion—creates humanity and virtue. The affective dimension of the French ideal of the self is prominent in, for example, the writings of Auguste Comte and Charles Renouvier; these theorists place sentiment at the center of the self, arguing that it is the basic motive force in life, that it imbues life with meaning, and that it alone fosters the coherence of an individual's personality. Both the Kanak and the Communards suffered allegations that their affect was perverted and their moral natures fundamentally sullied; the moralizing agenda they faced aimed to restructure their "selves." However, both these groups of so-called savages mounted campaigns of "self-defense"; they resisted as best they could the imposition of the government's moral vision and the colonial order. The comparison of these two groups of "savages" in their quest for rights vis-à-vis the French state deepens our understanding of the uneven historical progress of human rights for both male and female Communards and Kanak. The ideal of the sanctity of the individual, the realities of group identities and affiliations, the double-edged role of affect, and the determining influences of governmental policies—these elements interacted in France and New Caledonia to produce a mixed history of success and setbacks for human rights.

THE REVOLUTION OF 1871 AND MORALIZATION

The Paris Commune of 1871 was the fourth big revolution of modern France. The year of its eruption joined 1789, 1830, and 1848 in the list of famous moments of upheaval, each date marking a time of violence when the French people rose up against authoritarian, repressive, and inept regimes. Each of these revolutions was fought to pursue political and human rights, and each pushed the demands of earlier revolutions further toward social democracy. Begun in a street riot on March 18, 1871, the Commune ended in the mass slaughter of Parisians by government troops during Bloody Week, May 22–27, 1871. It was distinguished from other French revolutions by its short life and by the fact that France at that time was a nation occupied by a conquering army. In September of 1870 Prussian troops, led by Otto von Bismarck, had invaded France, forcing the abdication of Emperor Louis Bonaparte and placing Paris under siege. As a hastily elected government pursued a treaty with the Prussians, the people of Paris remained resolute in their resistance to capitulation. When the authorities of the French national government, known as the *Versaillais*, attempted to disarm the Parisian militias, known as the National Guard, the uprising of the Paris Commune began. This conflict divided French Republicans since some Republicans had been elected to the Versailles government and most of the Communards favored a republican form of government.

The Commune pursued rights for the working class, including fostering workers cooperatives, reducing the hours of work, and providing job education for young people. Legislation banning night work in bakeries stands out among the Commune's achievements, but a diverse array of further reforms were advocated. Secular education was mandated for all French children, including girls. The rights of women to equal pay for equal work were defended. Proposed legislation advocated subsidies for single mothers and day-nurseries for their children. Housing rights, including a moratorium on rents during the siege, figured prominently on the Commune's agenda. Self-government for the city of Paris was yet another goal of the Commune. The principles which guided these reforms were socialist: Most men in the government of the Commune professed a Prudhonian socialism; some were Marxists; others followed the French Jacobin tradition of Auguste Blanqui. Contemporaries described the exuberance of the revolutionaries as festive and carnivalesque; the workers celebrated their control of Paris and gleefully pursued their ideal society. Cafés and music halls sometimes rang with song and laughter even when the skies glowed red from exploding bombs. Laughter, according to the poet Villiers de l'Isle-Adam, was the people's last and most effective defense against the *Versaillais*.

The short-lived Commune was further distinguished by the fact that it was a revolution against a republican government. Most of the Communards favored some version of republican government, but they believed the Versailles government (which was *technically* a republic) incapable of guaranteeing the nation's integrity or the continuation of the Republican regime. In the hastily elected Constituent Assembly, Monarchists dominated by a two-to-one majority over the Republicans. The deep antipathy between Monarchists and Republicans made the fate of this provisional government highly uncertain and a Monarchist coup seemed very likely. Nonetheless, the form of the government was republican; an elected president, Adolphe Thiers, presided over an elected Constituent Assembly. As a revolution against a republican government the Paris Commune earned the admiration of international socialists across Europe. Karl Marx praised the Commune as the first dictatorship of the proletariat; Vladimir Lenin later studied the details of the Commune to better pursue the 1917 revolution in Russia. In Soviet-era Eastern Europe the names of major streets and plazas memorialized the Paris Commune as the precursor to successful socialism.

Ironically, the government that crushed the Commune so mercilessly lived on to become the first successful republican government on the European continent in modern times; it endured until the 1940 invasion by Nazi Germany. Indeed, it has been argued often that the success of the Third Republic grew from its resolute resistance to and punishment of the Communards. The republican sympathies of the Communards was not enough to win them the allegiance of the Republican members of the Assembly. Those in the Assembly voiced respect for law and order, while those in Paris preferred revolutionary resistance to a regime they thought traitorous. These divisions of loyalties ensured that the participants of the Paris Commune enjoyed the unenviable distinction of exciting the hatred not just of Monarchists and Bonapartists but also of some Republicans. As President Thiers was fond of asserting, in order to survive the French republic needed to be conservative. The final assault on Paris by the troops of the national government was merciless. Some 30,000 Parisians were killed in one week.

The government refused to recognize the Commune as a political event; in its eyes the Communards were criminal destroyers of French civilization, not actors in a political drama. Those arrested were tried as criminals by military courts. Hence, while the Third Republic constituted itself according to the principles of 1789, it simultaneously prosecuted the Communards for their criminal insurrection.

From 1870 to 1940 the Third Republic pursued governmental policies ostensibly based in the principles of 1789 but in fact heavily indebted to convictions about "moralization" and the "good citizen" that began developing in the mid-nineteenth century. The carnivalesque explosion of "rights" under the Paris Commune met its counterpart in the managerial practices of the Third Republic, where the desires for "order" and "morality" were allowed to limit the attainment of rights. Socialist goals, the goals of French women, the goals of colonized men and colonized women, all were circumscribed in the name of moral order. It is the peculiarity of the "Moral Order" that the constraints on each of these groups were defined and maintained according to different standards. The regime of Moral Order recognized difference; the managerial state categorized people according to their purported characteristics and capacities and assigned each category specific duties and rights. This historical reality contrasts to the Western ideal of government that grants the same rights and duties to each individual; such an ideal government would limit itself to establishing a legal framework within which each individual may pursue his or her own goals. Accepting this ideal of government without hesitation, however, begs the question, "What rights are human rights?"—i.e., what form of government best secures (what?) rights to (which?) individuals? The battles between the revolutionary Paris Commune and the national government of Moral Order was a struggle over such questions; the Melanesian opposition to French colonization was yet another contest over rights and ideals.

The 1789 French revolution swept away the old feudal order and instituted formal equality of all citizens under the law. In this revolution France groped toward a political solution to economic and social crisis and in the process produced the much celebrated "Declaration of the Rights of Man and Citizen." In response to the revolution of 1871 the French state chose a penal rather than a political solution. The nominally "republican" government of France responded to the 1871 revolution with management techniques: first to contain the revolution within the confines of Paris (a task made simpler by the presence of Prussian armies around the city perimeter) and next to "neutralize" the unruly and remove those still living from proximity to other citizens susceptible to the revolutionary contagion. After the slaughters of Bloody Week military courts sentenced about 4,500 of the Communards to deportation to New Caledonia. French penal colonization in New Caledonia allowed the large-scale management of unruly citizens along with state territorial expansion; rather than empowering

citizens by granting them rights this management technique attempted to foster the docility of the socially disenfranchised and the growth of state power.

In the revolution of 1789 the people rose up to demand innate and inalienable human rights against a decrepit monarchy. In 1871 the French state used
the alleged moral depravities of the people as a reason to revoke basic civil rights.
Above all, the French authorities viewed the Communards as attacking morality by

> denying the truths which up to this time have been the honor of mankind; they
> attack not only the secular bases of society, property and the family, they pit them-
> selves against the existence of God and the immortality of the soul. Rejecting the
> distinction between good and evil, between liberty and the moral value of human
> action, they attack humanity itself.[2]

The Constituent Assembly designed the deportation to instill in the
Communards belief in certain fundamental elements of "civilized" France: family, religion, work, property, and the state. The moralizing agenda of the penal
colony aimed to reform the Communards' characters, to turn socialists dedicated
to fraternal social bonds into "possessive individuals" who identified primarily
with property and work.

The exiled Communards suffered incarceration, caged transport to the penal
colony, and a closely controlled system of forced settlement in the colony.
Through long years of hardship, exacerbated by scant food, loneliness, and ran-
dom instances of torture by the prison guards, most of the Communards held
resolutely to their political convictions and resisted the "moralizing process" of
the penal regime. In letters, memoirs, novels, and newspaper articles Communards railed against what they viewed as the savagery of the French administration, revindicated their actions during the Commune, and proclaimed their
faith in socialist politics. They demanded over and over to be returned to France
so that they could resume their lives and their political activities. Finally, in 1879
and 1880 the government amnestied almost all of the deported Communards.
The hard-fought Republican conquest of the French Parliament—the Republicans dominated both the House of Deputies and the Senate by late 1879—made
this amnesty politically viable. Moreover, the amnesty signaled the
Communards's new ability to participate fully in French social and political life,
including holding elected office.

The amnesty of the Communards abruptly ended the project of moralization
and allowed their reintegration into French political life. If Monarchists had
maintained control of the French government and eventually suceeded in their
coercive attempt at character reform, one might argue that the extension of rights
to the Communards depended on a newly developed affective affinity between
the exilers and the exiled. In fact, however, the amnesty of the Communards
was unrelated to the feelings of Monarchist politicians; they simply no longer

possessed the political power to enforce their desires. The reintegration of the Communards into France renewed the socialist movement in the metropole; those who turned to politics upon their amnesty turned in the overwhelming majority to socialist causes and parties. Unless one focuses on women's rights (the few deported female Communards were no more capable of participating in French electoral politics than was any other female subject of the French state), the exile and amnesty of the Communards can be read as a protracted struggle to expand the boundaries of political discourse to include working class and socialist concerns.

COMMUNARDS AND KANAK

The comparison between the Parisian working class and the Kanak in their struggles for rights leads through similar terrain, but ultimately to a radical disjuncture. These contrasting histories demonstrate that a unified culture or history is a precondition for a successful human rights revolution. Without a shared cultural or political language, regardless of the possible affinities or dislikes between the disputing parties, the standard of "human rights" proves insufficient to bridge chasms of cultural difference and divergent values.

The lower classes in France had long lived within the framework of state government and concentrated property ownership. Their struggles for political and economic empowerment, of which the Paris Commune of 1871 is an excellent example, took shape within the French and European political culture. France had a revolutionary tradition dating to 1789, and the Paris Commune was a recognizable if redoubted descendant of this venerated ancestor. Even the carnivalesque dimension to the Commune had French roots in premodern festivals of unreason. If the Paris Commune was defeated, and if the plans of the Communards were viewed as the "savage destruction of civilization," and the deported revolutionaries treated as criminals, nonetheless, the political actors ultimately successfully claimed a commonality with the rest of France. The amnesty of the Communards in 1879 and 1880 allowed their assimilation into French political life; many sought and won electoral offices; others turned to political journalism to pursue their goals.

In 1878 a group of Kanak clans fought a concerted and prolonged war to throw off the colonial government. Chief Ataï forged alliances with several other Kanak leaders and planned a coordinated attack on the French settlements. The uprising began with a surprise attack on a settlement whose owners had grown familiar with Kanak on the premises and in their houses. Posing as friendly neighbors, Kanak surrounded the table at which some colonists were dining and began their attack with no advance warning. After the insurrection, the French press emphasized the diabolical nature of such an attack. Indeed, accepted European military practice did not include such surprise attacks on unsuspecting civilians. But the Kanak, who desired nothing less than complete independence, pursued their insurrection through their traditional methods. According to their own culture, such surprise attacks traditionally marked the commencement of hostilities. Trickery, quick attacks followed by retreat, and short campaigns characterized the Kanak expectations in war.

This insurrection drew on Kanak goals, Kanak culture, and Kanak techniques in warfare. Moreover, measured from a Kanak perspective the initial encounters pointed to triumph over the French. Among the Kanak the first deaths in battles were often the last; the loss of one or two warriors sufficed for the cessation of hostilities. The French, however, answered the Kanak surprise attacks with months of warfare. Seeing the chance to gain territory and members, Kanak clans that had been uninvolved in the initial conflict eventually joined with the French forces to defeat Ataï's alliance. The tribes of Canala took the lead in this Franco-Kanak alliance and tracked down and forced the surrender of Ataï's men. Although the victory would have been unlikely without allies among the Kanak, the French celebrated this event as a racial conquest and as the triumph of civilization over savagery.

The French response to the insurrection aimed to break up the Kanak clans by destroying their attachments to their lands and to their customs, thereby securing recognition of French state authority and of the "superiority" of French civilization. Retributive killings preceded the deportation of the surviving Kanak to other islands. These sanctions ultimately extended even to the clans who had allied themselves with the French. Throughout the following decades, the colonial government pursued the expropriation of more and more Kanak land; by the early twentieth century nearly all land was under European ownership. The Kanak were removed to reservations and subjected to a special legal code, the code d'indigénat, designed to address their allegedly depraved or atavistic moral condition. Worse than criminal, the Kanak morality was alleged to be "primitive" or "nonevolved." The land-hungry colonial administration conveniently decided that such morally undeveloped people could not possibly thrive in a political system that granted them the full rights of citizenship. Hence, the program for the "moralization" of the Kanak amounted to the institution of a feudal system in which the Kanak became serfs subjected to the authority of the local landlord-colonists and the police.

Not until World War II, when the United States and New Zealand used the islands as a military base, did this state of affairs improve. The militaries employed the Kanak on construction sites for their bases and treated the laborers fairly, awakening them to the possibility of ameliorated labor conditions. This heightened awareness of possible change led in the 1960s to agitation for legal reforms and even for independence. In the 1980s the long-festering discontent of the Kanak exploded in violent conflicts with the colonial regime. Significantly, this renewed Kanak independence movement incorporated such French repub-lican symbols as the revolutionary hat (the Phrygian bonnet), along with the slogan from 1789, "liberty, equality, and fraternity" (with independence tagged on). Independence was not won, but the Mitterand government negotiated a settlement that instituted political and economic power sharing between the Kanak and the Caldoche (settlers of European descent). The reforms divided electoral terrain, so that a Kanak majority was assured in at least one province and set a date for a referendum on independence. These rights, like those pre-viously won by the French working classes, were defined within the terms of French rule; in the spring of 1998 a new agreement negotiated with the conser-vative Chirac government postponed the referendum on independence for an-other twenty years.

In 1878 neither common historical nor cultural ground existed between the Kanak and the French to allow the reintegration of the defeated into political life. Unlike the Communards, whose claims to rights extended and broadened the tradition of 1789, the Kanak pursued claims exterior to the French state and French tradition. The French state, ostensibly anchored in the principles of 1789, appeared to the Kanak primarily as a conqueror and usurper of rights (most egre-giously, the right to own property). The French read Kanak resistance not as political action but as the manifestation of savage violence and destruction in the face of superior civilization. More than 150 years of French rule in the is-lands has produced a Kanak political class that operates within the terms of French political discourse. However, this participation is still tentative; the Kanak still preserve some of their indigenous system of governance even as they negotiate within the French system for greater empowerment.

KANAK RIGHTS: INDIVIDUAL AND TRIBE/MORALITY AND AFFECT

The first governor of New Caledonia remarked on the highly developed divi-sion of property among the Kanak saying, "There is not so much as a coconut tree without its proper owner." This early recognition of private property among the Kanak faded quickly from French consciousness; by 1867 a colonial law stipu-lated that all property held by the Kanak was held as communal, tribal prop-erty. Since the possessive individual is the fundamental building block for a re-gime of human rights, this colonial development portended harsh treatment of the Kanak in the years to come. Already in 1860 the government instituted a regime of forced labor for Kanak in the vicinity of colonial outposts. Phrased with a good deal of politeness, this legislation, out of "the great interest to civilize and soften the customs of the natives, to bring them closer to us without coer-cion," invited the heads of clans to furnish workers to the state.[3] Chiefs who did not comply with the order were subject to penal discipline. In 1867 the colonial government took another decisive step in removing the ("inalienable") rights of the Kanak by inscribing the "tribe" as "a collective moral being." The law described this being as a legal aggregation that possessed property and that was "organized in the only form which was and which will be proper to the state of the indigenous population."[4] This law on tribal identity revoked all rights to private property from individual Kanak; all the specific owners of coconut trees and plantations lost their property rights in 1867. This emphasis on tribal identity enabled the French colonial government to conserve resources while asserting authority over the Kanak. The government could wield both carrot and stick over the Kanak chiefs to ensure that they kept their subjects properly submissive to colonial rule. With the aid of these chiefs, the French authorities could dispense with the difficulties of establishing governmental authority over each individual Kanak.

Disruptive and disempowering as the law on collective moral identity was, its greatest evil lay not in the specific poverty it created but in the legal precedent it set. From 1867 the legal tradition in New Caledonia moved steadily away from recognizing the Kanak as individuals with rights; it developed an increasingly elaborate and harsh set of laws designed specifically for this allegedly morally backward people. The extensive legislation on citizenship and naturalization written in 1874 makes no effort to describe how a Kanak might become a French citizen (despite the liberal naturalization policies for immigrants from other lands); the collective identity of the tribe precluded citizenship.[5] In October of 1887 the *code d'indigénat*, prescribing crimes, punishments, and judicial authority specific to the Kanak, was set into place.[6] Like other "native laws" in the French Empire, this code identified specific "Kanak" crimes such as leaving one's reservation without authorization, carrying Kanak arms or going without clothing in areas inhabited by Europeans, practicing witchcraft or sorcery, entering a bar or any place that sold liquor, entering a European house or place of business without express invitation, and disturbing work in any habitation, workshop, construction area, factory, or shop. In 1898 the laws on *cantonnement* were strengthened and clarified; it was explicitly prohibited for a Kanak to live any place other than his or her assigned reservation, and European colonists were prohibited as well from allowing the habitation of Kanak in areas not designated as reserves. Within the capital city of Nouméa a law in 1888 had already made presence on the streets or in the suburbs after 8 P.M. illegal to any Kanak without an authorization from his or her employer. In 1898 the law was strengthened, prohibiting any Kanak to be in any European center of habitation after dusk. Violators were subject to immediate arrest and incarceration. In the 1890s land expropriations were again pursued with renewed vigor; by 1913 five-sixths of all land in the islands belonged to Europeans.

What can be said about this legislation is that it reflects a French interest in managing the Kanak as a *racial* group, rather than a commitment to instituting clear principles of rights-based government. In this instance, and in contrast to the "management" of the Paris Communards, the Kanak were denied rights as individuals and citizens into the second half of the twentieth century. Drawing from the Enlightenment rationalist tradition, the colonial administration employed various human sciences to achieve governmental goals. The government exploited the ethnographic understanding of "tribe" to render the Kanak tractable and to pierce the intimacy of their village counsels. Demographic and geographic surveys of the clans and their lands facilitated the creation of the reservation system. Medical doctors employed by the government documented the endemic illnesses among the Kanak, and included as well analyses of their sexual behavior, their eating habits, and their proclivity toward alcoholism.

As the legal fiction of "collective moral identities" took root in New Caledonia law, the conviction that the Kanak lacked individual indentity and rationality spread. By the end of the nineteenth century the legal idea of collective moral identities had helped to produce a widespread popular conviction that the Kanak possessed a "primitive" or "feudal" morality that prohibited them from understanding or desiring individual rights. The Kanak individual, from this perspective, seemed somehow deficient; writers from that period dwelled on the perversions of Kanak sentiment and linked these perversions to broader criticisms of Kanak culture and society. We know, however, that the precolonial Kanak did possess private property. Moreover, colonial records contain numerous instances of Kanak complaints against French colonists who ignored property boundaries and allowed their cattle to graze on laboriously cultivated yam and taro fields.

Colonial law and colonists' opinion held that the Kanak had no sense of individual rights. However, the instances of Kanak revindication of their rights are numerous. This conflict is exemplified by the Wagap Affair of 1899. On November 13, 1899, a group of Kanak sent telegrams to the head judicial authority in New Caledonia complaining of the harassment of their chiefs for nonpayment of the head tax. On November 14 three of the chiefs, Kéla, Robert, and Silveri, were indeed hauled off to prison, each sentenced to serve fifteen days and fined fifty francs. These arrests raised a crowd of some 200 Kanak men to protest, traditional clubs (*case-têtes*) in hand, at the police station. Why did the Kanak put up a show of armed resistance? The simple answer is that the head tax was a heavy tax, worth far more than the productive capacity of the land granted to each Kanak through the reservation system. Without hiring out to colonists as day labor, they could not pay the tax. Moreover, the tax was highly inequitable in comparison with other populations on the islands; it forced Kanak to pay between four and twenty times the land tax to which colonists were subjected.[7]

Government officials in charge of investigating the Wagap Affair asserted, however, that the Kanak were incapable of conceiving of protest, much less of organizing such an event. They insisted that Kanak were incapable of writing and that surely some other conspirators had dictated the letters. Unless one places this episode within a larger colonial environment in which intimidation, exclusion, and repression were carried to such an extent that telegrams demanding protection and justice were simply unthinkable, that is, a situation in which no Kanak would ever seek redress for wrongs committed, it is difficult to take seriously the government's assertion that "no Kanak" could dictate such a telegram. A trace of the colonial present lives in the government officials' claim: one can read in it the transformation of the Kanak into the stupid and servile savages the colonial administration so reviled.

Moreover, the government officials' explanation of the Kanak protest reveals a deep fear held by the colonial regime; as the officials explained, the reason for the protest was

> that (and if they [the Kanak] have not understood this, others have understood it for them) opinion reigns supreme under a regime of liberty like ours; in reality, moral forces govern our nation, and the simple *simulacre* of action, when it is supported by sufficient forces in the press and in the general public, can lead to significant results. Their demonstrations, negligible in themselves, are the necessary point of leverage that could be an irresistible force if wielded in Paris.

Liberal political activities threatened the colonial policies toward the Kanak, and the colonial government wanted to ensure that the Kanak were viewed, even in France, as incapable and brutish "savages." The government emphasized that the Kanak "are only the absolutely unconscious actors in a drama which has been staged and even scripted by authors who want to remain anonymous."[8]

The so-called anonymous playwrights and stage directors were supposedly none other than the group of local Catholic missionaries. This accusation was a savvy political ploy on the part of the colonial government, which resented the power of the missionaries in Kanak communities. Catholic theology did offer powerful ideals for the protection of the Kanak people. The Thomistic tradition of natural law coupled with the Christian belief in the innate dignity of the human soul closely fit the Enlightenment paradigm for human rights; indeed, the Christian message of the sanctity and dignity of human individuals is one of the roots of European human rights philosophy. However, despite these theological ideals (no doubt sincerely held by most of the missionaries) the realities of colonial politics ensured that the missionaries respected administrative authority. The priests vigorously denied any role in the protests and marshaled evidence proving they had advised the Kanak to pay the tax. In this way they defended themselves against attacks on their loyalty to France and the colonial project. The allegations of "anonymous authors" of the affair acted as a smokescreen to distract contemporaries from more invidious processes at work here: the denial of the moral sense and political agency of the Kanak and the repression of liberal public opinion both in New Caledonia and in France.

This relatively simple series of events formed part of a broader process of conceptually cordoning off the majority of the Kanak from "French" New Caledonia through emphasizing their savagery and their inassimilable characters. One product of these practices was a widely accepted language of inherent and coexisting prehistoric and feudal characteristics of the Kanak people, so that even their defenders worked within the discourse of primitivism and feudalism.

Though the code d'indigénat denied the Kanak human and civil rights, we should also consider the possibility that the effects of this legislation were not necessarily more or less destructive toward their culture than a strictly liberal legal system would have been. Tribal councils retained some juridical authority, mainly in areas of family law and inheritance. The legislation constituting the Kanak as tribes preserved social and family groups among the Kanak, in this way encouraging Kanak solidarity and identity. This is evident even today in New Caledonia, where life in the tribe is experienced as warmly sociable and emotionally gratifying; the center of emotional loyalty for many Kanak has remained the clan, rather than the individual. (However, important exceptions to this preference for living with their tribes are found among Kanak women, some of whom seek to escape rigid patriarchal authority by opting for life in the French-dominated city. Kanak women who seek redress against sexual violence and who seek divorces are leading a Melanesian exodus away from tribal authority to the jurisdiction of French civil law.) The use of money by those living in the tribe is only necessary to pay taxes and to buy manufactured items, such as alcohol or books for school. Communal administration of property and distribution of agricultural products ensures that needs are otherwise met. Evidence of intermarriage between Kanak and French in the nineteenth century suggests that the populations may well have formed a predominately hybrid community if the tribe legislation had not singled the Kanak out for restricted legal status. Those who "assimilated" to the Kanak were subject to treatment as a Kanak. As immigrants from Southeast Asia and other Pacific islands settled in New Caledonia, the restrictive legislation on the Kanak again inhibited the mixing of bodies and cultural identities. The legislation, by constituting the Kanak as a people apart from the general colonial population, helped preserve the strong sense of separate identity from which the Kanak have led their recent independence movement. Ironically, while only individuals could attain human rights and citizenship, the "collective moral being" of the Kanak clan provided an alternate basis for cultural and political empowerment. Defined by the French in derogatory and racist terms, within their clans and broader communities the Kanak nurtured reverence for their traditions and cohesion among their people.

THE LIMITS OF HUMAN RIGHTS DISCOURSE

The legislation that constituted the Kanak into tribes ("collective moral beings") cut in two directions: On the one hand it precluded individual Kanak from reclaiming their rights, while on the other it fostered a Kanak identity strong enough to support an independence movement. Contemplating this historical record, we are confronted with a limit to the applicability of the human rights standard. The ability of human rights language to act as a vehicle for racist sentiment points out another limit of the discourse. In the mid-1880s a humanitarian discourse began to emerge in France regarding the events of the 1878 insurrection. The new humanitarianism flowed from the pens of Leon Moncelon and Charles Lemire, both of whom had served on the committee that created Kanak reservations, as well as from former Communard prisoners Charles Amouroux and Henri Place. Through writing political polemics and ethnographic literature from a humanitarian perspective, these men helped to create a counterdiscourse that sought to defend the Kanak against extinction, to valorize *métissage* in the colony, and to secure rights to education and inalienable rights to property. To this day, human rights are widely considered one of the highest forms of ethical recognition within the political domain; yet we should remember Hannah Arendt's assertion in *Eichmann in Jerusalem* that "the compromised phraseology of the rights of man . . . were claimed only by people who were too weak to defend their 'rights of Englishmen' and to enforce their own laws."[9] When these Frenchmen revindicated the "human rights" of the Kanak they presumed the obviation of an independent Kanak sociocultural system. To enjoy "human rights" the Kanak needed first to concede that their culture was lowly and unworthy, then they had to accept a tutelage in "French civilization" from which eventually they might emerge in full possession of human and civil rights.

In an article with the admirable aim of supporting property rights for the Kanak, Moncelon pursued a lengthy criticism of the affective dimensions of Kanak life and derided the morality of the Kanak.[10] Moncelon insinuated that homosocial (if not homosexual) proclivities of the Kanak men prevented them from seeking sexual companionship with Kanak women and that this was the fundamental reason for the recent drastic decline in Kanak population. In another article, Moncelon advocated assimilation of the Kanak people and praised the rising number of mixed children in the colony, while indulging a racist impulse by calling Kanak children "vermin."[11] Lemire, who contended that he and Moncelon (among others) had been consistent defenders of Kanak property rights on the committee in charge of delimiting reservations, summarized his views on Kanak rights by asserting that "it would not be wise to sacrifice the interests of European colonization to those of the Kanak. We should protect these minor children, we should not emancipate them."[12]

Amouroux and Place characterized the Kanak as "these primitive men with their underdeveloped brains." They asserted that "the Kanak race is scientifically inferior to the white race, and even to many of the black races. On this point, we believe, everyone agrees." They also testified to the widespread conviction that the Kanak would soon die out, calling them "a decadent race, destined to disappear by the law of evolution that insures the progress of humanity." The authors demanded that "French law should be applied to everyone." In apparent contradiction they argued that "the colonists should not forget that morally, at least at this time, the Kanak is inferior, thus he must be made to feel this and be treated as a minor. However, the guardian should respect the rights of the Kanak. . . . Each French colonist is an active member of a republican country that has proclaimed the abolition of slavery and the equality of races, each is thus a natural guardian of the Kanak until the day he is emancipated by education." The paradox of unequal equal races here was settled, at least in terms of policy recommendations, by the idea of "education." "Moral education" was the duty of each French citizen toward the Kanak. "Under our Republic composed of citizens, each has the responsibility to participate in moral and intellectual government, and to ensure the rights of all are respected."[13]

This racism mirrors the humanitarian ideology with which the whole process of colonization began. A humanitarian promise to uplift the Kanak dominated the Catholic missionaries who began arriving on the islands in the 1840s and the colonial government installed in 1853. Yet the promise to uplift the Kanak always rested on the appraisal of these people as a fallen or nonevolved race. The missionaries viewed the Kanak as sinful; they speculated whether some horrible transgression had prompted God to curse the whole people by removing their access to the universal moral code known as "natural law." Eugene Alcan, in a book written to generate support for the Catholic mission, argued that "it is impossible to imagine the profound chasm into which this unhappy people has fallen." An upright and educated heart could not shrink from the duty of battling such savagery, contended Alcan, "letting them live freely, you all understand, would be a grave sin against humanity."[14] The colonial administrators, for their part, preferred to cast the Kanak as unevolved in their customs and their minds rather than as "sinful." In the eyes of the missionaries the immediate benefit of "moralization" for the Kanak was eternal salvation. This bore relevance in the political domain since, as mentioned previously, Catholic theology offered powerful ideals for the protection of the Kanak people. In the 1853 treaties for government between Kanak clans and the French, the administrators assigned the Kanak the status of "children" in relation to the state. Such attitudes toward the Kanak led to the indiscriminate denigration of all their attributes in the all-out effort to secure their subordination to the French.

It can be stated unequivocally that the first step of the moralizing and civilizing process did not ameliorate the condition of Kanak lives in some way, but consisted in forcing the Kanak to recognize their "fallen" state. Only if the Kanak acknowledged their own inferiority vis-à-vis the French, if they accepted the label "savage," could they embark on the long process of acquiring "civilization." The humanitarian defense of Kanak rights contrasts starkly to the Kanak "self-defense" mounted in its independence movements; the good sought in independence cannot be reconciled with nor replaced by the good offered by (even the best) humanitarian efforts of civilization.

VIEWED INVERSELY:
KANAK AND COMMUNARDS SEEKING RIGHTS

For the Kanak the empowering potential of human rights and humanitarianism was stymied by the radical differences between the Kanak and the French. The moralizing intent of the governmental state worked for 8 years on the Communards and for 140 on the Kanak. Henri Rochefort-Lucay, one of the most prominent Communards in New Caledonia, created a testimony to the unachieved desire to escape the boundaries of the state in his 1880 novel, *L'évadé; Roman Canaque*. In this fictional domain we discover that the Kanak and the Communards were natural allies against the expansionist state; the logic of colonization is revealed to parallel the logic of capitalist oppression of the working classes. The Kanak heroine of this novel, Ratouma, forms an alliance with the daughter of a Communard to free their men held captive by the French authorities. Ratouma attempts to seize power; she does not wait to be moralized or civilized before asserting her claim to rights. The pair eschew the submission thought proper to revolutionaries, primitives and women and pursue a daring assault on the main prison of the colony, freeing their fathers, sons and lovers.

For our purposes it is of little concern that this fictional revolt ends in bloodshed and failure. What matters is the heroism demonstrated through the alliance of "savages" and revolutionaries. Within liberal political discourse, the individuality of the Kanak is suppressed out of a greater desire to subject them to French rule. From the humanitarian point of view, the Kanak was always viewed as inadequate and misguided. Similarly, from within the precincts of the "moral order" the Communards were criminals, savage destroyers of civilization. Rochefort's novel memorializes the oppositional potential of Kanak and Communards; his characters seek their goals, their good, their truly valuable "rights" beyond the governmental boundaries established by the state.

Rochefort's iconoclasm goes deeper than this already searing criticism of humanitarianism. The Kanak and Communard who seize power in his novel are women. Two previous allusions to the position of women have been made in this essay, the first to women Communards deported to New Caledonia, the second to Kanak women faced with the choice of living with their clan or in French-dominated cities. Communard men were amnestied and allowed full political activity in France while Communard women were amnestied but still excluded from official political processes. Kanak men express high satisfaction with life in the quasi-traditional clan; women criticize the same life as oppressive and even humiliating. However, despite the difficulty of accommodating women within a language of human rights (because of a governmental commitment to preserving male familial authority), Kanak women have long sought out French locales in order to free themselves from clannish-patriarchal authority. Even in the early days of colonization Kanak women willingly established households with French men, reputedly because they were better treated there than in their own culture. Kanak women I have spoken with express respect for the tribal life and leaders, yet remain firm in their decisions to live subject to French law in Nouméa. Life in Nouméa offers an escape from the injunction to defer to men and to do their bidding in daily matters, just as it comes with the risk of racist tensions and discrimination.

What these women want, they insist, is the right to speak. Speech, *la parole*, for Kanak is weighted with ritual significance. Speech is the means of creating compacts, alliances, and trade agreements; in other words, far from being simple self-expression, in Kanak culture it represents the authority to act in the social realm. Traditionally this right is reserved for Kanak men. In contemporary New Caledonia, the French state does guarantee a certain degree of education and civil liberties for Kanak women and men. Working within this sphere of liberal rights, a small group of women is reinterpreting Kanak culture through art and literature. However, this right is gained at the expense of the transformation of the "speaking" from a Kanak social act to liberal self-expression. The Kanak women cannot claim to speak for their clans, nor can they easily transfer their cultural successes in Nouméa into authoritative status within their clans. Liberal human rights, one sees yet again, have clear limits; they can only deliver a good within the sociocultural framework of the liberal state.

Historically, class, sex, and race have been the most frequent grounds for disqualifying persons from the coveted status of citizen-individual. The histories of the so-called savage Communards and Kanak highlight the role of the *governmental* state in relation to the struggles by those belonging to a specific class, race, and/or gender to attain human rights. In this struggle the idea of the individual as the "rights-bearing subject" is inadequate for understanding the historical dynamics and empathy falls short as a standard for historical evaluation. We must recognize the historical role of collective identities, based in class, gender and "tribe," as the grounds for special status laws and rights. "Governmentality"—the complex of administrative and regulatory institutions providing controls, assistance, welfare, hygienic aids, education and discipline— expresses this model. Populations, not just individuals, played a central role in the nineteenth-century history of human rights in France and its colonies.

CONCLUSION

The language of human rights appears particularly ill suited to situations of radical cultural difference, yet this essay does not seek to relativize human rights or standards for their evaluation. Rather, it points to the limits beyond which human rights cannot act as an empowering discourse. In nineteenth-century language "savagery" marked such a limit. It would be a grave error to accept the unqualified condemnation of indigenous Kanak culture as sinful, immoral, and historically superseded by European civilization. Denied status as political agents, these people gained little or no protection from human rights. Unlike the Communards, indigenous to French culture and schooled in the processes and symbols of French politics, the Kanak existed exterior to "civilization." Their most fundamental demand was to retain this exteriority. Their incorporation into the French Empire—denoted as moralization and civilization—entailed loss of property and of autonomy. If we are to judge the French legacy of rights in the nineteenth century, the growth of racist sciences by which the Kanak were governed must be tallied alongside the expansion of working-class rights. The expropriation of Kanak lands must be considered alongside any measurement of their educational gains. Finally, the question of patriarchy and women, discussed only briefly in this essay, must be granted due consideration. With the limitations of human rights language kept securely in view, with the tactics of governmentality exposed, we can begin to evaluate the positive potential of human rights.

NOTES

1. For a more detailed examination of affect, colonialism, and rights, Alice Bullard, "The French Idea of Subjectivity and the Kanak of New Caledonia: Recuperating the Category of Affect," *History and Anthropology* 10, no. 4 (1998): 375–405; "Self-Representation in the Arms of Defeat: Fatal Nostalgia and the Surviving Comrades," *Cultural Anthropology* 12, no. 2 (May 1997): 179–211; and "Kant in the Third Republic: Charles Renouvier and the Constructed Self," in *Selected Proceedings of the Western Society for French History*, vol. 25 (Greeley, Colo.: University of North Colorado Press, 1998), pp. 319–328.

2. *Enquête sur l'insurrection du 18 mars*, 3 vols. (Paris, Imprimiere du parliament, 1871), pp. 189–190.

3. "Arrêté relatif au recrutement des travailleurs indigènes pour les services publics (4 janvier 1860)," *Bulletin Officiel de la Nouvelle-Calédonie* (Nouméa: Imprimerie du Gouvernement, 1861), pp. 213–215. Refined legislation of 1887 omitted the mediation of the "chiefs"—who by then had suffered substantial loss of power—relying instead on French regional administrators to guarantee that Kanak labored for local colonists, particularly at harvest time.

4. "Arrêté déclarant par voie d'interprétation des actes législatifs antérieurs, l'existence légale de la tribu indigène dans l'organisation coloniale de la Nouvelle-Calédonie," in *Lois, Décrets, Arrêtés et instructions formant la législation de la Nouvelle-Calédonie*, vol. 7 (Nouméa: Imprimerie Calédonienne, 1900), pp. 442–448. (du 24 dec. 1867: Vu le jugement du Tribunal criminel de Nouméa, en date du 17 decembre 1867; ensemble, les conclusions du Procureur impérial, sur lesquelles a statué ce jugement), p. 448.

5. "Loi portant promulation aux colonies des lois sur la naturalisation (29 mai 1874)," in *Lois, Décrets, Arrêtés et instructions formant la législation de la Nouvelle-Calédonie*, vol. 4 (Nouméa: Imprimerie Calédonienne, 1900), pp. 618–629.

6. "Décret relatif à l'administration des tribus et à la répression, par voie disciplinaire des infractions spéciales aux indigènes de la Nouvelle-Calédonie, du 18 juillet 1887, promulgué dans la colonie suivant arrêté du 12 octobre 1887," in *Lois, Décrets, Arrêtés et instructions formant la législation de la Nouvelle-Calédonie*, vol. 5 (Nouméa: Imprimerie Calédonienne, 1900), p. 665; and "Décision du Gouverneur: Organisation du service des affaires indigènes du 9 août 1898," in *Lois, Décrets, Arrêtés et instructions formant la législation de la Nouvelle-Calédonie*, vol. 5 (Nouméa: Imprimerie Calédonienne, 1900), pp. 96–99.

7. *Commission d'enquête nommée à l'occassion des troubles de Wagap, Ina et Tiéti (arrêté du 18 November 1899)*, *Dossier complet* (Nouméa: Imprimerie Calédonienne, 1900), pp. 1– 2 and 3; *Spoliation des indigènes de la Nouvelle-Calédonie, Mémoire du comité de protection et de défense des indigènes* (Paris: Constant-Laguerre, 1901), pp. 30–31.

8. *Commission d'enquête . . .Wagap*, p. 14. A similar contention is found in Marc Le Goupils, "Colons et Canaques," *Revue de Paris* (October 1 and 10, 1909), pp. 449–471 and 775–796; here Le Goupils recorded with dismay that Chef Samuel, "profoundly imbued with *de droit canaque*" as established by the colonial administration, accepted with equanimity the forced transfer of several Kanak families to his clan at Nassirah. The Kanak forced to resettle, Avit and Isidore, demonstrated quite a different "political morality"; they objected strenuously to the Chef du service des Affaires indigènes, claiming that they were "free and that they would do what they wanted." In face of this protestation, the colonial administrator had the impression that the Kanak had recited a lesson given to them, probably, so he thought, by a missionary of Touaourou or of Saint-Louis. "'It did not seem possible to me that the Caledonians, even those of intelligence, *tirassent cela de leur propre cru*.'" However, Le Goupils did not share these doubts, he felt strongly that like himself, Avit and Isidore operated with "another conception of the law than Samuel." Quoted from pp. 460–462.

9. Hannah Arendt, *A Report on the Banality of Evil: Eichmann in Jerusalem* (1963): (New York: Viking-Penguin, 1983), p. 271.

10. Léon Moncelon, "Un peuple qui s'eteint," *L'Homme, Journal illustré des sciences anthropologiques* 4, no. 4 (February 25, 1887), p. 100.

11. Léon Moncelon, *Les Canaques de la Nouvelle-Calédonie et des Nouvelles-Hébrides; La Colonisation européenne en face de la sauvagerie locale* (Paris: Imprimerie des écoles, 1886), pp. 30 and 13.

12. Charles Lemire, "Examen des propositions formulées par Monsieur Moncelon délégue de la Nouvelle-Calédonie dans son rapport à Monsieur le Ministre de la Marine et des Colonies sur les mesures à prendre vis à vis de la population Canaque," dated "seven years after the suppression of the 1878 Insurrection" (so 1885), ANSOM, N.C. 171, reproduced in Christiane Kasarherou, *Contribution a l'étude de démographie historique de la Nouvelle-Calédonie; 1853–1920* (Nouméa: Centre Territorial de Recherche et de Documentation Pedagogiques de la Nouvelle-Calédonie, 1984), p. 113.

13. Charles Amouroux and Henri Place, *L'Administration et les Maristes en Nouvelle-Calédonie, Insurrection des Kanaks en 1878–79*, 2d edition (Paris: Imprimerie P.Worms, 1881), pp. 7–8, 161, 163–164.

14. Eugene Alcan, *Les Cannibales et leurs temps; souvenirs de la compagne de l'océanie sous le commandant Marceau, Capitaine de Frégate* (Paris: Delhomme et Briguet, 1887), pp. v, 84, 88.

6

A European Experience: Human Rights and Citizenship in Revolutionary Russia

Yanni Kotsonis

Histories of the Russian Revolution are dedicated to identifying what went wrong and when, and almost all historians agree that massive violations of basic human rights were the main manifestation of the degeneration.[1] Many argue that Bolshevism was wrong to begin with and point to one or another alternative that was more promising, be it the liberals who formed the Provisional Government in February 1917, or the moderate socialists who took over the Provisional Government later in the year. Others sympathize with the original seizure of power by the Bolsheviks in October 1917, and argue that the Bolsheviks betrayed a fundamentally good cause at some later date—if not during the Civil War, then certainly under Stalin in the 1930s.

The problem is that none of these groups—liberals, socialists, and communists—stood for human rights as we understand them today, because none of them applied the label "human" universally. This was true not only in Russia and China (as Jeffrey Wasserstrom argues in this volume) but also in Europe as a whole. Since the eighteenth century, the question of who was human was entwined with another term that arose simultaneously in the same Enlightenment, the citizen. The question of who was deserving of human rights and liberation depended in part on who was considered mature enough to accept the responsibilities of the citizen. In this sense, the Enlightenment did not tell us that all people were human; it gave us universal standards for deciding who was human, and much of the history of Europe ever since has entailed a struggle to decide where to set the boundaries. The Russian Revolution—roughly the first third of the twentieth century—was one element of this ongoing debate and struggle.

AMBIGUITIES OF ENLIGHTENMENT

The moment that historians and political writers locate as pivotal in the emergence of the idea of human rights is the French "Declaration of the Rights of Man" of 1789. But the men gathered in the National Assembly saw fit to append another word—so often lost in the shorthand used by historians—rendering the full title, "The Declaration of the Rights of Man and of the Citizen." The Assembly did not pursue the question of who the citizens would be—it was dropped in parliamentary negotiations and overshadowed by other events—nor did it need to. The question had already been debated for some decades. As the historian Michel-Rolphe Trouillot points out in his discussion of the Haitian revolutions of the early nineteenth century, the boundaries of citizenship and humanity had been and would be debated for many decades to come in constitutional deliberations in France, Europe, and the Americas. In state after state, political actors expanded and contracted the boundaries of political citizenship to examine, case by case, the rights and obligations of women (the obvious question posed by the rights of that ambiguous term, "man"), non-Europeans (slaves and laborers of African descent spread across empires, dependencies, and metropolises, as well as the colonial populations themselves), nonnationals, non-Christians, the propertyless, and the illiterate.[2] We may well assume that each of these groups was human or deserving of human rights, but to contemporaries it was a matter of debate. All men were born with rights, American revolutionaries declared in 1776, by the very fact that they are men, but they meant that all adult, property-owning white males are citizens. For they also told us that anyone without enough property could not participate in politics, debated whether women were permanent children and politically immature, and considered whether Native Americans and Africans were human at all. Human rights are absolute, as Lynn Hunt points out in her contribution to this volume, but it was a long time before they were recognized as universal even in rhetoric, and a long time before the boundaries of humanity were expanded to include all people.

The "citizen," then, was equally the product of the Enlightenment as secular "man," and it was entwined with notions of rationality that (contemporaries assumed) not all possessed. To the extent that "man is rational"—one of the basic propositions of the Enlightenment—then some could be more rational and more fully human than others, and others not rational or human at all. In this light, human rights and its pair, citizenship, were not about claiming an inherent right (the end point or deciding moment of most of our revolutionary narratives, be it 1688, 1776, 1789, or 1848, which can only make 1917 a huge disappointment), but about the achievement of a status and the attainment of qualities that would admit one to political society, civil society, and, indeed, full humanity. All of these discussions of rights and obligations were laden with anxieties about whether large groups of the population had the maturity, however defined, to share in political power.

A good deal of this thinking was related to how historical actors understood another novelty of the eighteenth century, "progress," and its implicit opposition, "backwardness." We are accustomed to thinking of progress as a framework for dynamic and positive change, whereby all people can and should be improved over time, making for the redeemability of all humankind in the long run. In the short run, it was just as easy to accept or insist that things should be as they are because parts of the population are simply backward and unprepared for politics. Conceptions of progress can be used to locate and fix difference, to suggest that a person is "backward" (rather than imply "progress"), and to posit and rationalize inequalities within a clear relationship of power. In other words, "progress" required "backwardness" to be meaningful, and certain people were rendered backward by the very idea of progress. Rather than use "progress" to anticipate dynamic change and universal progress, the concept can become a legitimizing or delegitimizing weapon in a rhetorical arsenal: the person who understands and wields "progress" and possesses "rationality" can direct, manage, and govern the person who is "backward" and "elemental"—in a word, illegitimate, unable to govern oneself, let alone govern others as part of an integrated political system. From this comes the paternalism and benevolence that will underpin and legitimize so many commonplace relations of power and much more blatant dictatorships: a ruler denying rights to a person because that person is not prepared to use them wisely, and a government maintaining authority over people for their own good because they do not know what is good for them. It was this line of reasoning that underpinned formal European and American imperialism in the nineteenth and twentieth centuries and animated their resistance to decolonization. Peasants would become Frenchmen by the twentieth century with the spread (actually, standardization) of reason and rationality, but colonials would remain colonials until the 1960s.

If we look at "human" in these terms—the possession of rationality and enlightenment—then it appears that the Enlightenment did not give us universal human rights; it gave us universal standards for deciding who was human and who was a citizen. Russians shared in this European experience, not as the European exception, but as the extreme manifestation of a modern duality: human rights understood as the product of having attained humanity.

A RUSSIAN ENLIGHTENMENT

Early in the twentieth century, Russia's small, "enlightened" elite was fractured into different political ideologies, different legal estates, and different property-owning categories, and these antagonisms erupted during the mass revolutions

of 1905 and 1917. But the consensus easy to miss in the enumeration of differences was that this elite considered itself enlightened, while the mass of people
over whom they fought were "benighted." These frameworks of thought were
shared by the reformist tsarist minister who defended the autocrat's monopoly
on power on the grounds that subjects of the tsar were unprepared to rule themselves; the Marxist labor agitator who bemoaned the lack of "consciousness"
among Russian factory workers that required (as Lenin argued in 1902) a "vanguard" party to lead them; the liberal lawyer who took it upon him or herself to
defend the helpless and oppressed masses who had little understanding of the
written law; and the populist physician who attacked not disease but the people's
"ignorance" and "benightedness" that were, it seemed, the real root of epidemic.[3]
Far from being a matter of liberation—the release of a free people from an anachronistic and oppressive autocracy—this discourse on humanity perpetuated a
politics of legitimacy and subordination, in which different groups of "civilized
people" debated what to do about the obvious and uncontested backwardness
of "the people."

The fact that "the people" was always in the singular was also suggestive, for
we tend to pose questions of human rights as the recognition of individuality,
of autonomous humans reaching their full potential. It is true that the idea of
individual liberation imparted a sense of sovereignty on certain groups of people,
such as liberal noblemen, professionals, and political leaders who found the tsar's
monopoly on political power incompatible with their emerging senses of self-
worth. This development made for well-known conflicts within the elite, as liberal, populist, and Marxist battled autocracy, and Marxist battled populist and
liberal over how to battle autocracy. But when these groups turned their atten-
tions from each other and addressed "the people," their differences seemed less
stark. They tended to create new collectivities that lacked a face and a personality, "the people" of populism, "the masses" or "the proletariat" of Marxism, "the
peasantry" of all political discourse, and, from the pens of the very same people,
"the dark people" to which writers and activists of all political orientations referred. This was particularly true at those same revolutionary moments, 1905 and
1917, when the popular revolutions many had anticipated spun out of their control and became, they believed, "anarchic" and "elemental," one more proof that
"our people" was unprepared for the responsibilities of freedom.

In these circumstances, the question that divided contemporaries was not so
much how to liberate but who had the right to govern a people that could not
govern itself. The historical question that concerns us is not whether we consider workers, peasants, and national minorities as human and mature; the question that concerned these political elites was how to compensate for a "backwardness" that all took for granted. These conceptions informed interactions
large and small, events well-known to historians and others more obscure, and
allow us to consider old facts in new light.

The Problem of Property, 1906–1918[4]

Take, to begin with, large events with which most casual students of Russian history will be familiar. Following the Revolution of 1905, Prime Minister Stolypin determined that the crisis demanded extreme measures. He focused on the peasantry as the largest group of the population and the key to political stability. More specifically, he concentrated on the issue of property which had been central to European political, economic, and legal thought for a century. Since the serf emancipation of 1861, peasants did not own their land individually; they farmed land that was controlled by the commune, a meeting of (usually male) heads of household, which in turn was required to ensure that all member households had enough land to survive and pay taxes. Stolypin proposed to make the land the personal property of peasants, and like many reformers before him drew on a liberal rhetoric of freedom and individual autonomy: By holding the land as individual property (rather than a possession controlled by the commune), peasants would have the freedom to buy or sell, mortgage and risk—in short, to make their own decisions and mistakes and be responsible for their own futures. Ultimately, all property owners would have the right to vote based on their property, as was done in so many European countries and in the United States in the nineteenth century. At a time when peasants appeared in literature and political and economic rhetoric as elemental children, Stolypin proposed that peasants treated as adults might begin to act like responsible citizens. The great objection of his opponents of various political shades, liberals, populists, Marxists, and members of his own government, was that peasants would be thrust into a land market where most would be dispossessed. Rather than expropriation, capitalism, and inequality as experienced in western Europe, many of Stolypin's opponents proposed that communal relations should be maintained as the better guaranty of social equality and fairness.

On the surface both approaches seem to fit neatly into classic debates on human rights and political rights—Stolypin arguing for liberation through property, his antagonists for the real material equality at the base of certain European socialisms; Stolypin championing the individual, his opponents defending a distinct collectivist identity. The scene is set, it would seem, for a debate comparable to the later clash between certain Western governments arguing for a political interpretation of universal human rights (and sidestepping the blatant economic inequalities they countenance) and certain Asian and African governments retorting that material, collective, and spiritual issues must be addressed first if not exclusively (and thus legitimizing dictatorship). But a rather different debate is discernible if we immerse the Russian debates into context following a huge revolutionary movement, and notice that all of these groups were addressing a shared anxiety about the maturity of peasants and "the people." For in addition to liberal and traditional populist arguments, all of these groups expressed doubts about the capacity and ability of peasants to take control of their own futures and determine the disposal of their land and livelihood. The populist economist Nikolai Oganovskii declared in an argument against private property that Russian peasants were not a citizenry, would not be for some time to come, and should not be treated as one. By giving peasants all the rights, autonomy, and power that private property imparted, the government would only insulate peasants in their backwardness and empower them in their benightedness—this at a time when peasants needed the guidance and management of enlightened educated society. In a similar vein, agronomists, hydrotechnicians, and land surveyors, the people who were asked to implement the land reform but refused, objected that giving private property rights to peasants would be an obstacle in the work of reapportioning land as the specialist saw fit and interfere with the task of "reorganizing the peasant household" along rational lines. It would, in short, blunt the power of the enlightened professional over peasants. Since communal land belonged to no one person, they argued, communal land relations were a better way for the professional to implement a vision of economic and social rationality, unfettered by peasant "tradition" and resistance to "progress."

At this point it would seem as if Stolypin and his allies had more confidence in the capacity of peasants to manage their own affairs, in the sense that they were willing give peasants the rights and autonomy arising from private property. But in their responses to their opponents, they did not insist that private property was meant to empower its owners. Instead they pointed out that the material and legal implications of private property was a mortgage—that ubiquitous, commonplace, and seemingly mundane institution of twentieth-century economies—and the right to stake the land as collateral and receive credit from a bank. And a mortgage, Stolypin's supporters pointed out, was not about freedom but control. "Credit is power," declared the director of a state bank in 1913, and the state as creditor would gain power over the borrower. It allowed the creditor to decide what was an appropriate use of the money, what was an appropriate use of the land, to force certain types of amelioration over others, and, ultimately, to give the state and its agents a powerful if quiet coercive weapon in the structuring of the society and in the maintenance of the social order. In the end, the discussions on both sides of the issue were about how property, be it private or communal, might affect the power of one or another educated group over the peasant "masses," not how the peasants as such should be liberated.

The land question was settled by the Bolsheviks in 1917 with the famous Decree on Land, which nationalized the land and redistributed the holdings of the nobility among those who actually tilled it with their own labor. Peasants would hold on to that land until Stalin forcibly collectivized agriculture at the end of the 1920s. But the Decree on Land actually involved two separate processes and entailed two separate declarations that should not be confused. The first was redistribution, to which most of the literature refers as a concession to peasants. From the point of view of Marxists who believed in large economies of scale, a large estate was more efficient than a small peasant plot, so that redistribution was indeed a concession to the peasant movement and a way to diffuse the massive rural rebellion that was taking place in late 1917. Yet, "nationalization," as the text of the decree stated, meant that the land belonged to "the whole people" represented by, or at least reflected in, the state, which once again meant that the land belonged to no one person, and certainly not to individual peasants. If the land was to be the possession of a small holder, ultimate control of the land was a matter of state authority. Not only Bolsheviks believed in such control, but also the moderate socialists from whom the Bolsheviks borrowed the program. To put it another way, the Soviet government did not give the land to peasants and then take it away in the late 1920s; it had always declared that the land was too important to be made the property of peasants.

Witte, Lenin, and Chaianov, 1900–1924

If the Enlightenment was not a matter of universal liberation, it *was* about universalism. Consider the way three well-known historical actors representing mutually antagonistic ideologies understood "the people" and specifically the "peasantry," which highlights the similar ways in which they universalized their gradations of humanity. Lenin, of course, was the founder of the Bolshevik Party, the main agitator for the Bolshevik overthrow of the Provisional Government in October 1917, and the leader of Soviet Russia during the Civil War. In 1923, following the Soviet victory, shortly before his death, and surveying the ruins left by successive social upheavals and wartime catastrophes, a pensive and anxious Lenin wrote a series of essays on culture, where he proposed to a thoroughly militarized Communist Party that the Soviet peoples needed cultural revolution before they would be ready for socialism—understood in this context as a higher cultural form. In his last piece, "On Cooperation," Lenin the revolutionary-turned-statesman showcased the most reformist and unrevolutionary of institutions, cooperatives, as "schools" that would teach peasants "civilization" and "culture," rather than the "spontaneous" ways to which they were accustomed. Writing as one "cultured European" to a readership of other "cultured Europeans," he argued that it was their duty to teach peasants to act (and specifically to conduct their economic affairs) as "Europeans, not as Asians" (*po evropeiski, ne po aziatski*). The rhetorical slip collapsed all peoples into a single, culturally determined category of "backwardness," alike because they were so different from "the cultured European." Time as a physical property was prominent in this text, as Lenin contended that the two opposites—peasant/Asian and cultured/European—were separated by "an entire historical period." Lenin was hardly the first to do this; in the 1890s the founder of Russian Marxism, Giorgii Plekhanov, used "peasant," "barbarian," and "Asian" interchangeably, and he in turn drew on and contributed to a long tradition that included Voltaire, Hegel, Herder, and Marx. All of these figures drew on and contributed to a West-East cultural gradient from "civilization" to "barbarism," whereby cultures, societies, and people could be understood (or, actually, not understood) according to a single, universal, and secular standard of measurement.[5]

Obviously one did not have to be a Marxist to think in these universal terms. Exactly twenty years earlier, in 1904, a famous minister of finance, Sergei Witte, one of the last statesmen to attempt to modernize the autocracy, had written the *Memorandum on the Peasant Question*, which turned to "culture" and specifically discussed the importance of the acculturation of "backward," "semiliterate," and "primitive" peasants. These people, he wrote, in their current culture and economy, were like "wild fruit," distinct from the "cultured fruit" of advanced European institutions (as in English, "cultured" was both botanical and intellectual). Like Lenin after him, he wrote that the distance between the two was "an entire historical period," which could be bridged by "ideology, not reality." In this and other writings Witte implied that birth, religion, and nationality might not be important if they were supplanted by the universal categories of "progress" and "backwardness." His successor as minister of finance (and later Stolypin's successor as prime minister), Vladimir Kokovtsov, explicated some of the universal implications in 1904 and 1905, when he was asked to decide whether cooperatives—a new mass movement sponsored by the state—were suitable to Jews, who were so often painted in official rhetoric and policy as exploiters, "too advanced," and likely to use the institutions to dominate "undeveloped" Russian peasants. He answered in the affirmative in what seemed to be an affirmation of the equality of all peoples. But his reasoning was less than a resounding affirmation of human potential: What made these peoples alike was not their equal rights but their equal backwardness and helplessness before the march of predatory capitalists and exploiters, making them all needy and deserving of state protection from their enemies and from their own self-destructiveness. For as was the case with peasants, Jews comprised a "laboring mass" along with only a few "advanced" strata, making the stereotype of the squalid, ignorant, and helpless peasant indistinguishable from the stereotype of the squalid, ignorant, and helpless Jew.[6]

This was universalism, of course, because it rejected differences of language, religion, and ethnicity. But it replaced bigotry with one large universal difference based on gradations of "culture" and "advancement." It could be argued that little more could be expected from Witte, the defender of autocracy, or from Lenin, whose vision of the dictatorship of the proletariat left little room for peasants, and little room for the proletariat. Consider, therefore, the writings of a person we think of as a "democrat," Aleksander Chaianov. Chaianov was a contemporary of both Witte and Lenin, though he outlived them both and witnessed the rise of Stalin. He was one of the most articulate theorists of the peasant economy in any country and any time (he was a founder of the labor-production school before 1914) and was considered the leader of so-called Neopopulists of the 1910s and 1920s. From the 1960s he was revived in Western sociology, peasant studies, and historiography as a "pro-peasant" alternative to liberals and Marxists who saw humanity's future in cities and industry. He was revived in Russia in the late 1980s by scholars and publicists who sought alternatives to Stalinism in their historical narratives. That Chaianov could accommodate peasants in an economic and social vision is beyond doubt, and his vision of a ruralized future was sufficiently subversive in Stalinist Russia for him to be put on show trial and shot in the 1930s. Yet, we should reconsider what we mean by "democratic" and "pro-peasant" in this context. His vision of a new agrarian order was already in ruins in his mind in 1918 and 1919, and not simply because the contest came down to supporting either a Marxist government or what seemed to be plainly restorationist White armies. (He chose the former.) His real lament did not even concern Reds and Whites but "the people." Having worked for so long with so many other radicals for a national assembly that would be the culmination of the emergence of a new citizenry, he saw in January 1918 how the Bolsheviks dispersed the Constituent Assembly with no popular resistance at all. He watched as his students and colleagues were chased out of villages as "outsiders" by the very "people" he had hoped to help and represent. And his explanation? "Our people," he lamented in his handbook for agronomists in 1919, is but "a *demos*, a dark human mass," whereas "it should have been a democracy, a people conscious of itself." "The Russian Revolution revealed this truth with bold clarity, showed that we still do not have a nation"—in the sense of a coherent and integrated polity—"and even the Constituent Assembly cannot transform the Russian *demos* into a nation." Some of his colleagues in agrarian economics chose a different route in 1918 and helped found an anti-Bolshevik government in Archangel in North Russia; unable to mobilize "our people" into an army and effectively resist either Reds or Whites, they went into exile and into prison camps lamenting "the darkness of the people."[7]

Who informed whom? Chaianov's *Theory and Practice of Peasant Cooperation* was at Lenin's bedside when he died in 1924; and Witte and Lenin shared whole phrases, not to mention the spirit of what they each wrote. But the point is that, as striking as many of these terms and affirmations might be to a reader in the year 2000, they were not at all strange to a reader in 1900, 1919, or 1923. The terms permeate writings on politics, economics, and society and comprised part of the common cultural language and fabric of early twentieth-century Russian educated elites. Much as a student of the United States in the twentieth century will soon become accustomed to outrageous language on all sides of the debates on race, or a historian of interwar Europe will have to come to terms with the language of imperialism, so the student of Russia has to come to terms with the dehumanizing language with which so many Russian educated elites treated the vast majority of the population.

So much for ideas and rhetoric. But the writers mentioned above were powerful in different ways, as leaders of states, governments, parties, and schools of thought. Their ability to make their assumptions meaningful and to put them into practice were considerable. Having assumed that large groups of the population were backward, they fully expected to find backward people in their daily interactions. Some examples are mundane but nevertheless disturbing in the ways in which they demeaned and degraded. Peasants petitioning for investment funds from the government in the years 1900–1914 often claimed that the funds would be used well because the applicants were "entrepreneurial" and showed "initiative." Many of these petitions were rejected with the commonsensical statement, formulated by a professional and approved by the state credit committee, that only an exploiter could show these qualities. When the same groups of people resubmitted their applications and recast themselves as ignorant, poor, and backward, the petitions were approved. Or consider the peasants on the White Sea coast who found themselves in territory held by anti-Bolshevik populists and Whites during the Civil War, and who were to be conscripted into the White army for service against the Reds in 1918. Told by recruiters and in official publications that their reluctance to serve was a sign of their "undevelopment" and "lack of consciousness" as citizens and Russians, an agitated and war-weary village assembly agreed: Yes, read the petition, "the people" are "benighted," and therefore would be unfit material for an army serving such an important cause.[8]

Some of these cases are amusing in that peasants were able to manipulate the language of authority figures, but any way we look at it, the process was fundamentally dehumanizing because people were forced to admit to their inferiority. In different circumstances, similar assumptions underpinned one of the most violent episodes in modern Russian history, the collectivization of peasant agriculture and of peasants. The ongoing refrain of this and so many other policies of Stalinist Russia in the late 1920s and 1930s was a generalized assault on backwardness and its human manifestation—peasants and other populations of Russia and the Soviet Union—who were, after all, too backward and ignorant to understand that it was for the better. Estimates of the death toll resulting from military action, deportations, and famine range from the hundreds of thousands to the millions.

COMPARATIVE IMPLICATIONS

There is a tendency among historians of both Russia and western Europe to narrate how the modern West was born in the Enlightenment to tell the story of the liberating dimensions of the Enlightenment that were entrenched in

Europe and gradually carried to the rest of the globe. True, as far as it goes, and it is the story I prefer in the sense of "ought to be." "What was" is something different. Undesirable aspects of the Western experience, of which historians are becoming increasingly aware—gender exclusiveness, racism, bigotry, chauvinism—are in effect removed from the narrative (where the teleology will lead inexorably to the present democracy and recognition of human rights) and consigned to the non-West. Much is carried east to 1917, with the end point not yet apparent. I have argued here that the idea of human rights and liberation was dual from its very inception, and emerged with sincere and open doubt about the inclusiveness of "man" and "human," and therefore about the universalism of human rights. If we consider "man" alongside "citizen," and append "rational" to "human," then we can better understand why all these terms were exclusive and were used to exclude large segments of the population from the political nation.

If enlightenment and rationality could justify unidirectional management of people in Russia, then it bears remembering that the same dynamic was at work on a much larger scale, and at the very same time, in the formal imperialism practiced by the European imperial powers and the United States into the period after the Second World War, making for the management of most of the world's population who were deemed unprepared to manage themselves. These elements, in other words, were not detached from western Europe and sent east; they were carried to and practiced on the rest of the globe until very recent times.

NOTES

1. Three standard and distinct views of the Russian Revolution are Richard Pipes, *The Russian Revolution* (New York: Knopf, 1990); Sheila Fitzpatrick, *The Russian Revolution*, 2d ed. (New York: Oxford University Press, 1994); and Martin Malia, *The Soviet Tragedy: A History of Socialism in Russia, 1917–1991* (New York: Free Press, 1994).

2. Michel-Rolphe Trouillot, *Silencing the Past: Power and the Production of History* (Boston: Beacon Press, 1995). For a discussion of the Declaration of 1789, see Marcel Gauchet's contribution to *A Critical Dictionary of the French Revolution*, ed. F. Furet and Mona Ozouf (Cambridge, Mass.: Belknap Press, 1989).

3. John F. Hutchinson, *Politics and Public Health in Revolutionary Russia, 1890–1918* (Baltimore: Johns Hopkins University Press, 1990).

4. Material for this section is drawn from Yanni Kotsonis, *Making Peasants Backward: Agricultural Cooperatives and the Agrarian Question in Russia* (London and New York: Macmillan, 1999), chs. 3–4.

5. V. I. Lenin, "On Cooperation," *Collected Works* (Moscow and London: Progress Publishers, 1966), vol. 33. For a critical summary of the history of the East-West gradient as it emerged in the eighteenth and nineteenth centuries, see Larry Woolf, *Inventing Eastern Europe: The Map of Civilization on the Mind of the Enlightenment* (Stanford: Stanford University Press, 1994).

6. For a summary of Witte's pronouncements, see Kotsonis, *Making Peasants Backward*, ch. 2; on Kokovtsov, see ch. 5.

7. Kotsonis, *Making Peasants Backward*, epilogue.

8. Yanni Kotsonis, "Arkhangel'sk 1918," *Russian Review* (October 1992).

Part IV

Colonial Contexts and the Problem of Imperialism

7

An Enlightenment for Outcasts: Some Vietnamese Stories

Alexander Woodside

Where the Vietnamese are concerned, the debate about the differences between Asian values and Western ones was promoted in a particularly pressing way almost thirty years ago, not by Marxists in Hanoi, but by Henry Kissinger.

As the leader of the American side in secret negotiations with the Vietnamese communists to end the second Indochina War, Kissinger published an apparently magisterial book in 1969 about American foreign policy. In it he argued that the West and underdeveloped Asian countries were divided not by the former's wealth and the latter's poverty but by two different "philosophical perspectives." The West's perspective was "Newtonian," Kissinger claimed. American policymakers such as himself wrongly seemed to Asians to be "cold, supercilious, and lacking in compassion" because, as good Newtonians, they were committed to accurate knowledge classification and to the notion that the real world was external to the observer. Economically underdeveloped Asians such as the Vietnamese, in contrast, were allegedly "pre-Newtonian." They were inclined to think that the real world was almost completely internal to the observer. Their epistemological immaturity allowed them "great flexibility" in altering the perceived realities of "revolutionary turmoil," to the detriment of American policymakers.[1]

Contrast Henry Kissinger's wartime pronouncements with the way in which the Vietnamese worldview was defined more recently by Vietnamese elite figures themselves. The occasion was a 1994 Hanoi conference on "Asian Social and Cultural Development," sponsored by the Toyota Foundation and the Vietnamese Social Sciences and Humanities Center. In his summarizing speech at this conference, Professor Hoang Trinh, a senior Vietnamese scholar, singled out one great thinker from the past as rightly having special authority for Asian peoples. This was not Confucius but Francis Bacon (1561–1626). Bacon,

113

according to Hoang Trinh, spoke from his grave in warning the Asian "dragon" economies that mastery over nature must be combined with respect for nature's laws, in the modern form of environmental planning.[2] And indeed Bacon, as the English father of experimental science and of the scientific belief that knowledge is power, has been a major inspiration to both the modern Chinese and Vietnamese revolutions ever since Yan Fu, the great Chinese translator of Western thought, named him back in 1895 as the founder of the West's material superiority over Asian civilizations. Contrary to Kissinger, Descartes and Newton have been celebrated right along with him.

Certain predictable reflexes appear and reappear when the world talks about human rights these days. Westerners from outside the United States keep reminding their Asian conversational partners that the "West" is not the same thing as the United States, whose possibly pre-Newtonian addiction to capital punishment, for example, is no longer shared by Canada or Europe. Asian spokesmen for their part keep demanding a more pluralistic approach to human rights, not one based entirely on Western history, in which locally practiced notions of economic and cultural rights will be given attention along with civil and political rights. We oscillate between a naive universalism and a plaintive relativism. But in present-day Vietnam, the official state ideology is still communism. And communism began its life as a creed that embodied many of the values of the eighteenth-century Western Enlightenment. These included the desirability of the overthrow of mentally enslaving authority by the experimental philosophy that Francis Bacon advocated and for which major Enlightenment thinkers such as Voltaire were to praise him.

When Ho Chi Minh announced the independence of his Democratic Republic of Vietnam to Hanoi crowds in September 1945, he publicly invoked the French Revolution's "Declaration of the Rights of Man and of the Citizen"; and its secularizing determination to separate political authority from divine authority, in the name of fighting human ignorance, was almost immediately combined by Ho with the offer of a mass literacy campaign. Its utopian objective, not fulfilled even now, was to impart literacy to all Vietnamese by the end of 1946. The literary campaign was to create an awareness in all Vietnamese, including women and such marginal groups as fishermen, monks and nuns, and prostitutes, of their rights (*quyen loi*) and duties (*bon phan*) in the new republic. The Vietnamese revolution has never been a haven for local moral philosophers of the skeptical Western Alasdair MacIntyre type who assert that human rights are merely moral fictions, intrinsically no more credible than witches or unicorns.[3]

Of course Ho Chi Minh's association of his revolution with the French Revolution's faith in the rights of man was partly designed to manipulate the sympathies of foreign public opinion, especially French and American. And for a Western scholar to explain the Vietnamese communist revolution almost entirely in terms of an unnaturally idealized Marxism would be a little like a Tibetan with a theoretical knowledge of progressive Christian theology trying to explain from a distance the behavior of a complex Western country such as the United States. But there is little doubt that human rights ideas and practices in the Vietnamese revolution have not been determined exclusively or perhaps even primarily by the residual "Asian" values of premodern Vietnam. They have been determined by a very particular indigenous experiencing of the originally Western Enlightenment. Indeed, Francis Bacon and the specific ideals of scientific mastery and experimental reasoning that he bequeathed to that Enlightenment may mean more in Hanoi at the end of the twentieth century than they do in London or Washington, where Baconian thought was tamed, domesticated, and pigeonholed centuries ago. We are not dealing with starkly contrasting Asian and Western civilizations, as Kissinger so self-servingly pretended in 1969. But we may be dealing with a Baconian Asia confronting a tired, post-Newtonian West that is losing its faith in foundational certainties.

The ways in which the Vietnamese experienced the Enlightenment and the revolutionary programs that descended from it were critical. This is no doubt generally true of other Asian countries, too. Human rights in them cannot be elucidated without an understanding, not just of local practices and traditions, but also of the compromises and even the pathologies involved in the imperfect global diffusion of Enlightenment values, by Westerners and non-Westerners alike. The general term for "human rights" (*nhan quyen*) itself probably entered Vietnamese thought at the end of the 1800s. It would have been imported from China and Japan; the Chinese version of it appears as early as 1878, in the diaries of the famous scholar-official Guo Songtao, and its meaning was assessed in terms of its early applications in Japanese politics in a celebrated Chinese book about Japan (which Vietnamese scholars could read) by Huang Zunxian, published in 1890.[4] But the Enlightenment values that stood behind the term were dislocated at the outset by French colonialism (lasting from 1885 to 1954). The French conquest of Indochina brought with it the works of Rousseau and Victor Hugo and the claims that French civilization could cure Vietnam of the "leprosy" of its Chinese-style mandarinate (as Edouard Petit characterized the old-fashioned Confucian elite, in a book about Vietnam published in Paris in 1887). Precolonial Vietnam's mandarins, or ruling scholar-officials, educated in classical Chinese, were further vilified in French colonial propaganda as being at best as backward as "medieval" European scholastics, and at worst the torturers and murderers of French Catholic missionaries and Vietnamese Christians. But the French colonists themselves were to practice racial discrimination outside their schools while teaching Rousseau and Hugo inside them.

The Enlightenment in Vietnam was thereby undermined from the start by the colonizers' own ambivalence about it or daily contradictions of it. Such a circumstance could almost be said to resemble the coexistence of Jeffersonian democracy with black slavery in the early United States. There were differences. Unlike black slaves, a small number of venturesome Vietnamese could make limited escapes from the mocking false universalism of the colonizers'

Enlightenment by going to France itself, where they were sometimes better treated and where they discovered that colonialism's double standards were not written in the stars but were situational. A famous Vietnamese novelist traveled to France for the first time, before he had become famous, in 1927. He described graphically what it was like to leave behind in Vietnam an Enlightenment that had metabolized into a manipulative colonial civilizing mission:

> The farther the ship got from Vietnam and the closer it got to France, to the same degree the more decently the people aboard the ship treated me. In the China Sea they did not care to look at me. By the Gulf of Siam they were looking at me with scornful apprehension, the way they would look at a mosquito carrying malaria germs to Europe. When we entered the Indian Ocean, their eyes began to become infected with expressions of gentleness and compassion . . . and when we crossed the Mediterranean, suddenly they viewed me as being civilized like themselves, and began to entertain ideas of respecting me. At that time I was very elated. But I still worried about the time when I was going to return home!

Other Vietnamese were ludicrously reputed to have tried to circumvent racially based justice in French Indochina by asking court-appointed doctors to certify that they had enough French flesh and skin to merit French citizenship.[5]

So to ask why human rights ideals have remained stunted in the Vietnamese communist revolution is to ask, in part, why they were stunted in the practice of the colonizing West itself during the high noon of colonialism. Ho Chi Minh, the architect of this revolution, began it by being one of the young Vietnamese "mosquitoes carrying malaria germs to Europe" who wanted to rethink the Enlightenment's message in the freer air of Paris, French Indochina's colonial metropolis. As a fiery communist journalist living in Paris in the early 1920s, Ho helped to organize an "Intercolonial Union" of the France-based representatives of oppressed peoples in French colonies such as Algeria, Morocco, Senegal, Guinea, Madagascar, Guadeloupe, and Vietnam itself. Ho also edited, published, and personally sold on Paris streets a journal, *Le Paria* (*The Outcast*), with titles in French, Arabic, and Chinese. It aimed at preparing the way for an anticolonial reinvention of the Enlightenment, this time an Enlightenment for the world's "outcasts." The journal supplied its outcast readers, and anyone else to whom it could be sold, with articles Ho had written himself on such subjects as racial hatred, the sufferings of Vietnamese women, Algerian martyrs, and the evils of torture in colonial jails. *Le Paria* was secretly carried back to Vietnam by Vietnamese (and other) sailors who worked for international shipping lines. They played the part of pilgrims spreading the word of masterless freelance preachers such as Ho, in a manner—though secular and much more far-flung geographically—not without similarity to the missionary groups of the Protestant Reformation in Europe.

In his writings at this time, Ho's major theme was the West's systematic betrayal of its own eighteenth-century Enlightenment in its colonies. The French goddess of justice, he wrote, had lost her weighing scales and had kept only her sword when she traveled to Indochina. Choosing examples from different kinds of French colonists—high officials, railway service employees, priests—Ho tried to show how they all debased French claims to be enlightened by their abuse of the peoples they ruled. Read today, the charges that Ho made against French colonialism in the pages of *Le Paria* seem monotonous in tone and substance, cartoons of infamous behavior rather than a solid documentation of it. They are presented with an irony so overwrought that it is hard to believe they could have been very persuasive to the few French readers who came across them. Ho's journal for "outcasts" had a run of only about 5,000 copies and ceased publication in 1926.

But we may forget that the abuses actually happened; we also forget what energies of mythmaking were devoted to the presentation of Western colonialism as a benevolent enterprise, before World War II, by the leaders of the Western countries that had Asian colonies. Crude as he was in literary style, Ho was a Vietnamese Marxist precursor of the Western thinkers, two or three decades later, who were also to be shocked by the sinister discovery of the West's own falsification of its Enlightenment values. After 1945 many Western writers were to note, bitterly, that Voltaire had celebrated the beginning of the end of torture in eighteenth-century Europe, but that it had returned to Fascist and Nazi Europe; they were to lament as well the intimate geographical proximity of the centers of central European humanism to centers for the mass murder of Jews. But the West's subversion of its own Enlightenment was first demonstrated in the prisons of Western colonies before it became obvious in the West itself. And the young Ho Chi Minh was a witness.

Ho promised in the 1920s that the Enlightenment could be saved by being transferred to Asia by revolutionaries. This makes bitterly ironic, or worse, the subsequent history of the Vietnamese communist republic which Ho inaugurated in Hanoi in 1945 and which has ruled all Vietnam since 1975. But as some pessimistic Western thinkers themselves had come to see, systematized Enlightenment had always had "totalitarian" potentialities.[6] In Vietnam itself before the communist rise to power, Buddhist thinkers had criticized the Western Enlightenment differently. They had argued that its natural-law egalitarianism was too narrow in scope, and thus dangerous if it were treated as an end in itself rather than as a means, given its relativist and discriminatory tendencies by Buddhist standards. They tried to replace it with a more broadly egalitarian renewed Buddhism, in which the central right of all creatures was to escape from suffering. But they foundered in their inability to provide plausible techniques for Vietnam's political decolonization. Instead, some of them took refuge in a romantic nostalgia for an alleged golden age of Vietnamese Buddhism (back in the eleventh to the fourteenth centuries) in which emperors had supposedly married humble farm girls.[7]

After decolonization came a global Cold War in which each side divided the planet into areas that were saved and areas that were damned, with paranoia flickering like lightning behind all the geopolitical calculus. In this period, from the 1940s to the 1980s, the Vietnamese communist state attempted a smaller tropical reproduction of the structure and history of the Soviet Union. This involved the terror of revolutionary tribunals, secret police, and prison camps and the use of class warfare as an instrument of governance, rather than as the tragic necessity Marx might have thought of it as being. Even the state funerals of Vietnamese communist leaders in Hanoi resembled their Moscow counterparts, right down to the processions, gun carriages, flowers, military uniforms, and serried rows of official mourners. Ho Chi Minh's own embalmed body in its mausoleum in Hanoi today imitates Lenin's in Moscow. The peculiarity of this imitative political body snatching is made all the more apparent by the fact that the Lenin body worship in Russia was designed by the Bolsheviks in the 1920s to be a politically correct counterattraction to the mass veneration of saintly relics by the old Russian Orthodox Christian church—for which Vietnam knew no equivalent.

One of Ho's most eminent political prisoners, the poet Nguyen Chi Thien, evoked the ghostly, tubercular atmosphere of the countless "reeducation camps" in which he had been imprisoned by Ho's regime in a remarkable 1972 poem, "The Swampland." In the poem he commented that "Uncle Ho" had really become the cunning seducer "Uncle Fox." (The Sino-Vietnamese term for "fox," *Ho-ly*, resembles the "Ho" in Ho's name.) Ho was the "king of the devils," whose rubber sandals really had the weight of a hundred pairs of iron boots.[8] But in contrast to this Vietnamese characterization of him as an evil revolutionary who understood very well what ideals he was betraying, hostile French intelligence analysts back in 1945 had apparently thought that Ho and his associates were merely pitifully confused. They assessed the speech in which Ho had invoked for Vietnamese the French "Declaration of the Rights of Man and of the Citizen" as "a bastard combination of bookish internationalism and chauvinistic patriotism, a melange of intellectual Marxism and primitive social demands, corresponding exactly to the aspirations of a section of the backward masses of these Asiatic deltas."[9]

No matter what explanation of Ho himself will ultimately be found, the relics of the old Enlightenment universalism that he once proposed still nonetheless survive in Vietnamese life, even if they are like the debris from some great shipwreck floating on the ocean's surface. In the early 1990s, for instance, the World Publishers Company in Hanoi, whose function is to disseminate information about Vietnam to the outside world, was still publishing tracts in Esperanto, for Esperanto was the language that Asian revolutionaries of years ago once thought could undergird what the young Ho Chi Minh himself praised as the only thing that could save humanity and bring universal compassion: a "genuine world republic" without capitalist boundaries.[10] Visitors to Vietnam in the early 1990s also encountered English-language customs declaration forms inscribed with the terms "Independence, Liberty, Happiness"—not language one would find on the customs declaration forms of neighboring revolution-free countries such as Brunei or Singapore.

It is safe to assume that the "Enlightenment project" culture still overlies Confucian–Taoist–Buddhist civilization in Vietnam, feebly or not, in roughly the same way that that civilization overlay Cham Hindu civilization in central Vietnam centuries ago, in the late medieval period. Internal as well as external pressures compel the communist republic to explore the legal definition of "civil relationships" in its society (as in its first civil law code, approved in 1995, some fifty years after Ho's "rights of man" speech) and to search for an ethical post-revolutionary sense of purpose that will minimize corruption, and which must come in part from below. The pressures are revealed in the communist regime's encouragement of a rapid increase in the numbers of the country's newspapers and journals (from 185 in 1993 to 450 in 1996), in the name of the old Enlightenment goal of elevating the "people's intelligence" (*dan tri*), the theme as well of Ho's not completely successful literacy education blitzkrieg in 1945. There are even finely statistical public discussions of how backward Vietnam still is, with respect to its neighbors, in the popular accessibilility of print journalism. The theoretical journal of the Communist Party Central Committee, for example, complained to party cadres in 1997 that the average annual per capita consumption of newsprint in Vietnam was still less than one kilogram per person, as contrasted with Japan's fourteen kilograms. (Here is a good example of what Horkheimer and Adorno call the Enlightenment's conversion of mathematical procedures into rituals of thinking.[11]) But the press is still controlled. Amnesty International still has all too little difficulty in compiling lists of the names of Protestant churchmen, Buddhist monks, and Catholic bishops whom Vietnam is imprisoning for their religious beliefs. Communist Party theoreticians still warn ominously of how "negative" newspapers destabilized the "systems" of Chile in 1973, Romania in 1989, and the Soviet Union itself in 1991.

Perhaps a discussion of how long hypocrites can remain uncrippled or undisturbed by an awareness of their own hypocrisy—a question not unknown to the history of human rights in the West, too—would require the services of a theologian. All historians can do is suggest that the Jekyll-and-Hyde, split personality nature of the Vietnamese revolutionary regime has been the product both of theory and contingency. In general terms, the regime is the blurred reenactment of a marriage originally consummated elsewhere between the Enlightenment vision of human perfectibility and the less happy conviction that political life is a lethal conspiracy and revolutionary politics are the theoretical dignification of a justified paranoia. Marxism, it is worth recalling, was a theory of liberation. Part of its liberating impulse was directed against nature. (Enlightenment, Horkheimer and Adorno grumble, "behaves toward things as a dictator toward men."[12]) Through technologies of various kinds, human beings could conquer nature and master their own existences better, making them yield more plentiful economic surpluses. The conquest had to occur through collective means and collective economic ownership, which alone could transcend the reflexes of endless accumulation, whatever the human costs, of capitalism and its class-divided societies.

To this Lenin added the notion (not entirely original with him) of a vanguard political party, bent on such liberation, that must be designed as a counter-conspiracy to fight the conspiracies that it saw threatening its constituents. If the entire structure of the hostile political and social order, whether Russian tsarist or French colonialist, was imagined as an all-embracing enemy plot, the revolutionary party opposed to it would have to model itself upon its enemy to succeed. In fact, because of the ambitions inherent in their ideology of liberation, the Leninist party dictatorships that seized power in Moscow and Hanoi went beyond the Russian tsars or the French colonialists. They required not merely obedience but public enthusiasm and active mobilization in the name of their ideology. People who rejected the ideology and its party would have to be crushed.

Bullying purges became a specialty of the Vietnamese party during its resistance war against the French from 1945 to 1954. Imitating Lenin, Pham Van Dong—usually regarded as one of the more mild-mannered elders of Vietnamese communism—told a party congress in the borderlands of north Vietnam, in early 1950, that all means had to be used to "exterminate" enemies and reactionaries who harmed the communist cause. He explained that he spoke for a "people's democracy" that could be "dictatorial" toward its enemies because it was "democratic" toward the "people" (*nhan dan*). At that point the "people" were defined, more liberally than later, as workers, peasants, petty bourgeoisie, patriotic bourgeoisie, and progressive landlords. But in the next breath, Pham Van Dong complained that party members had little idea of what governmental power was or how to create a state, either during their struggle or for the future when the French were defeated.[13]

Here unfavorable contingencies played a part. The Vietnamese communists were not merely using Maoist methods to create a supposed revolutionary consciousness where its social class basis did not exist; they were also trying to construct political power, in the forest, with even fewer reference points than the Chinese Maoists had as to what modern administrative machinery or modern management methods looked like. French colonialism had preserved a mummified premodern monarchical order in northern and central Vietnam, behind which French power lurked. The Vietnamese missed the experimental constitution making of Sun Yat-sen and his successors in Nationalist China, let alone the "German phase" of state building of late nineteenth-century Japan, in which German legal thought had been imported and indigenized enough in Japan to begin to allow the creation of a "hard," rationalizing political order. Thirty years of war with the French, and later the Americans, induced the Vietnamese communists to exalt war, as well as class struggle, over concern with state formation. In this they were encouraged by the dictum of Stalin (the architect of their Soviet Union ally's victory over Germany in 1945) that the decisive test of a "system" was its success in warfare, not the quality of its law-based administration. By one calculation, even in the early 1990s more than half of Vietnam's state functionaries were military people (*quan nhan*).[14] The state itself, as the embodiment of a higher good to which all are subject, remained chronically underconceptualized.

The expansion of patterns of global connectedness, it has been said, encourages the prospects for individual self-actualization.[15] At first this sounds a little like an economist or a sociologist whose job is safe talking about "restructuring." But the principle has not been fully tested. The era of world history that has recently ended was, for Americans, an era of New Deal liberalism and racial segregation, for Vietnamese an era on the one hand of Victor Hugo and Rousseau and on the other of French colonial contractors buying Vietnamese peasants for twenty-five francs a head and shipping them to mines in the South Pacific. It was not an era of real globalization either in the universal accessibility of its advanced thought or in the moral wholeness of its master narratives. The threat was always that it might suffocate in the normative ambivalence of its own practices. This was true even for communism. The Vietnamese revolution was based upon mere fragments, largely Leninist and Stalinist and Maoist, of communist thought. (In the 1990s, the Vietnamese government is finally publishing the complete works of Marx and Engels in Vietnamese.) Such fragments, in turn, were first imparted haphazardly to many revolutionary partisans in makeshift classes in the forest, or secretively in French colonial prisons. As recently as the fourth Party Congress in 1976, an astonishing 200 of the 1,008 delegates claimed to have spent time in colonial prisons, including the ex-carpenter and painter from Hanoi (Do Muoi) who was to become party general secretary in the 1990s.[16]

Cold War politics brought a misplaced taste for seclusion from the noncommunist world, which further deepened the provincialism of the Vietnamese revolution. This trend and an American trade embargo imprisoned Vietnam until the late 1980s in a largely European, Moscow-directed trading system whose remote markets and high transportation costs removed much chance of real economic growth. Even Vietnam's critical shortage of freshwater fish in the 1980s had to be repaired with imported fish stocks from Cuba, the Ukraine, and Hungary. This long and severe circumstantial parochialization of what were supposedly global doctrines and forces of emancipation is the soft foundation upon which new approaches to human rights have to be attempted as Vietnamese revolutionaries enter a less Manichean period.

Western liberal intellectuals cannot help but be concerned with counterpart intellectuals in other countries who are denied freedom of speech. But the way in which societies treat their least privileged, least accepted members may well be an even better test of human rights in them than the way they treat their intellectuals. Nowhere was the Vietnamese revolution's parochialization of

Enlightenment values more obvious than in its treatment of the country's real underdogs: not just Vietnamese peasants, but ethic minority ones. The mountainous and midland regions of Vietnam where the non-Vietnamese minorities live occupy about two-thirds of Vietnam's national space. Vietnamese revolutionaries armed themselves with the belief that the traditional highland economy was primitive, but that the highland peoples themselves could not only be made to speak Vietnamese but also could be liberated by lowland elites' evangel of collectivized farming. From the 1960s to the early 1980s, therefore, state planners imposed agricultural cooperatives the size of larger lowland Vietnamese villages upon mountain villages whose inhabitants had historically had different, and smaller, conceptions of the proper size of community structures. The special economic and cultural characteristics of the Hmong, the Tai, the Nung, and Yao societies were resisted, for attempted homogenization on Vietnamese terms. In this false universalism era of Esperanto and reeducation camps, it turned out to be a very short jump from the Enlightenment belief in a preformed universal humanity to the self-deceiving identification of that humanity with purely Vietnamese traditions and values. But here retribution did not come at the hands of Amnesty International. Severe rice deficits in the eight mountain provinces north of Hanoi forced the beleaguered Vietnamese state not only to begin to accept the principle of "local knowledge" in mountain region economics, but also to ship 250,000 tons of scarce rice and cereals of its own each year to these provinces in the early 1980s to ward off famine.[17]

The Vietnamese communist oligarchy to which Ho Chi Minh's revolution has led, at the end of the twentieth century, is not representative of its people. Since it is not really elected, its unrepresentativeness cannot be compared to that of the many millionaires in the U.S. Senate, even if they are as remote from Tom Paine as the oligarchy is from Ho Chi Minh's outcasts. We see here rather a neotraditional unrepresentativeness, like that of the premodern patriarchal Vietnamese scholar-gentry. Committed to legal gender equality, the Vietnamese Communist Party's membership was only 16.9 percent female in 1995; committed to the rescue of the poor and the young, party members are becoming wealthier and older. Almost half of its members joined it before 1975.[18] Postrevolutionary oligarchies may nonetheless choose to be more enlightened about human rights than their more militant revolutionary predecessors. But if treatment of social underdogs, not intellectuals, is the greatest test of human rights, the ways in which the powerful imagine the less powerful and the powerless, or are compelled to imagine them, will be crucial in determining the immediate future of human rights in Vietnam (and elsewhere).

It has not been a good century in which to have been a Vietnamese peasant. Some evidence even suggests that between the 1940s and the 1980s—the years of war with the French and the Americans and of failed economic experiments and embargoes and malnutrition—the average size of young Vietnamese actually shrank while that of their Thai and Japanese counterparts was growing.[19] In the eyes of the more powerful "others" who rule them or who influence their lives, Vietnamese peasants' imagined essences or externally imposed identities have changed dramatically in this period, far more rapidly than their real substance. They have gone in a few years from being the "filthy *nhaques*" of the French colonalists to the communalistic revolutionary warriors of the Viet Minh to the objects of the fledgling "macroeconomics" management of *doi moi* reformers. A variety of would-be foreign custodians of their identity have come and gone: Rodgers and Hammerstein (the Vietnamese peasant "Bloody Mary" in *South Pacific*), Lenin, Chaianov, the World Bank.

But the Vietnamese revolution has also produced on its own soil thoughtful and sympathetic interpreters of the past and future of Vietnamese peasants. One of them suggested at the end of the 1980s that the real defeat for Vietnamese peasants would be defeatism itself, either in their own eyes or in the eyes of their rulers. Looking at the densely populated Red River delta of northern Vietnam, where the struggle to produce sufficient rice was engendering pessimism if not defeatism, Dao The Tuan warned that the "Green Revolution," with its high capital investment, chemical fertilizer demands, and irrigation requirements, could not by itself save the Red River delta peasants. But if such peasants were imaginatively reconceptualized one more time—this time as being the potential equals of the Japanese and Dutch family farmers who successfully farmed even more densely populated parts of the world than northern Vietnam—defeatist assumptions about the eternal poverty of the Red River might, with hard work, eventually turn into a mirage.[20]

Here the residual hope of the revolution blends with the much greater accessibility now of global ideals and means for vernacularizing them. An era in which their rulers really thought of them as potential Dutch polder farmers might be remarkable in its human rights significance for Vietnamese peasants, since most Dutch polder farmers are the economic embodiments of a more general knowledgeable historical capacity to create middle-class citizenship, with all its qualities of self-empowerment.

The twentieth century ended as a century of liberation movements that hadn't entirely liberated, in which people seeking to make themselves and others into angels became bureaucrats if not beasts instead, and in which cautious improvers killed fewer people than utopia-seeking perfectionists. The problems of the Vietnamese revolution, however, have had little to do with what Kissinger called "pre-Newtonian" non-Western resistance to the Western Enlightenment or the scientific culture that lay behind it. Even at its more autarkic, the Vietnamese communist revolution usually tried to remain open to as much global thought as seemed manageable and understandable to its mostly poorly educated leaders, who have had to move, in a few kaleidoscopic decades, from speaking French to speaking Russian to speaking English and to speaking French again. It never took rhetorical refuge in tribal "Asian" values to the same degree as some of its nonrevolutionary neighbors. Even the primitively Russified icon worship of Ho Chi Minh's mausoleum reflected a debased or muddled universalism more than a self-contained tribalism.

The problem has been, rather, the attempt to attach the wings of an eagle to the body of a sparrow. This was the attempt to apply a Marxist version of the Enlightenment ideal of the designed society, and one much more intense and historically condensed than the versions of the ideal in the wealthier West itself, to a poor, overpopulated, preindustrial society in which the better side of the Enlightenment ideal had already been confused by Western colonialism. The search that resulted for an earthly paradise led Vietnamese revolutionaries into far too many "swamplands," with far too many victims. But their revolution still has harbored what most revolutions harbor and what may be an important human right in itself. That is the right to hope. The denial of hope about the future, and total despair about building earthly paradises, might lead to swamplands of a different kind. Even the nearly always-deceived optimism in which revolutions seem to specialize may be better than unrelieved pessimism.[21]

NOTES

1. Henry A. Kissinger, *American Foreign Policy: Three Essays* (New York: Norton, 1969), pp. 48–49.

2. Reported in *Nhan dan chu nhat*, Hanoi, December 4, 1994, p. 6.

3. Alasdair MacIntyre, *After Virtue* (Notre Dame, University of Notre Dame Press, 1984), pp. 69–70.

4. Xiong Yuezhi, *Zhongguo jindai minzhu sixiang shi* (A history of modern Chinese democratic thought) (Shanghai: Renmin chubanshe, 1986), pp. 11–12.

5. Alexander Woodside, *Community and Revolution in Modern Vietnam* (Boston: Houghton Mifflin, 1976), pp. 4, 22.

6. Max Horkheimer and Theodor W. Adorno, *Dialectic of Enlightenment*, trans. John Cumming (New York: Continuum, 1975), p. 24.

7. Nguyen Trong Thuat, "Nghia binh-dang cua Dao Phat" (The meaning of equality of Buddhism), *Duoc Tue* (The torch of enlightenment), Hanoi, August 1 and 15, 1937, pp. 6–12 and 3–10.

8. See the masterful translation by Huynh Sanh Thong: Nguyen Chi Thien, *Flowers from Hell* (New Haven: Yale Center for Area and International Studies, Council on Southeast Asia Studies, 1984), pp. 73–99.

9. Quoted in David G. Marr, *Vietnam 1945: The Quest for Power* (Berkeley and Los Angeles: University of California Press, 1995), p. 539.

10. *Ho Chi Minh toan tap* (Collected works of Ho Chi Minh), vol. 1 (Hanoi: Su that, 1980), pp. 115–116.

11. Ho Bat Khuat, "Nhung van de cua mot nen bao chi dang phat trien" (The problems of a developing press), *Tap chi Cong san* (The Communist Journal) 12, no. 6 (1997): 25; Horkheimer and Adorno, *Dialectic*, pp. 24–25.

12. Horkheimer and Adorno, *Dialectic*, p. 9.

13. Pham Van Dong, *Nhung bai noi va viet chon loc* (Selected speeches and writings), vol. 1 (Hanoi: Su that, 1987), pp. 37–53.

14. Hoang Chi Bao et al., comp., *Co cau xa hoi-giai cap o nuoc ta: ly luan va thuc tien* (The social class structure in our country: theory and practice) (Hanoi: Thong tin ly luan, 1992), pp. 181–187.

15. Anthony Giddens, *The Consequences of Modernity* (Stanford: Stanford University Press, 1990), p. 158.

16. Le Mau Han et al., *Cac dai hoi dang ta 1930–1986* (Our party congresses, 1930–1986) (Hanoi: Su that, 1991), p. 88.

17. See the article by Lam Quang Huyen in *Tap chi Dan toc hoc* (Journal of ethnology), Hanoi, 1 (1983): 23–26.

18. Le Quang Thuong, "Mot so van de ve cong tac dang vien trong tinh hinh nay" (Some problems with respect to the work of party members in the present situation), *Tap chi Cong san* 14, no. 7 (1996): 14–20.

19. See the assessment by Dr. Nguyen Ky Anh in *Nhan dan chu nhat*, Hanoi, August 1, 1993, p. 5.

20. Dao The Tuan, "Dong bang song Hong co the san xuat du an duoc khong?" (Can the Red River delta produce enough to eat?), *Nhan dan*, October 21, 1988, p. 3. The author heads the Hanoi Institute of Agricultural Science.

21. E. J. Hobsbawm, *Revolutionaries* (New York: Meridian Books, 1975), pp. 136–141.

8

What Absence Is Made Of: Human Rights in Africa

Florence Bernault

Why is the human rights situation so dismal in Africa? Scholarly answers to this question have typically fallen into two categories. An *accounting* literature concerned with statistics generally proposes a disheartening list of human rights abuses, while offering poor hopes of progress on a continent described as submitted to increasing poverty, collapsing states, and spreading violence. A second literature reacts against such a perspective by arguing that human rights have a place in African philosophy and social practice. A common trend of this *defensive* literature, however, is to discard the universal validity of Western ideas of human rights by stating that they can neither account for nor be compatible with indigenous ideas of individual dignity and human value.

These perspectives convey the magnitude of the issue, but they usually end up stumbling over the evidence they both demonstrate and criticize: the absence, or exteriority, of human rights in Africa. Based on the underlying assumption that the continent is imprisoned into such absence, either by virtue of its political depravity or moral distinction, these approaches ignore the complex historical circumstances surrounding the emergence of human rights on the continent. From the end of the nineteenth century to the 1960s the representatives of colonial domination used human rights as political tools to exert control over local societies and to reserve political privileges to the whites. During this crucial period, therefore, human rights developed less as philosophical ideas of human dignity than as specific, historical relationships between emerging modern states (colonial governments) and reluctant civilians (the "natives"). Throughout the twentieth century, these relations shed light on the difficult emergence of a viable civil society in the context of an ever-enduring state oppression—a trend hardly stopped by postcolonial regimes.

FALLEN IDEALS: HUMAN RIGHTS AND THE COLONIAL PROJECT

Human rights served as a core principle during the colonial invasion in Africa. This implied a major distortion of the eighteenth-century ideas of human rights: instead of being equalizing and liberating concepts, human rights became a philosophical basis for racial hierarchy.

Historians have long studied how the colonization of Africa rested upon a composite set of economic and diplomatic factors. The European industrial and capitalist revolution required new markets for manufactured goods as well as cheap raw materials to supply factories. Diplomatic rivalries focused on securing strategic routes and fueling stations for steamers en route to India and Southeast Asia as well as on designing large "spheres of influence" in the largely unknown though potentially rich areas of the African hinterland. But less known is how those incentives were grounded in a large set of ideological assumptions that served to anchor the colonial project in European public opinions. African dependence was organized not only along the lines of global economic conquest but also through its relocation within master narratives that promoted a negative image of the continent and its peoples. By the end of the nineteenth century, Europe's interest in Africa had shifted from the abolition of the slave trade to the partition of the continent, from a debate framed by the universal nature of human beings and their right to freedom and equality to a project whose ideological bases depended on the assumption that African people were located outside (in chronological, geographical, or racial terms) the sphere of human rights. This ideological displacement was instrumental in legitimizing the colonial enterprise and answering its central contradiction: How could enlightened European nations engage into the forceful subjugation of an entire continent?

Beginning at the end of the eighteenth century, Europe progressively confined Africa to the sphere of cultural backwardness, social immobility, and historical impotence. Social Darwinists classified human beings racially, placing blacks at the bottom and whites at the top of physiological and cultural achievement. Historians and philosophers, reflecting on the human past and future as a linear progression toward complex social structures, began to perceive Africa as embedded in historical paralysis. According to this new spirit of theological classification, Africans were primarily organized in tribes (communities based on race and kinship) and Europeans in nations (communities based on a social contract between citizens and the state). Such perceptions stereotyped African societies as based on inequality and submission, symbolized by slavery. In contrast, freedom and equality constituted the heritage and political horizon of European nations, embodied by human rights. Innovation was therefore confined to the unique place where it could flourish and spread: Europe.

This powerful myth—studied by Edward Said under the name of Orientalism—emerged in direct connection with the intellectual needs of imperial expansion.

The scientific and philosophical necessity of bringing barbarian societies to civilization and history justified Europe's mission overseas. Colonial inequality could be envisioned as a necessary step to engage Africa on the path of freedom and modernity, and to build the conditions for the emergence of human rights in Africa. However, such a project completely transformed the notion of human rights itself, displacing them from the realm of essence to historical contingency. Freedom and equality were not essential, sacred features of the human condition, but a contingent stage of human history. In this altered form, they provided the core dogma of the colonial enterprise. Political and economic domination in Africa was organized around authoritarian state apparatuses, discriminatory laws, limited citizenship, and racial segregation. European propaganda and the popular imagination, however, pictured colonial rule as campaigns of "pacification," the ending of domestic slavery, the replacement of tyrannical rulers by benevolent administrators and enlightened chiefs, economic development, the diffusion of hygiene and medical science, literary education, Christianity, and the adoption of liberating codes of behavior such as monogamy and female emancipation.[1] The expulsion of Africa from the sphere of human rights betrayed in fact the tremendous alteration of European principles of human rights—a failure brilliantly denounced by the black writer Aimé Césaire.[2]

Accordingly, the expression "human rights" itself largely disappeared from the vocabulary of the colonial milieus in reference to Africa between 1885 and 1941. Neither in international debates about Africa nor in the colonies themselves was the term to be used again before the Atlantic Charter (1941); it was replaced by notions that carried the idea of historical accomplishment: usually "civilization" and "progress." The exclusion of Africa from the sphere of human rights had immediate consequences. On the judicial level, Europeans denied African peoples legal international existence. Consider the Berlin Conference Act (1885) that established regulations for free trade, missionary activities, and navigation on the continent, as well as the diplomatic rules for recognizing a Western nation's sovereignty over a colony. The meeting stands famous in relegating Africa as *res nullius* in international affairs, as not a single African representative was invited to attend. The treaty devoted a few passages to the fate of Africans. The "indigenous populations" did not hold rights, but were to be protected by the European rulers desiring "to promote [. . .] the most favorable conditions for the development of trade and civilization in certain regions of Africa." Chapter 1, article 6, was more explicit and assigned colonial powers the mission to preserve Africans as a backward human stock, worth primarily of material care, and marginally of benevolent moral paternalism: "All powers exerting sovereign rights or influence in these territories promise to protect *the conservation* of all native populations as well as *to improve their moral and material living conditions*, and to work toward suppressing slavery and especially slave-trading" (emphasis mine).

On the ground, the denial of Africans as equal human beings followed more complex lines. The colonized, it was argued, did not have a sufficient level of civilization to be granted rights. But Europeans were also influenced by pseudo-historical theories about African societies. Living in stateless societies, people were considered as having no need to develop individual rights against a potentially threatening central authority. European pacification having defeated predatory empires and rulers, the colonized would be protected enough by the customs as well as small size of their decentralized communities, "tribes," "clans," and the like—perfect examples of the primitive and happy natural societies that enlightened Europeans had imagined in their reflection on human rights at the end of the eighteenth century. The colonial mind constantly balanced between a vision of Africans as the "happy savage" and the "primitive barbarian." However, a more homogenous mind-set presided upon colonizers' image of their own government. They fantasized the colonial state (never named as such by them), in regards to Africans, as a benevolent "administration," a governing tool aimed not at organizing the sordid economy of domination upon conquered territories but at building material and moral progress for the sake of the Africans. As a consequence, no individual protection for the natives appeared necessary, while colonial states envisioned themselves as the primary vectors of modernization, civilization, and social reform.

In the African colonial empires the terms "revolution," "rights," and their colonial euphemisms "civilization" and "progress," became paradoxically some of the most important ideological pillars of the autocratic state. While the idea of human rights had emerged in Europe and in America from the bottom up, and worked historically as a new self-consciousness of civil society and as a challenge to the old regime's privileges and abuses, the colonial project bound the realization of human rights in Africa to a governmental enterprise of political tutelage.

INACCESSIBLE CITIZENSHIP

Besides the omnipotent state, no civil society was allowed to form as a licit counterpart of colonial governments, not even among Europeans. Local citizenship did not exist in the colonies, even for the whites, until after World War II. As a result, colonial states invaded the whole legal sphere and tried to monopolized most political initiatives.

At the time of their formation colonies had been given the facade of a nation: a central government, boundaries, and a "national" territory. However, sovereignty and legislative capacity belonged to the metropolitan government, delegated to the colonial administration (appointed by overseas government and not elected by local settlers). A double vacuum characterized citizenship. Whites were considered part of the larger metropole, not citizens of the colony. They retained their British, Belgian, or French nationalities and citizenship privileges in Europe, but they usually could not elect representants in the colony itself. The colonial administration, under tight control from the metropole, retained the entire monopoly of executive and legislative power and functioned as the only legal institution in the colonies. In French Equatorial Africa, local settlers became so frustrated with this exclusive state power that in 1944 they organized a lobby association and a conference, named after the first French Revolutionary Assembly, the *Etats généraux de la colonisation.*

Yet in all colonies, the state acted as the guardian of white domination. European rule rested upon the radical separation of whites and Africans, and this remained a fundamental configuration of the colony. Racial discrimination took many diverse forms, from spatial isolation to legal segregation, yet always confined Africans into subaltern status. In the British Empire, no assumption existed that Africans could eventually gain British citizenship and rights. Whites and blacks lived and developed in two different spheres. Under the principle of "indirect rule," Africans were supposed to govern themselves, under the ultimate tutelage of the white administration. Human rights were only marginally invoked in this context, while Africans were not supposed to share or to participate in the same historical development as colonizers.[3] In contrast, in French, Belgian, and Portuguese colonies, the separation between Africans and Europeans set off a different ideology: it consolidated the constituent gap between colonizers and the colonized by justifying the colonial mission through the principle of "assimilation," a vision of Africans evolving progressively to full integration as citizens into the white public realm. In fact, since successful assimilation would dissolve colonial domination, imperial policies took pain at reproducing and reshaping the racial faultline, while presenting it as a temporary, historically defined and contingent boundary.

In the French colonies for example, Africans were legal *sujets* (subjects), liable to special civil and penal laws, forced labor, and specific taxes. French administrators could sentence African *sujets* without trial to up to fifteen days of jail. No African political representation was allowed. Yet, to justify the colonial mission and comply with the assimilation ideals, access to the sphere of full citizenship had to be implemented. Examining how these channels opened for Africans helps one to understand how French colonization managed to retain full control of the racial hiatus. In theory, Africans could apply for full French citizenship, granted by a special decree of the French government in Paris. Only a handful of them achieved this before World War II, with the exception of natives of the four communes of Senegal.[4] Nevertheless, colonizers resented the possibility as too important a threat to their racial superiority. To prevent Africans from applying for full citizenship, intermediate but subaltern categories were designed in the 1940s. In the Belgian Congo, the administration devised a new status for Africans called *évoluants* (evolving persons). In Portuguese Angola and Mozambique, such categories existed under the name of *assimilados*. In the French colonies, the law defined the status of *évolué* in 1942, explicitly to prevent Africans from demanding full citizenship. *Evolués* were not French citizens, yet they were not *sujets* anymore. They could not be submitted to forced labor or to arbitrary arrest, and they could serve as appointed members of the few municipal councils allowed in African urban districts during the same period. However, they were still liable to customary laws and tribunals and not to the French *Code civil* and *Code pénal*. Acquiring the status involved holding a primary school diploma, writing a scholarly exam, and passing an administrative inquiry about personal habits, morality, and Westernized standard of living. Not only did the colonial state entirely control the process, but the administrations kept the number of *évolués* at significantly low numbers. In the two colonies of Gabon and Congo-Brazzaville, for example, fewer than 320 candidates were awarded the status between 1941 and 1946 from a total population of 2.5 million.

In 1946, the newly adopted French Constitution introduced a major rupture in colonial citizenship. Article 44 transformed all former *sujets* of the French Empire into citizens: "All natives of the French Union [the new name for the French Empire] enjoy the rights and privileges of human beings guaranteed by Articles 1–39 of the present Constitution. All national citizens and all natives in the metropole and overseas territories [the new name for the colonies] enjoy the rights of citizens."

The racial division between Europeans and Africans apparently dissolved. The new Constitution, however, located legal discrimination at a new level. Articles 80 and 82 provided that Africans would still retain a "personal status" while Europeans (whites) would own "civil status." Personal status submitted Africans to customary tribunals and restricted their voting privileges and political representation.[5] Legal provision established that Africans could freely renounce their "personal status" to acquire "civil status." In practice, none of the applications were examined by the French administration. As a former high-ranking civil servant of the government of Congo recalls: "The administration bureaus in Brazzaville received thousands of demands [for renunciation of personal status]. They stacked them in filing cabinets and never examined them."[6]

The colonial state's control over the formation of a citizenry remained seemingly undefeated even after Africans were granted access to citizenship and voting rights.

THE MYTH OF 1789 AS A CONTENDING SITE

Yet the existence of discursive frameworks concerning human rights, controlled and biased as they were, still provided Africans with a potential entry into the colonial system of references, and, more important, into its contradictions. In the French colonies, the myth of 1789 provided Africans with a surrealist episode of administrative self-celebration and a dramatic moment of *exposure*. French officials in all parts of the colonies carefully controlled the annual celebration of the 14th of July: it constituted a display of France's prestige and legitimacy as the "country of human rights."

Ceremonies began usually with a military salute to the French flag, in the town's public square, and were followed by marches led by scout organizations, associations, missions, etc. Fireworks and a torch parade formed the high point of the celebration at night. Throughout the day, administrators, officers, and guards kept a close watch for possible disturbances. The 14th of July ceremonies opened a place and time when the colonized could remember the discrepancy between French ideals and the practice of colonial rule and engage in physical confrontation and revolt. Such tension appears in reports of the 14th of July in the local newspapers, such as this one in the Congo colony: "We thank our two dynamic administrators for bringing more aura to the ceremony. We are also happy to note that no incident disturbed the manifestations."[7]

The French administration nominated a handful of Africans *évolués* and chiefs to win a trip to France, where they were greeted as official guests for the ceremonies of the 14th of July in Paris. They then spent a week or two touring France under official guidance and were expected to bring back to Africa living testimonies of the grandeur of the metropole. Most of the guests complied with these expectations, but some, publishing their impressions, brought up embarrassing questions. They wrote about a country where French men and women had shown attention and sympathy to the African delegates. In contrast, the general disregard and attitude of superiority Africans experienced in the colonies led a deputy of Chad to ask a crucial question: Were local colonists real Frenchmen?[8] This put the ideological premises of colonization upside down. The white men were not, after all, the guardians or the conveyors of better civilization and human rights. They proved an illegitimate extension of metropolitan France, organizers of domination and racism, unworthy of real French citizenship.

Within the white community itself, the subversive power of human rights promoted internal tensions and divisions. It is important to remember that colonial rule never achieved total and coherent domination over Africans and that the white community, moreover, was divided socially and by conflicting political and ideological projects. During the *Etats généraux de la colonisation* (1945), the conservative settlers used the rhetoric of the Revolution as a tool against colonial reforms. In contrast, missionary and liberal administrative reforms could point to African women as recipients of new rights and emancipation and launch new legislation on polygamy, bride wealth, marriage, and inheritance, but they did so by strictly limiting their initiatives to narrow, specific segments of the African population.[9] A more radical challenge existed among white liberals and Marxists, such as the *Groupes d'études communistes*, which in the early 1940s initiated the formation of local political workshops for Africans. Some used their positions as teachers to diffuse the concept of revolution and human rights among students and to inject it with a renewed invigorating power, such as this secondary school professor mentioned in a secret police report in 1948, who taught "tendentious opinions during her history classes" and identified "*montagnards*' ideas to the ones of contemporary communists."[10]

Such provocations proved exceptional. And the myth of 1789, while providing Africans and liberal whites with a potential tool to resist colonial rule, remained essentially ambivalent, used by conservative forces as well as progressive ones. For this reason, African nationalists proved increasingly reluctant to use it during the final period of colonization.

THE HESITANT RHETORICS OF INDEPENDENCE

The evolution of the tiny elite of African activists in France, nucleus of the first nationalists who would eventually lead independence movements, is revealing of this trajectory. During an early phase, in the 1920s, students such as Aimé Césaire and Léopold Sédar Senghor and workers such as Lamine Senghor and Tiémoko Kouyaté did not ask for independence but linked the promotion of Africans to the colonial concept of assimilation: access to the sphere of full citizenship, civil and political rights. Lamine Senghor founded in 1926 in Paris a Committee for the Defense of the Negro Race to lobby the government. As early as 1927, the committee split into two constituencies. One, increasingly isolated and weak, carried an enduring assimilationist program. A more radical branch, under the leadership of Lamine Senghor, and later Tiémoko Kouyaté, took on a new name as the Ligue for the Defense of the Negro Race. In 1931, the Ligue published a newspaper named *The Cry of the Negroes* in reference to the famous newspaper published during the French Revolution, *Le Cri du Peuple* (The Cry of the People). But the crucial move was that the Ligue had affiliated with the French Communist Party and was pressing for immediate self-government in the colonies.[11] Among the African intelligentsia in France—a trend that also held true among African nationalists in the British Empire—Marxist ideas proved a far stronger vehicle than the myths of 1776 or 1789 to formulate nationalist resistance.

Until the late 1950s, most colonial governments in Sub-Saharan Africa resisted the possibility of independence, even though they authorized the emergence of a constitutional life with political parties, trade unions, and partial elections. In this new context, born in part from increasing international criticisms of colonization, and in part from the local emergence of powerful political classes, all metropoles managed to prevent the radicalization of the opposition to imperialism. In French colonies, radical mass uprisings, backed by revolutionary intellectuals, such as the Madagascar revolt (1947) and the Sanaga rebellion in Cameroon (1955–1962), were immediately and forcefully smashed. In the Ivory

Coast, the administration harassed the politicians of the *Rassemblement démocratique africain*, a pan-African party whose deputies had allied themselves with the French Communist Party in the National Assembly, until its leader, Houphouet-Boigny, disengaged from the strategic alliance in 1950 and pursued collaborative policies. In Kenya, the Mau-Mau rebellion was ruthlessly repressed by British armed forces from 1955 to 1962. In these processes of controlled decolonization, independence was managed as a transfer of power from colonial governments anxious to avoid wars like those in Indochina and Algeria (France) to moderate African parties.

This is one of the reasons why, in the 1950s and 1960s, radical changes of regimes and/or social structures initiated by large mass movements were very few. Even later, no real popular revolutions happened in Africa. The violent independence wars in Angola, Mozambique, Zambia, and Zimbabwe (formerly Rhodesia) extended over long periods of time, and in the case of Angola and Mozambique, degenerated into armed civil conflicts among Africans. Mass resistance to apartheid in South Africa also lasted several decades, until its final victory in 1990. The final transfer of power between the Afrikaner government and the African National Congress embedded into, and carefully complied with, constitutional reforms and procedures. In most independence cases, if the dramatic changes in the government personnel, as well as the general democratization and the mass participation in civil and political life for Africans can be described as revolutionary, the process of change at the top of the government can hardly be. In other cases, radical changes triggered by popular uprising soon transformed into the monopolization of power by a restrained political elite (Ethiopia, 1974) and a top-down, authoritarian imposition of social reforms over society. It is therefore difficult to trace the role of human rights ideas in a context where the emergence of strong civil mass movements almost never existed.

Even when political uprisings were labeled "revolutions," the rhetoric of human rights proved to back extremely conservative changes. One striking example is the Hutu uprising in Rwanda in 1959, misread as a democratic "revolution" by Belgian administrators. Instead of promoting the emergence of a vigorous, homogenous civil society in this small country, the 1959 revolution locked Rwanda into racial hatred and dehumanization. In the mid-1950s, young Hutu intellectuals from the Parmehutu party, backed by dissatisfied Hutu peasants, denounced the political and social domination of the Tutsi. The Tutsi, imagined as the "natural" elite in Rwanda by Europeans at the end of the nineteenth century, had been granted extensive privileges and had been transformed from a fluid socioeconomic category into a racial group monopolizing authority over the Hutu, perceived by colonial experts as an inferior race of peasants. Cast in ethnic terms directly derived from the ethnicized structures of public power organized by colonialists, the 1959 Hutu mobilization won the paradoxical support of the Belgians. While the Belgians continued to see the Tutsi as the natural patricians of Rwanda, they became convinced that a democratization process was necessary. Such a shift would lead to the decline of the nobility (the Tutsi minority) and transform the Hutu majority into the natural and legitimate source of political sovereignty. The problem, of course, was that these two categories were still cast in racial terms. In November 1959, when Hutu militants organized violent uprisings against the Tutsi, the Belgian government appropriated a revolutionary analytical framework to promote access to central and local power for the Hutu. Colonel Guy Logiest, the key man of the Belgian armed forces in Rwanda, declared later: "Some among my assistants thought that I was wrong in being so partial against the Tutsi . . . Today, twenty-five years later, I ask myself what was it that made me act with such resolution. It was without doubt the will to give the people back their dignity. And it was probably just as much the desire to put down the *morgue* and expose the duplicity of a basically oppressive and unjust aristocracy."[12] The revolution that ended in 1960–1962 with the political victory of the Hutu and the independence of Rwanda led to mass killings and mass exodus of Tutsi to neighboring countries and constituted a key phase in the racial gridlock of Rwandan politics.

By and large, African independences created regimes that reproduced the features of colonial power. In most countries, the state retained a disproportionate amount of authority, and within the dominant ideology of decolonization, Africans were still perceived as collective groups and legal communities rather than persons with individual rights.

THE STATE'S ANNEXATION OF HUMAN RIGHTS
IN THE POSTCOLONY (1950s–1980s)

The political project that dominated African decolonization rested upon the consolidation of unified, viable nations and the promises of economic development. In this context, the goal of nationalists was to promote the right of Africans to become legal communities: Parties and leaders focused primarily on "peoples' rights," not on individual rights. Colonization had ruled over Africans perceived as collective, backward masses. To some extent, decolonization fought back along the same framework, promoting the rise of the colonized as oppressed communities. The 1955 Bandung Conference organized in Indonesia by Nehru unfolded as an anti-Berlin event, to overturn the moment when colonized continents and peoples had been rejected from legal international existence. Bandung participants condemned colonialism in terms that combined Marxist influences and eighteenth-century revolutionary rhetoric: "The Afro-Asiatic man should conquer a world citizenship, from which he had been exiled by colonization. Afro-Asiatic peoples are the world's proletariat."[13] The fusion of these two revolutionary traditions encouraged a vision of rights as those of communities and nations taken as a whole, a vision shared by Western liberals or conservatists since the days of the 1941 Atlantic Charter.[14]

This agenda successfully legitimized the rise of authoritarian regimes claiming to protect the consolidation of their fragile nations and denying rights to any political opposition that could weaken national unity. In the first years of independence, strong anti-imperialist statements warned against neocolonialist plots and stressed the necessity for the continent to free itself of all economic, political, and cultural Western influences. For decades, many African intellectuals along with the international community brought their support to this project.[15] The trend culminated in the creation of the Organization of African Unity (OAU) in 1963, whose first task was to recognize and freeze all national frontiers and reinforce the stability of existing governments. The OAU refused to adopt the UN 1948 Universal Declaration of Human Rights and wrote its own declaration, known as the Banjul Charter, twenty years later (1981). The charter recognized the rights of the individual and his or her freedom of conscience, religion, information, and speech. The document, however, also spelled out duties for every individual, "towards his family and society, the State and other legally recognized communities and the international community." Article 29 specified that "every individual must also preserve and strengthen positive African cultural values" and should "contribute to the best of his ability, at all times and at all levels, to the promotion and achievement of African unity."[16]

The Banjul Charter's invocation of the individual's duty to defending his or her community was less a liberation from Western hegemony than a culminating moment in the state's tentative monopoly over human rights. This pattern had been established by colonial rule. What human rights exist when individuals are denied the right to stand against their own community? Can human rights subsist when the state claims to be their only legitimate provider and arbitrator? In numerous African countries governments use human rights as an ideological tool directed toward civil society as well as a convenient facade to placate international scrutiny. In Congo-Brazzaville, for example, the government established in the early 1990s a Ministry for Democratic Culture and Human Rights that claimed to promote information and action; however, human rights violations by the state did not decline during this period, nor were precarious individual rights significantly strengthened.

Here appears again the fundamental ambivalence of the concept. Implementing human rights can be a political project, a moral agenda, and a collective ideal. In this sense, state agencies can legitimately carry forth such a program. But the rise of human rights also emerged historically as a particular configuration of politics as a specific relationship between the state and citizens. In the West, they helped articulate the rights of individual citizens as a powerful protection against potential state abuses. Today, African states largely function as dictatorships. Concentrating wealth and retaining a monopoly on legitimate violence, they present considerable threats to the freedom of individuals, while claiming to bear the sole initiative in handling human rights. The fact that some try to channel and capture legal recourse against state violence is, in this perspective, deeply troubling. The argument that human rights belong to a European project of cultural imperialism, and as such should be refused by Africans, is generally beneficial to dominant, not to dominated, categories within modern African nations.[17] For many observers of African politics, the main continuity of the nationalist period was not an enduring, neocolonial influence of the West over Africa but a more surreptitious neocolonialism from within, that of an authoritarian, unchallenged state rule.

THE LIBERATION OF CIVIL SOCIETY?

The late 1980s and early 1990s witnessed momentous changes in Africa. Apartheid came to an end in South Africa. Elsewhere, authoritarian regimes were overthrown, and in a number of countries (Gabon, Congo-Brazzaville, Congo-Kinshasa, Benin) a wave of national conferences debated the refashioning of national politics, public life, and civil liberties. Scholars predicted a "second independence" in Africa: After the "nationalist paradigm," political initiatives were to be based on the liberation of civil society and the democratization of politics. Visions of the future moved from the postindependence ideas of nation building at any cost, while considering human and civil rights as an unnecessary luxury. Local intellectuals strongly denounced the abuses of dictatorial regimes, and many withdrew their support or remained silent.[18] A dynamic, autonomous and outspoken press flourished in countries where only official newspapers had been previously authorized.

International pressures also contributed to a changing human rights environment. Western financial and technical aid has become increasingly contingent on democratization efforts in Africa. Humanitarian initiatives discounted previous hesitations that had prevailed in interfering directly in domestic affairs: In Somalia or Liberia, aid interventions proved more and more visible and publicized, contributing to a general phenomenon labeled as "a proliferation of humanitarian aid" by political commentators on African affairs. More important, aid provided by Western governments, nongovernmental organizations (NGOs), and UN missions clearly targeted helpless individuals and civilians. Multilateral support adopted a new facade, bypassing intergovernmental deals to publicize direct access to citizens.

By the mid-1990s, however, bright hopes gave way to strong feelings of pessimism. From April to August 1994, the presence of UN, and later French, troops, who had been instructed not to interfere in Rwanda during the genocide, gave a terrible picture of the powerlessness of humanitarian structures. The Rwandan tragedy unfolded as a dramatic moment of ultimate denial of human rights through the systematic dehumanization of the victims and their ruthless killings orchestrated by Rwandan political extremists. International aid created further problems. When a Tutsi army took power in Kigali, millions of Hutu left the country. Refugee camps opened in eastern Zaire a few kilometers from the Rwandan frontier and unwillingly, but unavoidably, gave shelter to perpetrators of the genocide. Within a few weeks, extremists had managed to intimidate refugees, channeled food and drugs to buy weapons, and organized guerillas to attack the new government in Rwanda. In 1996, Rwandan and Zairian soldiers attacked the camps in retaliation, killed thousands of refugees, and forced hundreds of thousand to flee in Zaire, many of whom starved to death. An apocalyptic failure had presided over the Great Lake crisis—a crisis that raised questions about the lack of political vision, historical advising, and clear agenda among international humanitarian agencies. No wonder recent conferences on humanitarian aid in Africa have placed the problem of "impunity" and the crisis of humanitarian aid on the agenda.[19]

CONCLUSION

In other parts of Africa, the 1990s' democratization waves have often ended up reinforcing previous regimes and strengthening state violence over individuals and communities. Numerous ethnic, political, economical, or ideological conflicts suggest that individuals, too, can impede human rights. The new European wars demonstrate that this is hardly, of course, an African particularity.

With the exception of South Africa, where human rights movements are strong, do such failures point out toward a structural weakness of African civil societies? If the mobilization around human rights is a good indicator of the strength of civil society and its capacity to crystallize against the state, does the apparent absence of recent victories condemn African citizenries to failure? Some scholars think so, and argue that African societies are primarily organized along patron/client relationships, reinforcing the strength of the powerful and preventing an autonomous civil society from challenging the state's authority. But this is far from certain. The daily battles of African NGOs, intellectuals, and journalists remind us that Africa is no more constrained by determinist trends than any other parts of the world. And to a large extent the long and ironical development of human rights on this continent demonstrates that the reinforcement of civil societies in the face of state violence is first and foremost bound to changing, historical *rapports de force*.

NOTES

1. The fact that historians and social scientists still have tremendous difficulties presenting these facts to most Westerners, who are usually ready to acknowledge the shortcomings of Western rule but remain strongly convinced of the positive integration of Africa in the global world, is a tribute to the power and endurance of the civilizing mission myth.

Chapter 8

2. "First we must study how colonization works to decivilize the colonizer, to brutalize him in the true sense of the word, to awaken him to buried instincts, to covetousness, violence, race hatred, and moral relativism . . ." Aimé Césaire, *Discourse on Colonialism*, 1st ed. (Paris: 1955; trans. New York: Monthly Review Press, 1972), p. 13.

3. They were primarily invoked to forbid any paramount chief and indigenous judicial system to use punishments that did not comply with European "civilized" moral standards, such as torture, mutilation, or death sentences. Because French ideology explicitly used human rights and the myth of the 1789 revolution to impose its domination in Africa, we will use this case in a more extensive fashion.

4. In 1918, natives of the four communes of Senegal were granted French citizenship for complex historical reasons, the main one being the participation of African soldiers of French West Africa in World War I. They remained a tiny minority in French West Africa.

5. Whites under civil status and Africans under personal status voted in two separate colleges. Each college elected one deputy to the National Assembly in Paris. As local assemblies were organized in the colonies, the white population (civil status) was granted a disproportionate number of local deputies (usually twelve against eighteen for the total African population). In the black electoral college, voting privileges were restricted to a minority of Africans who enjoyed personal status.

6. Interview with Pierre Bas, Paris, 1989.

7. *Semaine de l'AEF* (Brazzaville), August 21, 1954, p. 103. See Marc Michel, "Mémoire officielle, discours et pratique coloniale. Le 14 juillet et le 11 novembre au Sénégal entre les deux guerres," *Revue française d'histoire d'outre-mer* 77, no. 287 (1990): 145–158. On British rituals and ceremonies in Africa, see Terence Ranger's chapter in *The Invention of Tradition*, ed. Eric Hobsbawm and Terence Ranger (Cambridge: Cambridge University Press, 1983).

8. Tao Thomas, "Souvenir du 14 juillet," *Le Progrès politique, économique et social du Moyen-Congo* 12 (1956): 1–4.

9. However, most administrations worried about the emergence of free and "amoral" women in the colonies. They prevented women from settling in the cities and promoted patriarchal control in the countryside.

10. Daily Report, Sûreté, Direction des Affaires politiques, Government General of French Equatorial Africa. December 21, 1948. Archives Nationales, section outre-mer, Aix-en-Provence, 5D 241. *Montagnards* refers to the most radical constituency of French revolutionaries between 1792 and 1795.

11. In 1933, after the Nazi victory in Germany, the Communist International generally backed a strategy of building a common antifascist front. The Ligue for the Defense of the Negro Race returned to neoassimilationism, defending French ideas of universalism against the fascist threat. For details, see the excellent study of Philippe Dewitte, *Les mouvements nègres en France, 1919–1939* (Paris: Karthala, 1985).

12. Quoted in Gérard Prunier, *The Rwanda Crisis: History of a Genocide* (New York: Columbia University Press, 1995), p. 49.

13. Malice Beanbag, quoted in Elikia M'Bokolo, *Afrique Noire, Histoire et Civilisations*, vol. 2: *XIXe-XXe siècles* (Paris: Hatier-Aupelf, 1992), p. 451.

14. In August 1941, Roosevelt and Churchill pronounced the Atlantic Charter and proclaimed the right of self-determination for all peoples.

15. One example is the Nigerian political scientist, Claude Ake. See his *Social Science as Imperialism: A Theory of Political Development* (Ibadan: Ibadan University Press, 1974).

16. The second part of the Banjul Charter established a Commission on Human and People's Rights (Articles 30–62). *The African Charter on Human and People's Rights* (New York: United Nations, 1990).

17. Goran Hyden, "The Challenges of Domesticating Rights in Africa," in *Human Rights and Governance in Africa*, ed. Ronald Cohen, Goran Hyden, and Winston P. Nagan (Gainesville: The University of Florida Press, 1993), pp. 261–262. Rhoda E. Howard in *Human Rights in Commonwealth Africa* (Totowa, N.J.: Rowman & Littlefield, 1986), particularly pp. 1–36.

18. Goran Hyden, chapter on academic freedom, and concluding chapter, in *Human Rights and Governance in Africa*, ed. Cohen, Hyden, and Nagan, pp. 235–280.

19. Human rights associations from twenty-two countries (seventeen from Africa) met in Ouagadougou (Burkina Faso) in March 1996 to debate human rights and impunity in Africa. See the report in *Politique Africaine* 62 (1996): 95–102.

Part V

Views from the Field

9

Acumen of the Irreconciled: A Few Conjectures on Dictatorship

Adam Michnik (translated by Jacek Dalecki)

The irreconciled man cannot regard it as "normalcy" when he is systematically lied to and his rights are violated. He detects the world of dictatorship with his senses: of taste, smell, and touch. He knows the taste of lies, the smell of fear, the touch of cruelty. Instinctively and unerringly, he has no trouble recognizing other irreconciled men: their heroism, determination, and courage.

In Rangoon, the capital of Burma, I listened to the arguments of eulogists who defended measures taken by the military regime, who talked about "reasons of the state" and "irresponsible and factious elements." I saw people so paralyzed with fear that they were unwilling to speak to a foreigner. Last of all, I witnessed the Burmese security apparatus at work, refusing to let anyone into the house of Aung San Suu Kyi, a leader of the National League for Democracy (NLD) and winner of the Nobel Peace Prize. In 1990, the NLD overwhelmingly swept national elections. A military coup followed, and the State Law and Order Restoration Council (SLORC)—a rough equivalent of the Polish Military Council for National Salvation—seized power.

In secret and at night, I visited other leaders of the NLD. Pawel, a colleague of mine from *Gazeta Wyborcza*,[1] kept repeating stubbornly: "Dic-tators and dic-heads"—and I kept thinking of police blockades of Lech Wałęsa's apartment in Gdańsk, unending police harassments, house searches, detainments and imprisonments, and neighbors, whose faces, frightened at first, would later light up with a furtive smile.

Déjà vu, I thought. In Rangoon, I felt twenty years younger.

ORDER AND CHAOS

Dictatorship grows out of the weakness of democracy, out of the lack of consensus about the rule of law in a democratic state, out of chaos. Those who break this consensus do so, and usually for good reasons, in the name of social justice, historical truth, or to thwart corruption. The Bolsheviks wanted to end the war and promised radical land reforms. The Nazis wanted to put an end to political anarchy, curb inflation and unemployment, and overcome the stifling humiliation of the Treaty of Versailles. Jaruzelski wanted to halt the growing decay of the communist state and save Poland from the threat of "Big Brother's help." The Burmese generals wanted to preserve the unity of the state, torn apart by ethnic wars, and restore order in the streets, where gangs and banditry enjoyed a free reign. For many, a difference between order and chaos matters much more than between democracy and dictatorship. All that is common knowledge, although democrats will not rush to admit it.

Nonetheless, to succeed in contending with dictatorship, one must first understand its arguments and claims.

SECURITY IN DICTATORSHIPS

Dictatorship means living in fear . . . and security. The opponents of dictatorship have had a difficult time understanding this paradox, and in their refusal to grapple with it lies the source of their powerlessness. The security of the world of dictatorship means freedom from choice. Others make decisions. I do not have to decide about anything. I have to obey. This is the key to happiness and success.

Yet, security also means danger. It is not a coincidence that the most feared communist institution was the Ministry of Public Security. This institution, which extorted obedience through fear, was the prime source of danger for citizens. The security apparatus of a dictatorial regime was indeed a state within a state. Its organs and informers became propagators of universal fear. In their presence, conversations subsided into silence and laughter died away. Security was turning into danger: A secret police colonel was hated more than a Mafia boss.

How can we then compare the fear of dictatorship to the fear of freedom? It can be done by comparing the impunity of a secret police colonel to the impunity of a Mafia boss. Which one should I fear more? If I wish to exercise my natural right to participation in public life, then I should fear the colonel much more. If I want to be left alone outside the realm of politics, then I will fear more the hideous Mafiosi who terrorize my town in the times of a fragile, corrupted, and powerless parliamentary democracy.

Dictatorship ensures that the streets are safe. Nonetheless, this assurance is coupled with fear that a doorbell in your home may one day ring unexpectedly.

In democratic times, taking a walk at night can be dangerous. Nevertheless, early in the morning, the only noise you will hear at your doorsteps is that of a milkman.

Democracy means living in incertitude, in risk, and with a sense of responsibility for your own decisions. Yet, democratic politics seldom resorts to violence, whereas dictatorship means daily violence, living in fear, humiliation, and silence. People cannot trust each other. Social bonds deteriorate. Lies, hypocrisy, and cynicism reign. Still, the allure of dictatorship consists in freeing a person from all responsibility because the state is responsible for everything.

Under dictatorship, a human being is not a citizen of the state but its property.

APPEAL OF DICTATORSHIP

Dictatorship always wins over new supporters because it formulates goals that thousands find appealing. Such goals may include a revolutionary change of property relations, expropriation of foreign capital, saving the sovereignty and independence of the state, or thwarting lawlessness in public life. Universal ideas and more detailed plans for action accompany these goals: With this, a process of building a national state against destructive ethnic minorities takes place; here a constitutional dictate that forces the heretics, sectarians, and atheists to respect religious values serves a Highest Good; hereby, the owners, exploiters, and bloodsuckers of yesterday are to be properly punished so visions of social justice will become real. What dictatorship needs for justifying its existence is an enemy—people of the ancient regime, who need to be brought to justice; anarchists, subverters, and troublemakers; foreign intelligence agents; individuals devoid of true national spirit. The language of accusations that the Burmese junta used in addressing the opposition is not much different from the language of the Polish secretaries and generals when they talked about the Committee of Workers' Defense or Solidarity.

Dictatorships always foster one belief: They see themselves as saviors of the nation and guardians of order. What about democracy? Dictatorships disavow democracy in the name of Higher Ideals—communism, national socialism, the theocratic state—or maintain that people are not mature enough to live in democracy.

Dictatorship may always count on the empathy of well-disposed observers. There will always be a British commentator ready to state that although democracy has worked wonders for the British, it will not work for the Poles, the Russians, or the Burmese because of different cultural traditions. Indeed, once democracy yields to dictatorship, arguing that the source of this defeat lies in the fragility of traditions of political independence and free citizenry seems easy.

REVOLT OF ASPIRATIONS

Economics sets the limits on any dictatorship. When the economy crumbles, desperate people take to the streets chanting "We want bread!" When the police start shooting at them, they begin to chant "Bread and liberty!"

Social tranquility usually follows economic booms. Tranquility, however, does not last forever. Once they have satisfied their elementary material needs, people—their children, in particular—begin to wish for democratic freedoms. This is a natural order of being: Economic collapse causes a revolt of despair, whereas economic prosperity—a revolt of aspirations.

A wise Burmese man explained it to me: "Oh, Europeans, you're so captivated by the economic growth of the Asian Tigers that you don't want to notice the incredible growth of democratic consciousness throughout these countries. Democracies are born in pain. They remain fragile and are always prone to failure. Nevertheless, democracy is a primordial human necessity at the dawn of the twenty-first century."

True, if the people of Burma had not wanted freedom, what would the tanks have been doing in the streets of Rangoon or the secret police in front of San Suu Kyi's house?

The revolt of aspirations penetrates into the inner circles of dictatorship. In the power apparatus, there emerge more and more individuals who no longer want to rule by rattling the saber and who are tempted to rationalize the system of power. Unfortunately, reformistic ideas in dictatorial inner circles share one thing in common: Reformers want to change everything so things can stay the same.

The dialectic of change rests on a peculiar encounter between the inner-circle reformer and the dissident reformer. In Burma, I met people associated with the junta, responsible for the crimes of marital law, and people of the opposition, political prisoners for many years. Both were asking me with hope in their voices: "So, how is this Jaruzelski of yours?"

General Jaruzelski is a positive symbol, of sorts. For some, he is a progressive Pinochet, who saved the country from a total collapse. For others, he is nothing more than a leader of the junta, who, capable of critical reflection, embraced the idea of the Round Table negotiations with the opposition and demoted dictatorship without spilling a drop of blood. This is what San Suu Kyi and people of the NLD are now setting their eyes on. Still, the SLORC has not yet produced its Jaruzelski. The Burmese generals speak in unison, yet, theirs is not a voice of national reconciliation.

Still, Jaruzelski did not start off with the Round Table.

RESISTANCE

Before the Round Table of 1989, Jaruzelski attempted to achieve accord without concord. This was precisely the point of establishing the Advisory Council in 1986. Despite the presence of selected oppositionists, the Council was but window dressing. Lacking any real prerogatives, it resembled a safety valve installed so the opposition could air out its frustration: A few chaps had a chance to harangue to the point of nausea but the entire mechanism of dictatorship remained intact. This explains why the leadership of the underground Solidarity called for a boycott of the Council.

Although a fictional creation, the Council assumed an important symbolic meaning. From the standpoint of dictatorship, the opposition, moderate and monitored as it was, made its presence known in the official arena. It turned out that there was room for people of the opposition outside the prison walls.

The Advisory Council was a pseudoinitiative, a trick that dictatorship played. At the same time, the Council's very presence meant that the regime symbolically recognized the role of the opposition. It is much the same in Burma. The National Convention convened by the SLORC continues to be a mere ornament. Although the NLD delegates withdrew from the Convention, those who remain are by no means alike. That is why the Convention may serve as a useful instrument for dialogue about democratizing the state.

Dictatorship always asks itself the same question: Why change? Why trigger a process that may bring about unpredictable and uncontrolled results? Dictatorship always senses the truth of the well-known adage of Alexis de Tocqueville that the most dangerous moment for a bad regime is just as it is starting on reform.

Consequently, dictatorship does not fancy reforms but worships "progress and improvement." Nevertheless, a reform knocks at the door. People begin to revolt, although one will never know why on that very day, in January, on Thursday . . .

The reaction of the authorities is stereotypical in such circumstances. The police, in close order, disperse the crowd. There are casualties: wounded, killed, and imprisoned. The nation has new martyrs—and new leaders, who emerge on a revolutionary surge, who "jump over the fence"[2] and speak at street meetings. Police batons and arrests give people a sense of togetherness, and new leaders epitomize this new awareness. They speak up about dignity and self-rule. They can be arrested, pulled to pieces, and slandered but they will live in public memory as symbols of hope, like Solzhenitsyn and Sakharov, Wałęsa and Havel, San Suu Kyi. No longer does social resistance resemble a shapeless mass of rolling stones that angered mobs throw at state buildings. The masses now have leaders who make political demands and with whom the regime can negotiate— if the regime and the opposition are willing to negotiate.

INTERNAL DISSENT

Now, disagreements within the regime and within the opposition are inevitable. Inside the regime's inner circle, the hard-liners clash with the reformers. We must pull together in face of danger, the hard-liners say. We must not change anything because any change will be interpreted as our weakness. The opponents, they say, talk about dialogue and reforms but what they really want is to get rid of us. Their success will lead to chaos and the downfall of the state, and we will end up in prisons or on the gallows. Our demise will make for a delightful gift to our foreign enemies, of which the domestic opposition is a mere agent. The opposition has no program other than to destroy. Unfortunately, our comrades-reformers have become the involuntary tools of this destruction. They dilute the fundamental principles, call for dialogue with criminals and enemies, and open the gate to destruction of the state.

The reformers face an equally difficult task—how to convince their comrade-hard-liners that the more unyielding and uncompromising they are, the more they work toward their own demise? The reformers ascertain, therefore, that not only has the dictatorship lost its ability to correct errors but it has also forfeited its potential to develop. Only reforms can make the system of rule more rational, modern, and, in effect, potent. Still, to embark on reforms, we must engage in a difficult and risky dialogue with the opposition. Otherwise, we will be confronting recurrent outbursts of social anger and will have to rely on the army and the police to suppress revolts. It is only a matter of time before the army joins the revolt. The scaffold and the gallows will be all that's left for the regime. Blind loyalty to a traditional doctrine of the camp of dictatorship will result in bloody rebellion, chaos, and destruction of the state.

The end result of disputes between the reformers and the hard-liners is not only contingent upon the politicking within the ruling camp. It also depends on signals that this camp receives from the opposition and from abroad. The opposition's unity, having been tested through its unremitting resistance to dictatorship, now begins to crumble under the pressure of new circumstances. A question is bound to arise: What is to be done? Intensify protests or seek ways to negotiate? Rely on revolutionary methods and demand sternly that dictators and their coteries be brought to justice? Or compromise, conciliate, and choose reforms?

The "revolutionaries" reiterate their arguments with calm: The hands of dictatorship are stained with the blood of the innocent. Dictatorship means Absolute Evil, and dictators and their followers are the carriers of Evil. One must call a spade a spade. The sense of justice demands that the propagators of Evil be eliminated—one owes it to the victims of dictatorship. The very attempt to compromise means, in fact, supporting Evil, polluting the purity of the Idea. It means treason, moral fraud, and political stupidity. Instead, one must await a Grand

Explosion, when people take to the streets, and, then, we must take the lead, in the vanguard of the rebellious masses, to overthrow the dictatorship. Only then will the truth and freedom triumph, virtue be rewarded, and crime and treason be punished.

The "reformers" think otherwise. To wait for a Grand Explosion—they say—may take time. Moreover, a social explosion involves huge risk: societal self-destruction, bloody civil war, new wrongs, and new victims. Meanwhile, life is short, the country is in ruin, and the nation is yet to recover from the effects of past revolutions. The revolutionary terror is sometimes inevitable, but one should always try to avoid it, and one should always try to overcome the lethal logic of revenge. One should, therefore, join negotiations to dismantle dictatorship peacefully.

For a revolutionary, compromise means opportunism and lack of principles; for a reformer, a necessity of life. So, the reformers discard the logic of revolution in favor of the logic of negotiations. Before, they sought all that separated them from the world of dictatorship; now, they seek something that binds the two. When the reformers seek compromising solutions, they expose themselves to charges of betrayal. Indeed, making concessions is in the nature of compromise. There is no such thing as total victory; one must respect the former enemy's right to civic freedoms and a place under the sun.

If the regime hard-liners gain the upper hand, compromise will not stand a chance. If the revolutionaries gain the upper hand in a democratic society, compromise will not stand a chance, either. If, in both cases, the reformers score a victory, the nation can say that the people hit the jackpot. Poles hit the jackpot in the spring of 1989. What will happen in Burma?

Politicians in foreign capitals carefully monitor transformations of a crackling dictatorship. They ask themselves what tactic to adopt. Maybe the harsh language of political boycott and economic sanctions? Perhaps a more flexible diplomacy of détente and "realpolitik"—while keeping silent about human rights abuses? Or, a complex strategy of a carrot and a stick to make the dictatorial regime tolerate the enlarged area of civil society?

If pressure from abroad—economic, political, or diplomatic—favors the reformers within the regime and the opposition, the chances for a peaceful transformation are real. (This is the Polish component of the "velvet revolution.") No one abdicates from power while confronting the specter of a guillotine. The people of the dictatorship must be assured some kind of security blanket. Otherwise, they will hold onto power to the bitter end, bringing on bloodshed on a nationwide scale. Only after they are defeated will true justice triumph—amongst the burned-down cities, parents who lost their children, thousands of new graves.

The route of negotiation causes much disappointment and bitterness. It fosters a sense of injustice but is free of casualties—people are disappointed but alive.

For negotiations are possible only when a democratic opposition is strong enough to defend itself against dictatorship, and when dictatorship is strong enough not to let the opposition seize power overnight.

The weakness of both sides becomes a chance for the people.

BURMA AND POLAND

Looking at Burma, I thought of Poland. Thinking about the Polish experience, I see Burma. In the NLD, Burma has already had its hope, its "Solidarity." It has its Military Council for the National Salvation, here called the State Law and Order Restoration Council. In the person of San Suu Kyi, Burma has its Lech Wałęsa.

Burma is still missing its Wojciech Jaruzelski A.D. 1989, although it has already gotten its Jaruzelski A.D. 1981. Will there ever be a Burmese Jaruzelski who will decide to convene a Round Table? Or, to put it differently, do the Burmese people understand freedom? Do they need democracy like the Poles?

I think that the answer is yes.

I belong to the "irreconciled men" and remember what dictatorship means. It means rule by force and falsehood. I am not tempted, not a bit, to relativize all that I have lived through: debasement, humiliation, and fear. I have never blurred the difference between truth and lie, courage and cowardice, virtue and vileness, freedom and captivity.

That is why I react so strongly to lies, vileness, and loathsomeness today, when a sovereign and democratic Poland is compared to "Bantustan"[3] and "Targowica,"[4] or when some talk about a "Round Table treason." I will not sit like a tongue-tied coward when I hear such rubbish.

NOTES

1. Michnik has been the editor-in-chief of the daily *Gazeta Wyborcza* since its inception in 1989. —Trans.

2. Wałęsa was said to have joined the 1980 strike by, literally, jumping over the fence of the Gdańsk shipyard. —Trans.

3. Bantustan, a nominally independent territory set aside by the Union of South Africa for blacks (who thus lost their limited rights as South African citizens), exemplifies a paradox of granting formal sovereignty to a region while simultaneously denying civil and political rights to its inhabitants. —Trans.

4. On the eve of the Second Partition of Poland of 1793, a group of noblemen, loyal to the Empress Catherine the Great and backed by a Russian Army, created a confederation in the village of Targowica with the intent to overthrow the Polish Parliament and the Polish Constitution. From then on, the name Targowica has been synonymous with national treason. —Trans.

10

Sendero Luminoso and Human Rights: A Perverse Logic That Captured the Country

Carlos Basombrío Iglesias

The doctrine of human rights as we know it today has a short history. It emerged as a reaction against the horrors faced by humanity as a consequence of fascism and World War II. The United Nations formulated the doctrine on 10 December 1948 in the Universal Declaration of Human Rights. Since then, there has been considerable progress in developing concepts, designing mechanisms of protection, and taking concrete action to protect human rights. It is well-known that this process has been essentially and almost exclusively directed toward controlling and sanctioning abuses that states have carried out against individuals and groups. This is the raison d'être and the principal feature of global and regional intergovernmental organizations that focus on human rights, and of the thousands of NGOs (nongovernmental organizations) that operate from civil society, in every country in the world, to pressure governments to comply.

The explanation for this consistent focus on the abuse of governments is obvious: States are responsible for protecting the rights of citizens. To achieve this, people concede authority to the state (or the state appropriates such authority). In addition, the state monopolizes the exercise of force. Therefore, when a state, rather than fulfill its protective role, opts to violate the rights of its citizens, whether incidentally or systematically, we find ourselves confronted with a special type of abuse against which individuals find themselves practically defenseless. This situation requires that the abuse be denounced before the rest of humanity, regardless of national frontiers, as a violation of human rights. Within the predominant conception of human rights, crimes committed by individuals and irregular groups should be prosecuted by the state, and in such cases, the human rights question only involves ensuring that the state follows the law and procedures of due process.[1]

In periods of violence the behavior of states and irregular groups received monitoring through what is known as International Humanitarian Law, which mandates minimum standards of conduct for forces engaged in armed conflict. Initially, International Humanitarian Law was intended to apply principally to international conflicts. Subsequently, the Additional Protocols to the Geneva Convention (which Peru signed) extended the jurisdiction of humanitarian law. These protocols elaborated on points already included in Article 3 of the original convention and established rules of conduct for actors in internal conflicts. The logic of action by the International Committee of the Red Cross, the institution charged with looking after the application of these accords throughout the world, is different, however from that of human rights organizations. Among other differences, the Red Cross's action is exclusively humanitarian and guards absolute secrecy; it addresses its reports and recommendations only to the parties involved.

Within this general context, let us turn more specifically to Latin America. Latin American human rights movements have emerged almost exclusively as responses to abuses by the state. For this reason, they have held the sympathy of armed rebel groups that, for reasons of principle or political convenience, found the conduct of such organizations to be positive. Demands for respect for International Humanitarian Law have, more often than not, emanated from irregular armies seeking to humanize conflicts. Governments, in contrast, have often resisted such demands out of fear that they would impede the effectiveness of repression.

The eruption of Shining Path in 1980 and its conduct over the succeeding years broke the schemes that had previously shaped the human rights theme in Latin America. For the first time in the region, an insurgent force on the Left developed a systematic practice of violence against the civilian population that matched, and perhaps surpassed, state-sponsored violence. Shining Path's profound disregard for human life, its contempt—in both theory and practice—for the discourse of human rights, and its refusal to ascribe to the norms and principles of International Humanitarian Law rendered it unique on the continent.

Nothing could be further from the intent of this essay than to justify the costly errors and atrocities that the Peruvian state has committed against human rights in recent years. We are diametrically opposed to the argument that human rights are relative and that one must grant a sympathetic latitude in the face of extreme circumstances. Nor do we in any way sympathize with those who attempt, nationally or internationally, to use denunciations of Shining Path's actions to mask the state's own crimes and responsibilities. I believe that my personal trajectory,[2] including more than a decade of human rights work in Peru during which I have clearly condemned and denounced all kinds of atrocities by the Peruvian state, should in any case block a misunderstanding of intent. We reaffirm here that the logic of conduct by the Peruvian state in matters of human rights has been, and in many ways continues to be, unacceptable and counter-productive. It is unacceptable because, in the name of suppressing armed sub-version, the state has incurred massive (some would say systematic) violations of human rights. Peru became a country of disappeared persons and torture victims, of people displaced and unjustly detained, of common graves and extraju-dicial assassinations, all with absolute impunity. The state's conduct is counter-productive as well because such repression has not only violated the rights of persons, who in the most cases were innocent and poor, but because it also has served as the "gasoline" that helped "to light a prairie fire."

Yet because this book aims to understand Shining Path and its effects on the life of the country, permit us on this occasion to invert the usual practice. Let us begin not with the logic of state conduct, but with that of Shining Path. This is to say, let us try to see how this movement influenced the form that the human rights debate took in Peru. Let us examine how Shining Path defined human rights conceptually and in actual practice, consider how this resonated with the state's own vision and practice of human rights, review what repercussions Shining Path had for the struggle for human rights in Peru and for the conscious-ness of the population. Finally, with the insurgency defeated, let us consider the new challenges that this heavy inheritance leaves for the future of the human rights question in Peru.

DIFFERENT FROM THE BEGINNING

Unlike other Latin American countries, such as Guatemala and El Salvador, that underwent intense processes of political violence during the 1980s, Peru neither lived under a seemingly unending dictatorship nor experienced grave human rights violations before the start of the insurrection. (Both circumstances, one should note, were important factors for understanding the upsurge in violence in the other countries.) In Peru, as we know, the incubation of Shining Path's politico-military project culminated toward the end of the 1970s, just as the military government was in retreat and a complex but real political transition toward representative democracy was emerging. In 1978 elections took place for a Constituent Assembly, in the midst of great social turbulence and with sig-nificant levels of political repression. But none of these limitations blocked the political presence of any sector that chose to participate.[3] The most obvious example is that of Hugo Blanco, the Trotskyist ex-guerrilla of the 1960s who had been a prisoner for many years and who obtained 12 percent of the vote with-out ceding any of his radicalism. Altogether the Left received a third of all votes cast.

But Shining Path remained totally aloof from the decision of the rest of the political forces of the country to participate in the political process that would bring the military government to an end. Shining Path abstained even though the political movements that opted to participate included those of the most radical Left. None of the parties that participated in the presidential elections encountered any significant obstacles. Even the Communist Party of Peru-Red Flag (Partido Comunista del Peru-Patria Roja; PCP-PR)—the most influential Maoist party in the country, whose slogan, "power is born from a gun," clearly revealed its worldview, and which chose to boycott the Constituent Assembly in 1978—ran its own presidential candidate in 1980.[4] In short, it was by choice that Shining Path excluded itself from participation in the open political process. Sendero demonstrated its opinion of the process by initiating armed action on 18 May 1980, the day of the general elections that brought President Fernando Belaúnde to power.

Shining Path also remained aloof from another equally important and real process of democratization. We refer to the emerging participation of popular social sectors in social and political life, a new phenomenon for the country that resulted from mass migration to the cities, increased access to education, and, above all, a generalized and multifaceted process of popular organization that provided new, once unimaginable mechanisms of participation. Of course, in the 1970s the process was still in its initial stages and had not wiped away the terrible imbalances and exclusions of the past. Yet it was rapidly becoming a complex yet interesting challenge to the formal institutionality of the country, traditionally so distant from the common people.

Thus, the surge in political violence in Peru, in clear contrast to the other countries we mentioned, cannot be explained by the impossibility of legal political participation by the future insurgents. Nor, we might add, did the start of the insurgency gain legitimacy from a situation of massive human rights violations. In Peru, despite the prolonged military dictatorship and despite a social storm of great proportions in the late 1970s, human rights violations paled in frequency and in form to those that convulsed countries such as El Salvador and Guatemala. Certainly, we did not live in anything even approaching the best of worlds. Restrictions of press freedom and political party activities were common practice, along with detentions, deportations, mistreatment of street demonstrators, and torture in prisons. But extrajudicial executions and forced disappearances were not yet part of our vocabulary, as they tragically would become just a few years later. Political crime was virtually unknown.[5]

An explanation for the emergence of this particular case of violence must therefore come from another angle. Perhaps relevant is something I heard Hubert Lanssiers say some time ago, in a debate with those who cited the terrible structural conditions of the country as the principal cause of the violence we were experiencing.[6] In his view, what such terrible conditions generated, usually and spontaneously, in the people that suffered them was not rebelliousness, but rather fatalism, passivity, or religious resignation. Lanssiers maintained that the explo-

sions of violence could only be understood if given social conditions came together with an ideology that deliberately and consciously proposed exercising
violence as a response.

According to Lanssiers, all ideology serves as an "arm of combat," an "instrument of power," a "mechanism of defense against objectivity," and a "pretext to
escape moral criticism." He adds that "the value [of ideologies] is not found in
the rigor of their construction or in the quality of their argument, which are
rather poor and schematic. . . . What is important is that they tell us essentially
what we need to think; they express what is needed to make a thought collectively operative. Their mobilizing energy is more useful than the content of their
concepts, the orchestration of the themes is more important than their richness."[7]

Shining Path provided an ideological reading of reality, totally independent
of the political process under way, and converted this interpretation into the
guide and fundamental motivation to initiate armed action. As we have already
suggested, the political changes of that time, which any analysis might consider
as pointing away from justifying armed rupture, were absolutely dispensable facts
for Shining Path, given the ideological edifice it had constructed. "The problem, *Señores* revisionists," Shining Path said disdainfully to the legal Left, "is not
whether those in government are wearing collars and ties instead of uniforms
and boots, or that they still sport beards and tie their pants with rope [a reference to Hugo Blanco], because this does not negate their reactionary position
nor does it make them revolutionaries. We are not talking about civilian dictatorships versus military dictatorships. We are talking about class dictatorships. . . .
*Do we not know that power is conquered with violence and maintained through dicta-
torship,* that 'revolution is an act in which one part of the population imposes
its will upon the other with guns, bayonets, and canons . . . and where the win-
ning party is necessarily obliged to maintain its dominion by the fear that its arms inspire in the reactionaries?' as Engels teaches?"[8]

Abimael Guzmán, only days before the ILA (the initials which signify the
Inicio de la Lucha Armada, or initiation of the armed struggle, in Shining Path
literature), pronounced the closing speech at Sendero's "First Military School."
Without a trace of modesty he entitled his speech: "We are the Initiators."
Among other things, he provided a preview of the practices Peru would have to
endure during the following years:

> Comrades: our labor with our hands unarmed has concluded. . . . A period has
> ended. Here we seal what has been done; we open the future, the key is action, the
> objective power. This we will do, history demands it, the class needs it, the people
> has foreseen it and wants it, we must comply and we will comply. We are the ini-
> tiators. . . .
> The people's war will grow more every day until it overturns the old order, the
> world is entering into a new situation: the strategic offensive of the global revolu-
> tion. This is of transcendental importance . . .

[A]nd the people gets up on its hind legs, arms itself, rises in rebellion, and places a noose around the neck of imperialism and the reactionaries, grabs them by the throat, tears off their flesh, and will strangle them. [The people] will tear the reactionary flesh, leave it in shreds, and drown these black wretches in slime; what is left will burn and the ashes will scatter to the ends of the Earth, so that all that is left is sinister memory of what will never return, because it cannot and should not return. . . . Marxist-Leninism-Mao Zedong thought, the international proletariat and the peoples of the world, the working class and the people of the country, the party with its bases, cadres and leaders, all the grand combined action of centuries has culminated here. The promise opens, the future unfurls. ILA 80[9]

At that time, only a few faithful followers knew of this important warning. Understandably, the rest, even those who might have known of it, still did not have any reason to take it seriously.

HUMAN RIGHTS AND PEOPLE'S RIGHTS

A comparative vision of other countries that confronted internal insurgency continues to be useful, as we enter into an analysis of how Shining Path dealt with the issue of human rights once it embarked upon the project of a "protracted people's war." Upon surveying the continent, we find that guerrilla movements in Latin America generally sought to have the cause of human rights on their side. Some doubtlessly held this position with great conviction and honesty; other embraced human rights with varying degrees of political instrumentalism, as a means to isolate the state nationally and internationally, and to justify the guerrillas' own course of action.

Therefore, denunciations of the state as the principal violator of human rights usually have formed an important part of the political discourse of guerrilla movements. At the same time, guerrillas either described their own abuses as inevitable costs of the confrontation or simply denied that they occurred. In reality, and without in any way justifying the crimes committed by insurgent movements, their violations generally seem to have been significantly less in number, importance, and frequency than abuses attributed to agents of the state.

In Peru, however, we lived a very different reality. Shining Path openly repudiated human rights in both doctrine and practice. To achieve its goals, Shining Path would not hesitate to attack the civilian population and to use varied methods of terror against persons uninvolved in the conflict. In the point of departure for this approach, we find, once again, an "ideological justification": Shining Path insisted that human rights originated in a bourgeois conception of the world and were opposed to "the rights of the people [*derechos del pueblo*]."[10] According to Abimael Guzmán,

For us, human rights contradict the rights of the people because we base ourselves in man as a social product, not in an abstract man with innate rights. "Human rights" are nothing more than the rights of the bourgeois man, a position that was revolutionary in the face of feudalism; thus *liberty, equality and fraternity were advanced bourgeois criteria in the past.* . . .

In so far as the people's rights are the rights that the proletariat and the immense popular masses conquer with their own struggle and blood, and that they establish as the guiding principles of the New State, in service of the interests of the classes that conform the people, *the rights of the people are the rights and obligations of class,* superior to so-called human rights in the service of the masses, the poor especially, of the New State, of socialism and of future communism; the people's rights [are ones] that only the People's Republic of Peru, in our case, will be able to guarantee.

Guzmán went on to explain that by people's rights he referred "principally to the supreme right to conquer Power and to exercise it in order to transform the old existing order, oppressive and exploitative, and to construct a New State and a New Society for the people and the proletariat" (Guzmán 1991).

With his usual conviction that what he said constituted incontrovertible truth, Guzmán maintained that "the Marxist-Leninist-Maoist Gonzalo-thought conception makes us understand the bourgeois, reactionary, and counterrevolutionary character of the so-called Human Rights that are so manipulated in the world today, and [shows us] how to understand the rights of the people." In Guzmán's rendition of the history of human rights, the Universal Declaration of Human Rights was an instrument to establish "the expansion, domination, and influence of imperialism," and the United Nations as "a pro-imperialism organism, guarantor of the superpowers and imperial powers." He concluded with a vision of human rights as anachronism:

And today as imperialism falls into general collapse, it recurs to the old bourgeois reactionary banners, to its old resurrected principles, because it can no longer create anything new or progressive, and it covers them with a "humanitarian" varnish to hide its counterrevolutionary class nature whereby it seeks to contain the principal historical and political tendency in the world, which is revolution; cunningly hiding that human rights are one instrument more for imposing its reactionary ideology (the core of which is idealism, and the most vulgar pragmatism, totally contrary to dialectical materialism) and its fallacious bourgeois democratic politics of bloody reactionary dictatorship. . . . And all for the defense of the expired imperialist system, bloody parasitic barbarism that scorches the Earth, contrary and totally opposed to the socialist system, the great innovation of the twentieth century, the only system that will lead humanity to the reign of liberty: Communism. (Guzmán 1991)

Before moving on to examine the practical repercussions of such belligerent opposition to the human rights perspective, one might add that this belligerence did not impede Shining Path from developing, when convenient, an absolutely pragmatic attitude regarding human rights. Thus, when human rights appeared useful for its political and military objectives, Shining Path demanded compliance with these principles and the laws that embodied them. Sendero's absolute attachment to legal technicalities to defend well-known leaders, who without any scruples denied their obvious leadership positions, became rather notorious. (Osmán Morote, for example, claimed to be only a "social researcher.") Sendero leaders attempted to exploit the deficiencies of the Peruvian legal system to their own advantage, and only later, in the event of a conviction, would they reassume their original positions.[11] Also well-known, to name another example, was their denunciation of violations of liberty of the press, whenever necessary to ensure that their mouthpiece *El Diario* could continue to circulate.[12]

FROM WORD TO DEED

This disdain for human rights, whereby Sendero reduced respect for the rights of others to the interest and necessities of "class" and "revolution" (read: the Party) provided a basis for Shining Path's cruel and relentless military conduct against others. In addition, it informed the scant value placed on the lives of their own militants.[13]

Shining Path's cruelty in war actions is widely known. Never, for example, have Shining Path guerrillas been known to carry out military operations in which they ended up taking prisoners or treating the wounded. Certainly, the same may be said about the operations of the Peruvian Armed Forces. Even worse, the military battles, per se, can account for perhaps 10 percent of the war's victims over the course of fifteen years. The immense majority of deaths resulted from unilateral actions against an enemy without any capacity for response, that was annihilated without contemplation. Shining Path assassinated hundreds of police for no other reason than to take their arms. The Armed Forces were responsible for numerous extrajudicial executions and forced disappearances.

I am interested here, in particular, in the role of Shining Path. Continuing the methodology of drawing comparisons with other realities in Latin America, note that in other countries, the guerrillas took great care not to produce victims in sectors that they considered potential allies for their cause: political parties on the Left, popular organizations, NGOs, and so forth. And, perhaps for this very reason, these groups suffered repression by the state. In Peru, however, this was not the case. Shining Path, because of its vision of human rights and its general conception of politics and war, perceived all such groups as direct enemies of its armed struggle and did not hesitate to use the most violent methods against them. One might argue that Shining Path, even more than the state, affected directly and systematically these sectors of civil society, or what was long known as the popular movement.

Thus, Shining Path guerrillas massacred peasants who dared oppose them. The most notorious case was that of Lucanamarca, where Shining Path assassinated more than eighty villagers, including women and children, with the purpose of sending a message to a third party, the Armed Forces. In Guzmán's words, this massacre was intended to give "a decisive blow to restrain them, to make them understand that the thing was not so easy." Always with intricate justifications, Shining Path killed many other people as well: humble local authorities ("representatives of the bourgeois state in the countryside"); candidates in any electoral process ("we warn all the electioneers that seek to run for office that if they persist in the farce we will annihilate them sooner or later"); politicians on the Left ("revisionism is the advance of the bourgeoisie in the bosom of the people"); labor and popular organizers of all kinds ("reactionary agents infiltrating in the ranks of the people"); members of different churches ("death to the worshipers of imperialism, death to the preaching dogs"); members of local and international NGOs ("they corrupt the popular leaders with foreign money and promote aid policies [*políticas asistencialistas*] to enrich themselves at the cost of the hunger of the people"); and so forth.

The flip side of this logic was evident in the attitude that Shining Path leaders assumed toward the suffering and terrible deaths faced by thousands of their own militants and supporters. Shining Path justified this attitude with the same notions of purity and ideological reinforcement. In his "Interview of the Century," Guzmán (1988) is very clear on this point:

The reaction attempts to use its armed forces and repressive forces in general to wipe us out (*barremos*) and disappear us. And for what reason? *Because we want to do the same to them*, to wipe them out and to disappear them as a class; Mariátegui had said that only be destroying, demolishing the old order can a new social order be created. In the last instance, we judge these problems through the lens of the basic principle of war established by President Mao: the principle of annihilating the forces of the enemy and preserving our own; and *we know well that the reaction has applied, applies, and will apply, genocide, on this we are absolutely clear. And, in consequence we face the problem of the quota, the problem that to annihilate the enemy and to preserve our own forces, and even more to develop our forces, it is necessary to pay a cost of war, a cost in blood, the necessity of sacrificing a part to ensure the triumph of the people's war.*

For Abimael Guzmán the crowning moment of this "vital and principal" sacrifice was the barbarous repression produced by the intervention of the Armed Forces in Ayacucho in 1983 and 1984. "*There took place the greatest show of massive revolutionary heroism and our greatest forging ahead as well.*"[14] The connection between the sacrifice of militants and the strengthening of the organization and political project is confirmed in senderista reference to the massacre of more than 200 senderistas in the prisons of Lima in 1986 as the "Day of Heroism." "The 19th of June," said Guzmán, "is a date that demonstrates to our people and to the world *what firm Communists and committed revolutionaries are capable of doing.*"

When analyzed from a perspective informed by respect for human life and the dignity of persons, Shining Path's conduct could not have resulted in a worse outcome. We cannot for this reason avoid mentioning how, when subjected to rigors much less harsh than those he himself imposed upon his enemies or demanded of his own followers, Abimael Guzmán broke weakly. In exchange for minimally decent prison conditions, he acceded to negotiate the same peace he had always described as the worst of betrayals.

WHEN COMBATANTS CONVERGE

Let us complete this complex panorama by noting that in Peru a perverse convergence emerged. We refer to the practical and conceptual appraisals of human rights by the Shining Path insurgents and the agents of the state who planned and conducted the counterinsurgency campaign.

For example, both sides would blame the preoccupation with human rights on unacceptable intervention by the United States for purposes of domination. In 1994, at no less an important occasion than the Fourth Summit of Heads of State in Latin America, Fujimori affirmed his "rejection of underhanded interventions with the pretext of defending continental democracy or human rights." He went on to sustain that "each people must resolve as best it can its own internal affairs," including in "the cases of Haiti and Cuba."[15] Guzmán was not outdone. He sustained that "today, imperialism, principally Yankee, uses human rights to impose international norms that justify its intervention in whatever part of the world and to submit everyone to its hegemony" (Guzmán 1991).

Another area of impressive convergence was the evaluation of the role played by NGOs in human rights. One very interesting poll asked more than 100 commanders and majors of the Armed Forces to provide their opinions anonymously regarding human rights (de la Jara 1994). In response to a question about human rights groups, nearly three-fifths (57.26 percent) of these military men replied that human rights organizations were only concerned with terrorists and only promoted the organizations' own interests or those of other countries. Nearly a third (31.62 percent) responded that although such groups have had laudable goals, in practice they favored subversive actions. Indeed, the respondents would have found it difficult to think differently since this is what they have heard from their superiors and successive presidents over the years. Fujimori, in particular, has made the denigration of human rights groups into a personal crusade.

Here I repeat only two of the many allegations made against us: "We know that the terrorists and their front organisms, or useful fools, are not going to give up and will use every resource to damage the image of the country arguing that the Armed Forces systematically violate human rights." In addition, "these professional organizations are not coherent in the defense of life and human liberty because, in some cases, *they are legal arms of subversion, but we will unmask them.*"[16]

The state's accusations that the human rights groups were biased, and did not understand the underlying reasons for what they did, mirrored accusations by Shining Path. "When in the context of developing the people's war, the PCP applies military actions of selective liquidation against informers, functionaries of the state, and others, as in the execution of María Elena Moyano ("Mother Courage"), the 'human rights defense organizations' exclaim: 'horror!' *But when the armed forces and police assassinate defenseless people, including children, the organizations do not say anything. They maintain a nauseating complicit silence.*"[17] Abimael Guzmán would maintain, in an epoch in which his utterances constituted virtual death threats: "We have not encountered until today among the NGOs [referring to human rights organizations], an organization that openly and valiantly defends the rights of the poorest people, much less advanced revolutionary positions; at most we find bourgeois humanitarian positions, *but the great majority are lackeys, conscious or unconscious, of imperialism*" (Guzmán 1991).

I still experience a certain chill upon considering Guzmán's references to the institution to which I belong. In the text just cited, he used this organization as an example to illustrate his point: "Among the NGOs: the Institute of Legal Defense (IDL), a nongovernmental organization that defends human rights in the service of mainly Yankee imperialism . . . always serving the demands of its imperialist masters and acting as their soft hand, against Marxism and the people's war, and marking off and even criticizing reactionary governments when imperialism necessitates."

Let us consider one last theme where both sides converge. At times, both recognize certain "excesses" against the civilian population and consider them acceptable in exchange for advancing the principal objective, finishing off the enemy. Martha Chávez, the most prominent pro-Fujimori parliamentarian, would sustain: "I weigh the balance between the war against terrorism and subversion on one side and, on the other, *the question of the human rights of some . . . it is painful, but I end up choosing the war against subversion.*"[18] Guzmán complements this idea from his perspective, when he analyzes the "excesses" that he admits his men committed in the Lucanamarca massacre: "Excesses might be committed, *the problem is to arrive at a point and not to pass it*, because if you pass it you go off track, it is like an angle that opens only to a certain degree and no more" (Guzmán 1988).

ENORMOUS CHALLENGES

By this point, it should be easy to imagine the difficulty of the work of human rights organizations over the course of fifteen years (1980–1995). It is worth adding, of course, that similar difficulties also faced those who expressed a con-sistent commitment to human rights in the communications media, in the Chris-tian churches, in the academic world, and (in this instance the numbers can be counted on one's hands) in the political parties.[19]

The accusations and threats under which the human rights activists worked are well-known and originated in the elements described previously: we are only concerned with the rights of terrorists and remain quiet when the victims are caused by the subversives; we tie the hands of the forces of order, impeding them from acting efficiently; we are "useful fools" (or *candelejones*, "silly ones," as Luis Bedoya Reyes once called us); or in more extreme versions, occult allies of ter-rorists. The other side called us embellishers of the system, accomplices of im-perialism, and so forth.

To face up to this political problem constituted the fundamental challenge of the Peruvian human rights movement. The first difficulty to overcome was to break with the inertia of following the usual quasi-universal schemes of defense of human rights, according to which our work should focus exclusively on de-nouncing the abuses of the state.[20] In spite of the fact that no human rights group or individual activist had any inclination whatsoever, at any moment, in favor of Shining Path—and on this I can give personal testimony—there was, particu-larly in the first years, an intense debate regarding our role. We debated whether it was our responsibility to denounce Shining Path in the same manner that we denounced the state. The doctrinal referent in these arguments was an interna-tional juridical tradition that viewed the state as the sole violator of human rights.

The process was intense and complex, but had clear results. In our favor was the fact that all of us united early in a common coalition, the National Coordi-nating Committee of Human Rights (La Coordinadora Nacional de Derechos Humanos, hereinafter "La Coordinadora"),[21] which all of us decided to use as our political voice at a national and international level. Little by little, La Coordinadora opted to leave aside any theoretical disquisition that could be interpreted as weakness in the condemnation of Shining Path. We decided to denounce each and every crime committed by Shining Path with the same en-ergy and conviction with which we denounced violations by the state.[22]

In addition, differentiating ourselves from most Latin American human rights groups, we broke with the idea of neutrality, or intent merely to humanize con-flicts. We announced with absolute clarity that we opposed Shining Path, that our struggle for human rights was intrinsically associated with obtaining peace, and that for this purpose, we felt solidarity with civil society's desire to defeat Shining Path and we supported legitimate efforts by the state to accomplish this goal.[23] In addition, we decided to convert our political choice into a matter of principle. We demanded that all groups and individuals who wanted to join our organizations adhere to four principles: repudiation of all forms of violence, revindication of democracy as the best political system, independence in regards to the state, and opposition to the death penalty.

This manner of addressing the issue of human rights had practical repercussions in our daily activities. The human rights groups consciously decided that our primary commitment was to the innocent victims of the confrontation, to whom we had to dedicate our best efforts. In cases in which senderistas were subject to human rights violations, we decided to act only if their lives were at risk. This of course did not mean in any case endorsing the crimes committed by the state simply because some or all of its victims might be senderistas. Many of the best known cases of disappearances and extrajudicial killings to which we dedicated so much effort included known Shining Path members among the victims.

The distinction was clearer in cases of detained persons. The human rights organizations decided expressly not to provide legal defense through our lawyers to people whom we considered with reasonable certainty to be members of Shining Path or the MRTA.[24] This decision certainly caused many conflicts of conscience, above all in the final stage, since in some cases we ended up turning ourselves, in a sense, into anticipatory judges. That is, we did not give the accused the benefit of the doubt, even though we knew that judges, in deciding the innocence or guilt of an accused person, considered it important to know who was behind the defense.

It is necessary to state clearly that this choice, which in my opinion was not only made out of conviction but also because it was the only choice that was politically viable, in effect silenced a response to certain abuses. Thus, while no one among us doubted the justice of convicting Abimael Guzmán and other Shining Path leaders, we never publicly stated with sufficient firmness the evident truth that they did not benefit from minimum guarantees of due process and that the legal validity of the trials was quite relative.[25]

Nonetheless, our declarations of principle and our daily conduct did not suffice to end accusations of partiality and complicity with subversion, accusations which persist today and have become, in great measure, popular common wisdom. Without underplaying our own errors and limitations it is important to consider the extraordinary difficulty of defending human rights, given the pressure from Shining Path and its effects on public opinion. One must add, however, that although this perception in the general public may have been, and may now be, honestly held, the political and military leaders with whom we argued all these years, and even sectors of the communications media, knew better. They understood perfectly well that the accusations were mistaken, yet purposely encouraged the confusion. What they sought was not that we take an impartial and balanced position, but rather to neutralize our capacity to denounce the state's violations of human rights.

INEVITABLE CONSEQUENCES

For human rights in Peru and for the struggle to ensure their enforcement Shining Path brought many negative consequences and, ironically, a positive consequence as well. The many negative effects are overwhelming, so let us begin with the effect that might be considered positive.

If one asks who were the victims of human rights violations in Latin America in those countries that recently or currently suffer armed internal conflicts (such as Colombia, El Salvador, Guatemala, and Nicaragua) one will find that the victims have been mostly peasants not directly involved in the confrontations, as in Peru. But in those countries, in contrast with Peru, the state's victims also frequently included activists in popular organizations, political leaders of the legal Left, student leaders, and members of human rights organizations. This generally did not happen in Peru. Over the years, the Peruvian cases in which these sectors suffered state repression have been quite isolated and never constituted a systematic pattern.[26]

In my view, this difference has to do principally with the type of movement that Shining Path was, and the clear division between the distinct camps in Peru. That is, Shining Path, according to its own ideas, did not have, did not want, could not have alliances with legalized sectors that would have served to broaden its political project or its social base. Sendero's fanaticism, expressed in an absolute and exclusive conception of its own role, facilitated this separation between the world of Peruvian politics and that of war. Thus, in contrast to the other countries cited, and despite the voices that (with more malice than ignorance) proclaimed the contrary, in Peru one could argue, even in the worst moments, that there were no ties between the legal Left (however radical its language) or between activists in all kinds of social organizations (however confrontational their practices or incisive their criticisms) and armed senderistas. This situation rendered it more difficult to justify systematic repression of the legal Left and activist social organizations. In the particular case of the human rights organizations, and in contrast to countries such as Guatemala or Colombia, this situation allowed us to continue and to develop further our labor over the course of this whole period, despite having to confront difficult situations and instances of violence, and despite having to work in a climate of repeated verbal aggression.[27]

The negative effects to which we alluded earlier were without a doubt very great. Shining Path's conception of human rights was a decisive factor that contributed to increasing contempt for human life in Peru. Such contempt applied to Shining Path's own victims in all social sectors as well as to those who had to suffer in retaliation. In my judgment, the type and magnitude of the violence that we had in Peru, and particularly the way in which Shining Path exercised violence with absolute disdain for its consequences upon the civilian population, generated in the great majority of Peruvians a cynical and pragmatic attitude toward democracy and human rights. Sendero, in short, induced a weakening of the consciousness of the population on the importance of respecting human rights and the dignity of persons.

By the end of the 1980s, when the sense of frustration and desperation had spread to the majority of the population, it became common sense that sacrificing democracy and human rights, and damaging the lives of innocent people, were costs well worth paying in order to get rid of Shining Path. According to this perspective, which today is lamentably predominant, any price was worth paying to overcome the threat of Shining Path. This view coincides with the beliefs of the senderistas that the ends justify the means.[28] The psychological climate was certainly encouraged and embodied by Alberto Fujimori and constituted one of the reasons for his popularity—for the support that he received in the "self-coup" of 1992 and for his overwhelming electoral victory in 1995.

With this sentiment so widespread among the population, the struggle for human rights became, and remains, much more difficult and complicated. The struggle for human rights, by its nature, only has an impact if national and international public opinion takes it up and makes it their own.[29] But we are still far from achieving the possibility of juridical, political, and moral sanctions against those who have committed human rights violations as part of the state. For example, Peru is far from obtaining a Truth Commission. Different versions of such a commission were established in Argentina, Chile, El Salvador, and in Colombia for one specific case, and will soon be established in Guatemala.

The experience of human rights groups when we denounced a massacre in the Alto Huallaga River in 1994 was very revealing. This was probably one of the gravest denunciations, and one of the best-documented with eyewitness accounts, that we have been able to make in recent years. In the early days of April 1994, on the left bank of the Huallaga River, in the localities of Moyuna and Moena, counterinsurgency troops of the army, after a show of rapes and other terrible acts of cruelty, assassinated dozens of peasants. The troops allegedly used artillery helicopters. Despite restrictions of access to the zone even for the International Red Cross, and despite not being permitted to go to the specific place where the peasants indicated that the majority of the victims were to be found, twelve cadavers were recovered.

La Coordinadora spearheaded the denunciation of the facts and produced a voluminous, detailed, and documented report that presented the testimony of more than thirty witnesses from the zone, including priests and nuns. Nonetheless, the government ably exploited the public's fears that such accusations might have a negative impact on the continued successes—already visible—of the counterinsurgency campaign. The government maliciously described our denunciation as a desperate attempt to stop the most important and final offensive against the guerrillas. My point is not simply to affirm my profound conviction that we acted correctly in making this denunciation. The point is that, for the reasons already given, the government managed to ensure that our action was negatively received, even by sectors that had traditionally identified with our cause. The government thus managed to bury, perhaps forever, one of the worst crimes committed in recent years in impunity and forgetfulness.

RETURN TO NORMALCY?

Even though all that we lived through with Shining Path and the war that it unleashed happened very recently, for many Peruvians those experiences already belong to the past. In our particular style of confronting national problems, the collective consciousness has preferred to forget what occurred among us.

It is not the intention here to inventory all the war has signified for the country. I note only that, in great measure because of the war, we have fallen decades behind in terms of democratic institutional development. The hope that Peruvians would construct a solid democracy, based on the initiative of sectors that emerged from below, is only a memory from the past. Today, we Peruvians have become more cynical and pragmatic about public affairs and politics, and about our own participation in them.

As one might easily imagine, there is tremendous unfinished work from a human rights perspective. In addition, new problems confront us and will demand our attention. Perhaps the most important task, however, will be to contribute to an understanding—and reversal—of the fact that even though Shining Path lost utterly on the military terrain, it achieved some unforeseen victories at the level of consciousness and values. Ironically for its authors, the amnesty law approved by the Peruvian government in June 1995 represented the triumph of this mentality.[30] Its first article is so revealing, that in place of an explanation, it merits an extensive excerpt: "General amnesty is conceded to military, police, and civilian personnel, whatever their police or military or functional role, who have been denounced, investigated, prosecuted, tried, or condemned for common or military crimes, under the common or military codes [of justice], respectively, for all of the events derived or originated upon the occasion of or as a consequence of the struggle against terrorism and that could have been committed in individual or group form since May of 1980 until the promulgation of the present law."

If this law is not an important indication of the emergence in Peru, as a consequence of this unwanted war, of a profound degradation of our appreciation for the essential dignity of human life, then what would be? One might find hope, however, that this is not an irreversible tendency in the unforeseen and massive repudiation that the amnesty law provoked among the Peruvian citizenry.

NOTES

1. The ideas in this introductory section have been amply discussed in other works. See for example O'Donnell 1988.

2. The author is a member of the Legal Defense Institute (Instituto de Defensa Legal; or IDL), a nongovernmental organization dedicated since 1983 to the defense and promotion of human rights, the strengthening of democracy, and the construction of peace. The IDL, like similar organizations in Peru, has had to work in very adverse conditions, openly confronting the practices of both the Peruvian state and insurgent groups.

3. In the elections for the Constituent Assembly the noticeable absence of Acción Popular was considered to be a highly risky political ploy on the part of Belaúnde, but one that was successful, as his party emerged triumphant two years later.

4. In fact, since then, the Peruvian political system attracted the participation of all of the political forces. The Left, including even the most radical sectors that continued to affirm armed struggle as their ultimate objective, participated in the electoral process, at times successfully, as in the Lima mayor's race in 1983.

5. As in other Latin American countries, leftist sectors were the most likely targets of these violations. Nonetheless, Peru, in contrast to many other places, did not witness significant and systematic state repression against the Left. We have to reach as far back as 1962 to find a massive round-up and imprisonment of leftist leaders.

6. Lanssiers is a priest of Belgian origin who has resided for many years in Peru, and is perhaps one of the most lucid minds in Peru today.

7. Cited in IDL 1992.

8. Document cited in Gorriti 1990. Emphasis in this and subsequent quotes is mine.

9. Cited by Gorriti 1990.

10. *Editor's note:* The word "pueblo" as people carried a connotation of "common people" or "people of modest means" in common Spanish usage.

11. This contrasts, again, with attitudes displayed by other guerrilla movements in Latin America, exemplified in the case of Peru by the MRTA. These groups refuted the political and moral authority of such tribunals, publicly revindicated their actions, and as "prisoners of war" refused to exercise their rights to defense.

12. In their favor we might add that they did not hide it: "As far as our violating human rights is concerned, our point of departure is that *we do not subscribe to the Universal Declaration for Human Rights, nor to that of Costa Rica. But we do use their legal mechanisms to unmask and denounce the Peruvian Old State,* its institutions and organisms, its authorities, beginning with those who lead it, functionaries and subordinates who violate human rights in defiance of their own international promises" (Guzmán 1991).

13. We should add that in contrast to other armed movements in Latin America, Shining Path has never demanded respect for International Humanitarian Law on the part of the Peruvian state. Nor has it practiced such principles in its own acts of war.

14. The Armed Forces' entrance into Ayacucho marked the beginning of what in Peru also has been known as the "dirty war," which escalated the conflicts to unforeseen levels. Thus, during 1983 and 1984 in just five provinces of Ayacucho (Huamanga, Huanta, Cangallo, La Mar, and Víctor Fajardo) there were 5,645 deaths, that is, 46 percent of all that were produced in Ayacucho during fourteen years of violence and, perhaps even more revealing, 20.5 percent of all that were produced in Peru during the same period.

Equally illustrative of the level of violence in this zone, "for Lima to have had the same proportion of casualties that Huanta suffered, for example, rather than 2,014 that really occurred, there would have to have been 213,453! And on a national level, rather than 24,117, there would have been 816,540!" (Basombrío 1994).

15. *El Comercio*, 15 June 1994 and *Expreso*, 14 June 1994.

16. Cited in IDL 1991.

17. *El Diario Internacional*, no. 18 (March 1993).

18. Declarations in *Panorama*, reproduced in *La República*, 12 July 1993.

19. It is hard to think of anyone in Acción Popular or the Popular Christian Party (Partido Popular Cristiano, or PPC) who worked for the human rights cause. In APRA, there is only one person, Javier Valle Riestra. The political discourse of various sectors of the Left referred to human rights, but only Javier Diez Canseco, Enrique Bernales, Rolando Ames, and Henry Pease carried out concrete and consistent action as protagonists of human rights. In Cambio 90, Fujimori's group, the only person who was sensitive to the issue was the second Vice-President Carlos García, who distanced himself from the regime almost as soon as it started.

20. Years later the journalist Guido Lombardi, who was not known for any pro-Shining Path inclination, publicly criticized us for not having persevered in this perspective: "I want to express my frustration over the fact that the human rights groups have ceded to the pressure from those who demanded similar condemnations for the violations committed by the state and those committed by terrorism . . . it is not a hindrance to keep thinking that those that proceed from the state are more grave and intolerable, because it is the state that should be the first guarantor of their protection" (Lombardi 1994).

21. La Coordinadora presently includes some fifty civic and religious organizations that work in the area of human rights in Peru.

22. We did this, according to our abilities and resources, through communiqués and notes for the press, through visits and private letters of solidarity with the victims, through international denunciations, and, increasingly, through humanitarian aid to victims of Shining Path. In fact, La Coordinadora has given concrete and effective humanitarian aid to many more of Shining Path's victims than has the state.

23. One could cite dozens of public communiqués that expressed this sentiment. The most revealing was, however, that which the human rights groups issued after Guzmán was captured, manifesting our satisfaction with, and approval of, the methods by which the capture had been achieved.

24. We should point out that as a rule they also preferred not to associate with us, and sought out legal assistance from the Association of Democratic Lawyers (Asociación de Abogados Democráticos).

25. In addition, Fujimori's authoritarianism impeded the trial against Abimael Guzmán from becoming a moment of political and moral sanction of his crimes, one that would have demonstrated the superiority of those who fought against him and judged and condemned him through strict adherence to the norms and principles of legality that Guzmán so disdained.

26. The most notorious exceptions to this rule were the assassinations of the peasant leader Jesús Oropeza and the mining leader Saul Cantoral.

27. The worst attacks against human rights organizations were the detention and subsequent disappearance of the president of the Comité de Derechos Humanos (Human

Rights Committee) of Huancavelica, Angel Escobar Jurado; the package-bomb that cost an arm, and almost the life, of the lawyer Augusto Zúñiga of COMISEDH; and the bombs that went off in the offices of the Andean Commission of Jurists and Amnesty International.

28. There is no element of sublime sacrifice for the nation in this reasoning given that, of course, the assumption was always that someone else would pay this price.

29. There were notable exceptions, however, when a particular set of events led many sectors of the Peruvian citizenry to join in a common cause and to corner politically the perpetrators of human rights violations. These events revealed the true nature of the regime and contributed to making sure that these types of violations could not be repeated. Such was the case, for example, of the massacre of nine students and a professor of La Cantuta University by a military death squad in July 1992.

30. For the amnesty law and human rights in 1995, see CNDDHH 1996.

ABBREVIATIONS

APRA   *Alianza Popular Revolucionaria Americana*/American Popular Revolutionary Alliance
COMISEDH *Comisión Nacional de Derechos Humanos*/National Commission on Human Rights
MRTA   *Movimiento Revolucionario Túpac Amaru*/Túpac Amaru Revolutionary Movement

REFERENCES

CNDDHH (Coordinadora Nacional de Derechoes Humanos). 1996. *Informe sobre la situación de Derechos Humanos en el Perú en 1995*. Lima: CNDDHH.
de la Jara, Francisco. 1994. "Militares opinan sobre derechos humanos." *Ideéle* 61 (March).
Gorriti Ellenbogen, Gustavo. 1990. *Sendero: Historia de la guerra milenaria el Perú*, vol. 1. Lima: Editorial Apoyo.
Guzmán, Abimeal. 1988. "Entrevista del siglo. Presidenta Gonzalo rompe el silencio." *El Diario*, 24 July.
———. 1991. " 'Sobre las dos colinas.' " Document in possession of author (Basombrío).
IDL (Instituto de Defensa Legal). 1992. *Perú Hoy. En el oscuro sendero de la guerra*. Lima: IDL.
Iglesias, Carlos Bamsobrío. 1994. "Para la historia de una guerra con nombre: ¡Ayacucho!" *Ideéle* no. 62 (April): 27–33.
Lombardi, Guido. 1994. "Puntos positivos y negativos." *Ideéle* no. 70 (November).
O'Donnell, Daniel. 1988. *Protección internacional de los derechos humanos*. Lima: Comisión Andina de Juristas.

Part VI

A Human Rights Revolution?

11

A New Age of Liberal Imperialism?

David Rieff

If anything should be clear from the Kosovo crisis, and, for that matter, from the unhappy experiences that outside intervention forces, whether serving under their own flags, the UN's, or NATO's, have had over the past decade in places such as Somalia, Rwanda, and Bosnia, it is that ad hoc responses to state failure and humanitarian catastrophe are rarely, if ever, successful. At the same time, the fact that there is now demonstrably a willingness on the part at least of the NATO countries to intervene militarily in the internal conflicts of other nations represents a radical change in international affairs. The conflict over Kosovo, the first war ever waged by the NATO alliance, was undertaken more in the name of human rights and moral obligation than out of any traditional conception of national interest. Indeed, had strictly practical criteria been applied to Kosovo, NATO as a whole might well have taken the same tack its European members did in Bosnia and attempted to prevent the conflict from spreading rather than trying, however halfheartedly, to reverse Slobodan Milosevic's campaign of murder and mass deportation.

The longer term implications of this further step in the post–Cold War moralization of international politics are not yet clear. Realists, whether they belong to the pure national interest school of a Henry Kissinger or the "lead by moral example" of a George Kennan, are alarmed, as well they should be, for it is now clear that half a century of campaigning by human rights activists has had a profound effect on the conduct of international affairs. The old Westphalian system, in which state sovereignty was held to be well-nigh absolute, is under challenge as never before. As former UN secretary general Javier Pérez de Cuellar put it in 1991, "We are clearly witnessing what is probably an irresistible shift in public attitudes toward the belief that the defense of the oppressed in the name of morality should prevail over frontiers and legal documents."

Whether it is really "irresistible" is of course debatable. Sometimes what appears at first glance as a prescient description of the future can turn out to be little more than an accurate diagnosis of the present. But Pérez de Cuellar, who, for all his grandee's aloofness, was a far abler diagnostician of his times than he is usually given credit for being, does seem to have discerned an essential shift and discerned it early. The Westphalian system in which he was formed as a diplomat now had challengers, many of whom spoke the language of human rights and derived from this language the belief that, in extreme cases at least, human rights abuses necessitated international intervention. The Franco-Italian legal scholar Mario Bettati and the French humanitarian activist and politician Bernard Kouchner even formulated a doctrine: the right of intervention.

And they and those who took a similar line had a profound effect on the thinking of Western governments. Human rights became an organizing principle for action in the 1990s the way anticommunism had been throughout the Cold War. The result was that most of the interventions of the 1990s, whether they were meant to protect civilians in states that had fallen apart, as in Somalia, or to shield an ethnic group from the murderous intent of its own government, as in Kosovo, were undertaken under the banner of preventing human rights abuses or righting humanitarian wrongs. Kosovo has been only the latest example of this, as President Clinton made clear when he said that NATO had acted to prevent "the slaughter of innocents on its doorstep."

ENDS AND MEANS

However, the fact that while the NATO powers are often willing to intervene they have also shown themselves almost never willing to take casualties suggests that this commitment is as much about having fallen into a rhetorical trap as about being guided by a new moralizing principle. The means employed simply do not match the high-flown rhetoric about ends. There have been times during the Kosovo crisis, as there were during the Bosnian war and the Rwandan emergency, when it has appeared that Western involvement came about because the leaders of the Western countries no longer found it politically possible to get up at a press conference before a television audience and say, in effect, "Sorry about the starving Xs or the ethnically cleansed Ys. It's just awful what's happening to them, but frankly they don't have any oil, nor are those that oppress them a threat to us. So you, Mr. and Ms. Voter, will have to continue to watch the slaughter on the evening news until it burns itself out."

Of course, that is precisely what members of the policy elites in Washington, Brussels, Paris, London, or Berlin say in private to one another all the time. But public language, along with public pressure, is often what drives policy. By now, commonplace expressions of realism in international affairs have become, to borrow the Early Christian theological distinction between elite and mass Christianity, an esoteric language restricted by and large to policymakers when they are out of public view. It is the language of human rights and humanitarianism that now stands as the exoteric language of public discourse about such questions. What this demonstrates is the degree to which there really has been a human rights revolution in the attitudes, though not to nearly the same degree in the practices, of the Western public and its poll-addicted, pandering governments.

The fact that it is all but inconceivable that a responsible Western leader could say of the Kosovo conflict what Neville Chamberlain said of Czechoslovakia, that this was "a quarrel in a far away country between people of whom we know nothing," should be demonstration enough—even though, strictly speaking, this would be no more than a simple statement of fact, all the rhetoric about Albania being in the "heart of Europe" to the contrary notwithstanding. To be sure, a politician or cabinet official will occasionally flout, intentionally or unintentionally, the new moral bilingualism. When, famously, then Secretary of State James Baker said of the breakup of Yugoslavia, "We don't have a dog in that fight," he was breaking the unwritten rule that held that, in public, representatives of the Western democracies were always supposed to insist that they stood ready to defend high moral principles.

But for the most part, what a human rights advocate would probably describe as the triumph of the categorical imperative of human rights—an imperative that, in extreme cases anyway, is held to trump all other political or economic interests or criteria—and what a realist might describe as the hypermoralization of international political action, has taken hold not just as a rhetorical but as an operating principle in all the major Western capitals on issues that concern political crises in poor countries and failing states. The fact that there is, as the writer Aryeh Neier has pointed out eloquently, a human rights double standard where powerful countries such as China are concerned does not mean nothing has changed.

The problem lies in separating the cosmetic from the fundamental, the makeover from the moral and political sea change. In all likelihood, elements of both figure in. It is not just that the possibility of any senior government official of any Western government speaking as bluntly as Baker did about the former Yugoslavia has receded, at least when the press microphones are on. The changes are deeper than that. The writer Michael Ignatieff is surely correct when he insists that "the military campaign in Kosovo depends for its legitimacy on what fifty years of human rights has done to our moral instincts, weakening the presumption in favor of state sovereignty, strengthening the presumption in favor of intervention when massacre and deportation become state policy."[1]

By "our," of course, Ignatieff means the Western public that is, as he says, perturbed by distant crimes in a way that it would probably not have been fifty or seventy-five years ago. Obviously, some sectors of public opinion in all Western states have viewed international affairs largely through a moral lens. U.S. relations with China before the Second World War, to cite only one obvious example, were highly influenced by the agenda of the missionaries. What is impressive is the degree to which these largely Christian missionary (and imperial) habits of thought and categories of analysis find their much broader echo in the secular human rights movement of the past thirty years, and how successfully that movement has been in persuading governments to act at least publicly as if they shared the same concerns and at least some of the same priorities.

MORAL AMBITIONS

Had the consequences of this ascendancy largely been beneficial, and had the actions undertaken by governments in the name of human rights and humanitarian imperatives been as successful as activists initially expected them to be, it would be possible simply to welcome the changed rhetorical and, perhaps, even moral circumstances in which international politics must be conducted. But this is not the case. From Somalia to Rwanda, Cambodia to Haiti, and Congo to Bosnia, the bad news is that the failure rate of these interventions spawned by the categorical imperatives of human rights and humanitarianism in altering the situation on the ground in any enduring way approaches 100 percent. Time and time again, our moral ambitions have been revealed as being far larger than our political, military, or even cognitive means. And there is no easy way out.

It is undeniable that the Western television viewer does indeed—and surveys support this contention—see some scene of horror in central Africa or the Balkans and want something to be done. But "something" is the operative word. Even in situations where the media pays intense attention over a long period of time, there is rarely a consensus that military force should be used, while there is usually a great deal of anxiety about involvement in any operation whose end point is not fixed in advance.

No matter how profoundly the influence of the human rights movement has led to a questioning of the inviolability of state sovereignty, the wish to help and the increasing consensus, at least in elite opinion in most NATO countries, that the West has not just the right but the duty to intervene in certain egregious cases is not matched by any coherent idea of what comes next. This is assuming—and as Kosovo has demonstrated, success is anything but ensured—that the intervention has succeeded in bringing the particular horror to an end.

Perhaps this is why, in Western Europe at least, the prestige of humanitarianism increased so dramatically over the past fifteen years. The humanitarian enterprise—giving help to people desperately in need of it—has seemed to cut through the complexities and corruptions of politics and national interest. Here at last, it seemed, was something morally uncomplicated, something altruistic, something above politics. Of course, what the humanitarian movement discovered painfully over the past decade (though many aid workers had understood this much earlier), starting in Bosnia and culminating in the refugee camps of eastern Zaire where aid helped not only people in need but also those who had perpetrated the Rwandan genocide, was that there was no transcending politics. Aid undeniably did good things. A vaccinated child is a vaccinated child. But at least in some instances, it also prolonged wars, distorted resource allocations, and, in Bosnia, where the humanitarian effort became the focus of Western intervention, offered the great powers an alibi for not stopping the genocide of the Muslims. And Somalia demonstrated that what the West saw as a humanitarian intervention might well be understood by the locals as an imperial invasion, which, whatever its intentions, to a certain extent it almost always is.

AN UNSTABLE MIXTURE

As the limitations of humanitarianism have increasingly become apparent, human rights has taken center stage in the imaginations of those in the West who continue to believe in human progress. Even many humanitarian aid workers have increasingly come to believe that they too must uphold rights, and most of the major private voluntary groups, such as Doctors Without Borders, Save the Children, or the International Rescue Committee, are taking bolder and bolder positions on the need to redress wrongs as well as build latrines, set up clinics, or provide food.

As aid becomes more and more of a business, and private-sector companies expert in construction projects increasingly vie with aid agencies for contracts from principal funders such as the U.S. Agency for International Development (USAID) and the European Commission Humanitarian Office (ECHO), some humanitarian workers are coming to believe that the more emphasis they place on human rights (something that private companies are hardly likely to have much taste or aptitude for) the more important a role they will retain. But it is more than a question of corporate self-interest; the way out of the crisis of confidence humanitarianism has undergone has seemed to lie in the quasi-religious moral absolutism and intellectual self-confidence of the human rights movement.

For Western leaders, these distinctions have very little resonance. The Clinton administration, like its European counterparts, routinely conflates human rights and humanitarian concerns. Kosovo is probably the most extreme example of this, but the pattern has been consistent. The best one can say is that most post–Cold War interventions have been undertaken out of an unstable mixture of human rights and humanitarian concerns. And yet the categorical imperative of upholding human rights and the categorical imperative of getting relief to populations who desperately need it are almost as often in conflict as they are complementary.

The human rights activist seeks, first and foremost, to halt abuses. Usually, this involves denouncing the states or movements who are violating the laws of war or the rights of their citizens. In contrast, the humanitarian aid worker usually finds that he or she must deal with the abusive government or rampaging militia if the aid is to get through safely and be distributed.

So far at least, there is more confusion than any new synthesis between human rights and humanitarianism. And the consequences of this have been immensely serious, both operationally and in terms of rallying support for interventions like the ones that took place in Rwanda, Somalia, or Bosnia. Somalia, in particular, revealed the difficulty of engaging in an operation that was supposed to end a famine but that ended up as a war between the foreign army deployed to help the humanitarian effort and one of the Somali factions. Americans were appalled to see soldiers killed in such circumstances, and their revulsion cannot be attributed solely, or even fundamentally, either to the pictures of a dead U.S. soldier being dragged naked through the streets of Mogadishu or to the trauma of Vietnam.

Soldiers are expected to die in a war, but the Somali operation was not presented as a war; it was presented as a humanitarian mission. And soldiers are not supposed to die in such circumstances. Even when the U.S. government declared Mohamad Farah Aideed its enemy, and set out to hunt him down through the back alleys of Mogadishu, it did so using the language of police work. Aideed was a criminal, U.S. officials kept saying.

The result was that the American public came to think of the hunt for Aideed, even though they knew it was being carried out by U.S. Army Rangers, not as war but as police work. Casualties in war are understood to be inevitable. Soldiers not only are supposed to be ready to kill, they also are supposed to be able to die. But casualties in police work are a different matter entirely. There, it is only criminals who are supposed to get hurt or, if necessary, killed, not the cops. Again, the fundamental problem has not been some peculiar American aversion to military casualties. Rather, there has been an essential mistake in the way such operations are presented to the public, and, perhaps, even in the way they are conceived of by policymakers. Under the circumstances, it should hardly be surprising that public pressure on Congress and the president to withdraw U.S. troops predictably arises at the first moment an operation cannot be presented in simple moral terms, or when the casualties or even the costs start to mount.

CONFLATING WAR AND CRIME

The emphasis, both in Bosnia and Rwanda, on tribunals and apprehending war criminals, however understandable, has only further muddied the moral and political waters, for it cements this conflation of war and crime. One deals with an enemy in war very differently from how one deals with a war criminal. And wars against war crimes, which is how Kosovo was presented at the beginning of Operation Allied Force, must either be waged as the Second World War was waged—that is, until unconditional surrender—or run the risk of seeming utterly pointless when, as in most noncrusading wars, a deal is struck between the belligerents that leaves those who have previously been described as war criminals in power. The tensions of such a policy were apparent at the end of the Bosnian war when Slobodan Milosevic, who had quite correctly been described previously by U.S. officials, at least in private, as the architect of the catastrophe, was seen as the indispensable guarantor of the Dayton Accords.

If the tensions are inevitable, so too is a crime-based outlook about war. Ours is an era when most conflicts are within states and have for their goal less the defeat of an adversary's forces on the battlefield than either the extermination or expulsion of populations. Actually, there are few wars that do not seem to involve widespread and systematic violations of international humanitarian law, so thinking about war as crime is not just an understandable but in many ways a rational response to objective conditions.

And yet the emphasis on the Yugoslav and Rwandan ad hoc international tribunals, and, more recently, on the International Criminal Court (ICC), has created not only false hopes but also false perceptions of what a human rights–based international order implies. The false hopes are easier to categorize. Such tribunals may, like the death penalty, deter the individual in question, breaking, as Michael Ignatieff put it, "'the cycle of impunity' for [certain] particular barbarians," but they cannot hope to seriously deter future criminals or crimes any more than the death penalty deters future murderers—a fact one might have expected the largely anti–death penalty, pro-ICC activists to have confronted more seriously.

But it is by insisting that there is no intellectual or moral problem with demanding that international law should be upheld as strenuously as the domestic laws of democratic states that human rights activists, and the governments that are influenced by them, however intermittently, are engaged in a project that almost certainly seems doomed to failure. Starkly put, its presuppositions do not withstand scrutiny. It is all very well to talk about these laws, or courts, or imperatives, as expressing the will of the "international community." In practice, however, the definition of this "community" is highly if not exclusively legalistic and consists of the states that sign various treaties and conventions and the activist nongovernmental organizations that lobby them to do so.

In finessing this fundamental problem of legitimacy—the ICC, as one of its American defenders once conceded, was largely the concern of "hobbyists and specialists"—and in asserting that a body of law that is the product of a treaty has the same authority as a body of law that is the result of long historical processes that involve parliaments, elections, and popular debate, the activists have in effect constructed a legal system for a political and social system that neither exists nor is likely to exist any time in the foreseeable future. Presented as the product of some new global consensus, it is in fact the legal code of a world government.

NO WORLD GOVERNMENT

But there is no world government. There is only world trade and national governments. To say this is not simply to indulge in nostalgia for the Westphalian system or to deny that, in the West anyway, there has been a shift in consciousness toward believing that certain conduct by nations within their borders should not be tolerated whatever the current legal status of state sovereignty may be. Obviously, the power of nation-states to control their destiny is less today than it was half a century ago. And in trade law, there has been a real ceding of sovereignty. Where politics and, above all, the conduct of international relations that can result in war are concerned, however, the picture is much more mixed. States must wage war, and only the state's inherent legitimacy can make it plausible both for young soldiers to kill and die and for their fellow citizens to support or at least tolerate such a tragedy.

The problem with the human rights approach—and in this Western governments that have eagerly seized on the rhetoric of human rights are, if anything, far more blameworthy than the activists themselves—is less that it is wrong than that it is unsustainable in the absence of a world government, or, at the very least, of a United Nations system with far more money, autonomy, and power than it is ever likely to be granted by its member states.

A UN mercenary army organized along the lines Brian Urquhart has proposed might well have been able to break the back of the Khmer Rouge in Cambodia or the warlords in Somalia. In places where the interests of the great powers are not involved, the Security Council may at times be willing to grant a mandate for intervention to the secretary general. And open-ended UN protectorates in those or similar places, backed up by military force and the mandate to use it, unlike such short-lived operations along the lines of the UN Transitional Authority in Cambodia (UNTAC) that have actually taken place, would theoretically have a chance of restoring the broken societies over which they had taken control.

But even leaving aside the question of whether such a move toward world government would be in humanity's best interest, it is obvious that no such option is now available. Even the prospect, seemingly quite realistic in the late-1980s, that UN peacekeeping would become a central instrument of international peace and security has receded over the course of the 1990s, with peacekeeping reduced to a narrower and more traditional role of postconflict cease-fire monitoring and truce enforcement. But if the United Nations has been marginalized, and if the demands of the emerging human rights consensus among the Western elites have proved to be not just hard to satisfy but hard even to define except in the broadest and most nebulous terms, it is equally clear that the current ad hoc-ism is also unsustainable.

"JUST DO IT"

Kosovo has seen to that. The conflict there has revealed more than simply the fact that NATO was willing to bomb but not—at least not before it was too late to prevent a second slaughter in the Balkans in a single decade—to take the kinds of military action that might have prevented the ethnic cleansing of almost the entire Kosovar population. In Pristina, before the NATO air war began, young Kosovars walked around wearing T-shirts with the Nike logo and their own gloss on the Nike slogan. "NATO," it read, "Just do it!"

In a sense, that is what important constituencies within the human rights community had been saying as well. Obviously, neither the activists nor the Kosovars themselves imagined the kind of limited, hesitant, politically hamstrung military campaign NATO would undertake when they called for action. And yet this was the predictable, perhaps even the inevitable consequence of not defining that "it." The new language of rights, so prevalent in Western capitals, has been revealed to be at least as misleading about what is and is not possible, what it did and did not commit Western states to, as it is a departure from the old language of state sovereignty.

It is not just that the issues over what the future of a postwar Kosovo would be were fudged from the start. Was the province to be liberated by force? If so, was it to be turned into a NATO or an Organization for Security and Coordination in Europe (OSCE) protectorate? Or was it to be given its independence? These are only some of the questions that were never answered satisfactorily in Washington or in Brussels before the air campaign began.

More gravely still, there is no evidence that a Marshall Plan for the Balkans, clearly a sine qua non for regional stability even before the bombing started and the mass deportation began, had been worked out. The World Bank was barely consulted; the UN specialized agencies, on whom responsibility for the predictable refugee crisis rests, were caught flat-footed. And most Western governments had to run to their parliaments just to get supplemental appropriations to pay for the war; they had no coherent plan for the future whatsoever. Thus, on the political level, the economic level, and the military level, the West was improvising from the start.

But war, even war undertaken on human rights grounds, is not like jazz singing. Improvisation is fatal—as the Kosovars have learned. Just do it, indeed! A country that ran its central bank this way would soon collapse. And yet it continues to be the implicit assumption of the NATO powers that they can confront the crisis of failed states by making it up as they go along. In Somalia, in Rwanda, and in Congo, the Western powers chose to respond with disaster relief, which both guaranteed that the political crises in those countries would continue and represented a terrible misuse of humanitarian aid. In Bosnia, the emphasis was on containing the crisis. In Algeria and Kurdistan, it has been either to ignore it or exploit it.

FINESSING THE DISASTER

And yet in Kosovo (this had almost happened in Bosnia), the West was finally hoist on the petard of its own lip service to the categorical imperative of human rights. It was ashamed not to intervene, but it lacked the will to do so with either vision or coherence. Kosovo is probably a lost cause; it is certainly ruined for a generation, whatever eventual deal is worked out, as Bosnia, whose future is to be a ward of NATO, America, and the European Union, probably for decades, has also been ruined for a generation, Dayton or no Dayton. What remains are the modalities through which this disaster can be finessed and its consequences mitigated.

It is to be hoped that in the wake of Kosovo, the realization that this kind of geostrategic frivolity and ad hoc-ism, this resolve to act out of moral paradigms that now command the sympathy but do not yet command the deep allegiance of Western public opinion—at least not to the extent that people are willing to sacrifice in order to see that they are upheld—will no longer do. To say this is not to suggest that there are any obvious alternatives. Even if one accepts more of its premises than I do, the human rights perspective clearly is insufficient.

As for the United Nations, it has been shown to be incapable of playing the dual role of both succoring populations at risk while simultaneously acting like a colonial power and imposing some kind of order and rebuilding civic institutions. The important Third World countries seem to have neither the resources nor the ideological inclination to intervene even in their own regions, as Africa's failure to act in Rwanda in 1994 demonstrated so painfully.

The conclusion is inescapable. At the present time, only the West has both the power and, however intermittently, the readiness to act. And by the West, one really means the United States. Obviously, to say that America could act effectively if it chose to do so as, yes, the world's policeman of last resort, is not the same thing as saying that it should. Those who argue, as George Kennan has done, that we overestimate ourselves when we believe we can right the wrongs of the world, must be listened to seriously. So should the views of principled isolationists. And those on what remains of the left who insist that the result of such a broad licensing of American power will be a further entrenchment of America's hegemony over the rest of the world are also unquestionably correct.

WHAT IS TO BE DONE

But the implications of not doing anything are equally clear. Those who fear American power are—this is absolutely certain—condemning other people to death. Had the U.S. armed forces not set up the air bridge to eastern Zaire in the wake of the Rwandan genocide, hundreds of thousands of people would have perished, rather than the tens of thousands who did die. This does not excuse the Clinton administration for failing to act to stop the genocide militarily, but it is a fact. And analogous situations were found in Bosnia and even, for all its failings, in the operation in Somalia.

What is to be done? The Office of the United Nations High Commissioner for Refugees cannot solve crises of such magnitude; these days, it is hard-pressed even to alleviate one without logistical help from NATO military forces. The humanitarian movement has even fewer means. In becoming dependent on NATO's logistical support, or, as in Kosovo, in effect serving as a humanitarian subcontractor to one of the belligerents, its intellectual and moral coherence, which is based on impartiality, has been undermined. And human rights activists, for the valuable work they do in exposing brutality and violations of international law, are demanding a regime of intervention whose implications they clearly have failed to think through seriously.

By this, I do not mean the issue of consistency—a debate that, these days, is usually framed, "If Kosovo, then why not Sierra Leone?"—although the distorting effect of concentrating exclusively on the south Balkans and channeling what monies exist for aid in its direction cannot but have a devastating effect on Africa in particular. To insist on this point is, when all is said and done, to make the great the enemy of the good. There will be no serious intervention in Sierra Leone; that is no reason for us to turn our collective backs on the Kosovars.

But Kosovo is an anomaly—a crisis at the edge of Europe that comes on the heels of the Bosnian crisis about which the NATO powers have a bad conscience. Even had the NATO countries responded more effectively, Kosovo would not have provided a model for how to do post–Cold War interventions.

A deeper problem is how to replace a chaotic post–Cold War disorder with some kind of order that does what it can to prevent both the worst sorts of repression and ethnic cleansing. A realist would say the effort is not worth it. For those who believe differently, whether it is simply because they find the suffering of people in places such as Kosovo or the Great Lakes region of Africa as unconscionable when their countries have the means to set it right, or because they believe that too much disorder, even at the periphery of the rich world, is a clear and present danger, the task is to think through how such an order might be imposed.

A more active, attentive, and consistent diplomacy will certainly be necessary, but so will the occasional use of force. Realistically, this means either NATO or the army of the Russian Federation, or both, since only these military establishments have the logistical capacity to move troops long distances in short periods of time. But it is hard to imagine, after the experience of Kosovo, that there will be much appetite for further improvisation. At the same time, it is evident that America's strategic partners will not be disposed to support a renewed Pax Americana in which the United States acts as the global policeman of last resort, even if America were willing to reassume that role. And it never will, since the American consensus is strongly against such an arrangement.

BACK TO THE FUTURE

Where does this leave us? One possible solution would be to revisit the mandatory system that was instituted after the Versailles Treaty. Its pitfalls are obvious. In practice, League of Nations mandates became thinly disguised extensions of the old colonial empires, with trusteeships distributed more on strategic than on humanitarian grounds, that neither improved the situation of the peoples of the territories in question nor brought about any great improvement in regional stability. Woodrow Wilson's warning during the negotiations at the Paris Peace Conference that "the world would say that the Great Powers first portioned out the helpless parts of the world and then formed the League of Nations" needs to be borne in mind.

But Wilson's original idea, which was, as he put it, to take temporary control over certain territories in order "to build up in as short a time as possible . . . a political unit that can take charge of its own affairs," may be one way out of the current impasse. The unhappy experience of the United Nations in Cambodia suggests that an ad hoc imposition of a trusteeship is doomed to failure, if for no other reason than supervisory control is simply too diffuse and too subject to political pressure. Had the United Nations stayed in Cambodia for a generation, as, to his credit, then Secretary General Boutros-Ghali argued that it should, it might indeed have improved that unhappy country's prospects; by staying two years, it provided little more than a short respite. Haiti represents a similar failure to stay the course.

To insist on this point is not to bash the United Nations. The structure of the institution, above all the cross-currents and conflicting interests that find their expression in the work of the Security Council, simply makes it the wrong organization to undertake to administer a new trusteeship system. Regional organizations and great powers are far likelier to be able to devise a system of burden sharing. For all its faults (and the "imperialistic" interests) involved, the Nigerian invasion of Sierra Leone has been a positive development. The problem was not that the Nigerians came; it was that once there, they had neither the will nor the money to follow up their military conquest with state reconstruction. Perhaps, if General Olusegun Obasanjo really does represent a return to democracy in Nigeria, such efforts will begin.

Obviously, behind the scenes the NATO countries and, above all the United States, would have to exercise some degree of supervisory control over the trusteeships and underwrite efforts at nation building. Funding would be politically controversial (obviously, most would have to come from the Western powers and possibly from the Bretton Woods institutions) and difficult to appropriate wisely. But, on balance, the costs would still be less than the astronomical figures that will be required to rebuild Kosovo or, for that matter, were needed to deal with the humanitarian crisis in central Africa in the mid-1990s. Waste and mismanagement are facts of life. They should not become the impediment to actually dealing with the current disorder and tragedy in so much of the poor world.

It is likely that, were such a system to be put in place, the role of American power might actually diminish over the long term, although in the short run it would probably increase. For the most part, however, except in emergencies, or where the rapid dispatch of troops is required, other, midsized nations—rather than NATO powers—could do the actual administrating and the policing. And a structure that would necessarily involve this degree of burden sharing between small, medium, and great powers might also serve useful purposes in other fields of international relations, although it would be foolish to expect too much on that score.

The central point is that a mandatory system could take the insights of the human rights revolution into account without overreaching; it could provide a framework for action that could only be an improvement over the current system—if it can even be called that—in which each crisis comes as a kind of lightning bolt from the blue; and it would not be constrained by the kind of divisions that make any sort of serious action through the UN Security Council all but impossible to imagine.

Is this proposal tantamount to calling for a recolonization of part of the world? Would such a system make the United States even more powerful than it is already? Clearly it is, and clearly it would. But what are the alternatives? Kosovo demonstrates how little stomach the United States has for the kind of military action that its moral ambitions impel it to undertake. And there will be many more Kosovos in the coming decades. With the victory of capitalism nearly absolute, the choice is not between systems but about what kind of capitalist system we are going to have and what kind of world order that system requires. However controversial it may be to say this, our choice at the millennium seems to boil down to imperialism or barbarism. Half-measures of the type we have seen in various humanitarian interventions and in Kosovo represent the worst of both worlds. Better to grasp the nettle and accept that liberal imperialism may be the best we are going to do in these callous and sentimental times.

Indeed, the real task for people who reject both realism and the utopian nihilism of a left that would prefer to see genocide in Bosnia and the mass deportation of the Kosovars rather than strengthen, however marginally, the hegemony of the United States, is to try to humanize this new imperial order—assuming it can come into being—and to curb the excesses that it will doubtless produce. The alternative is not liberation, or the triumph of some global consensus of conscience, but, to paraphrase Che Guevara, one, two, three, many Kosovos.

NOTE

1. Michael Ignatieff, "Human Rights: The Midlife Crisis," *New York Review of Books*, May 20, 1999.

12

Kosovo: The War of NATO Expansion

Robin Blackburn

NATO has established a Kosovo protectorate at the cost of great suffering for the peoples of the region and in a way that is likely to further poison the relations between different communities. The bombing by NATO set the scene for the expulsion of around one million Albanian Kosovars and devastated the social infrastructure throughout Yugoslavia. Thousands were killed in Kosovo itself and in the rest of Yugoslavia; those wounded or rendered homeless were very much more numerous. Most of the victims were civilians and refugees, not soldiers. Despite the claims for precision weapons, errors claimed many lives.

Some critics of the air war argued that a ground assault should have been mounted from the beginning. On this point the NATO high command had a more realistic grasp. The Serb army was well dug in and possessed thousands of rocket launchers, mortars, and artillery pieces. While the ultimate outcome would never have been in doubt, the casualties arising from an immediate invasion would have been very high, civilian as well as military. No sane commander would prefer a contested entry in such circumstances, amongst some of the most inhospitable terrain imaginable, to the prior destruction of the enemy's hardware, supply dumps, communications, and morale. Advocates of a ground assault might claim that it would have avoided sorties against civilian targets, the use of cluster bombs, and some of the errors. But the prior aerial bombardment had a perfect military logic, and it was the first week of bombing that precipitated the escalation of violence on the ground as hundreds of thousands were driven from their homes by enraged and murderous Serb soldiers and paramilitaries.

As the conflict developed both sides were frustrated at their inability to hit and hurt the enemy's military capacity so they hit civilian targets instead. As it turned out the NATO bombardment was, in fact, militarily even less effective than was realized at the time, with many of the targeted tanks, artillery pieces, and the like being plastic decoys while the real military assets were hidden in underground bunkers. Unfortunately the bridges, power plants, refineries, hospitals, and schools destroyed were the real things. The war was undertaken by NATO in the name of human rights but the conflict itself hardened ethnic animosity and blindness, ending with the terrorization and forced expulsion of the great majority of Kosovo's Serbs and Gypsies. The desire for revenge instilled in the minds of many Kosovar Albanians was, of course, very understandable. But the role of outsiders in perpetuating and aggravating the cycle of communal conflict is quite another matter, especially when the supposed champions of human rights are silent as women, children and old people are driven from their homes.

The West has a heavy responsibility for the bloody break-up of former Yugoslavia and for its prolonged neglect of the oppression of the Kosovar Albanians. But even as late as December 1998 or March 1999 it could have played a crucial part in promoting a peaceful settlement. The disastrous air war was wrong not because there was another military option, but because, from the outset, a deal was available providing for the withdrawal of Serb forces and their replacement by a UN or OSCE (Organization for Security and Cooperation in Europe) security force. This alternative foundered because it did not give NATO the protectorate it wanted. The Russian government, eager to please its Western creditors and play what it saw as its rightful part on the international scene, was amenable to a joint approach to Belgrade.[1] The UN Contact Group could have reached an agreement on a withdrawal of Serb forces from Kosovo at any time from March to December 1998 so long as the leading Western powers had lined up the Russians first. The Yugoslav government was on the brink of signing up to such a package at Rambouillet but when details of the provisions of the agreement imposed by the United States were disclosed it became clear that Russia had been by-passed. The provisions stipulated that the international security force would be NATO-led, that it would have the right of inspection throughout the Yugoslav republic, and that its members would be exempt from responsibility for their actions before local courts. Moscow attacked the proposal for a NATO-led occupation force and the Russian negotiator declined to be present when the agreement embodying it was signed by the Kosovar delegation on March 15. When news of the bombing came through the Russian prime minister canceled in midflight a visit to Washington. Milosevic was never going to accept an agreement rejected by the Russians, especially one which provided for a provocative expansion of NATO's sphere of operations. To do so would deprive him of vital support and make him vulnerable to internal opponents. But by the same token a settlement supported by Russia would be very difficult for him to reject even if it meant wholesale evacuation from Kosovo.

An item on the failed Rambouillet negotiations in the *New York Times* for April 8, 1999, observed: "In a little-noted resolution of the Serbian Parliament just before the bombing, when that hardly independent body rejected NATO troops in Kosovo, it also supported the idea of U.N. forces to monitor a political settlement there." The Serbian delegation, under duress, had been willing to accept the principles of the Rambouillet package save for the very detailed twenty-fifth chapter on the NATO-led occupation force.[2] When Milosevic made a deal at Dayton he implemented it punctiliously, accepting the forced expulsion of hundreds of thousands of Serbs from lands they had long inhabited. Even if implementation of a Kosovo deal had been more difficult, the relationship of forces, both in Kosovo and in the world, would have ensured compliance without the horrendous cost the war had entailed.

In late April and early May a new round of diplomatic mediation assisted by the governments of Russia and Finland again foundered on NATO insistence that the proposed security force should be built around a NATO "core." Following a meeting of the G8 the Russian Foreign Minister, Igor Ivanov, made it clear no agreement had been reached on this issue because Russia could not accept the transformation of Kosovo into a NATO protectorate. The Western insistence on a controlling role for NATO thus precluded a combined approach to Belgrade and doomed the prospects for a Security Council resolution on the question. This phase of negotiation was brought to an end by the bombing of the Chinese embassy in Belgrade without the West having made any concession on NATO's role.

Of course the willingness of Milosevic to strike a deal did not come from the goodness of his heart but because of his fear of NATO striking power, his wish for an end to sanctions and a craving for international respectability, precisely the motives which brought him to endorse the agreement at Dayton in 1995. It might be thought that the fear element in the Serbian leader's motivation itself justifies the air assault. But this would only be the case if the bombardment produced a result for the Kosovars very much better than that already available at Rambouillet in February, and after the exodus that could scarcely have been the case. The settlement eventually reached, notwithstanding a token Russian role, means that NATO will have acquired a better strategic emplacement in the region and the Kosovars will still have paid a heavy price.

The composition of the security force was the stumbling block in March and in early May because NATO opposed any security force in Kosovo that it did not wholly control. In public both sides were bound to overstate their position but the composition of the security force was always the sticking point. At all times the Russian stance was bound to be critical to Belgrade, not only because a Serbian-dominated Yugoslavia would always find it easier to go along with Russian mediation, enforced with the help of Russian troops, or because Russia had the resources to help Yugoslavia with fuel, arms and diplomatic comfort, but also because any Belgrade government authorizing a NATO protectorate in Kosovo would earn the enmity of Russia. Milosevic was always sure in the knowledge that all sectors of Russian opinion would oppose the conversion of Kosovo into a NATO protectorate.

Some Kosovars and their supporters argued that anything less than immediate and full self-determination for the people of Kosovo was unacceptable. But at Rambouillet the Kosovar delegation, after much pressure and agonizing, declared that they accepted a NATO protectorate and that the security force must be NATO-led. Of course, the composition and leadership of this delegation had been carefully vetted by NATO—the veteran KLA leader Adem Demachi was excluded and an inexperienced twenty-nine year old, Hashim Thaci, was recognized as leader of the delegation while the veteran Ibrahim Rugova was sidelined. NATO did not to allow the Kosovars to dictate its strategy. At no point did NATO ask Belgrade to renounce all claim to Kosovo. The Kosovar delegation was eventually persuaded to sign up to Rambouillet despite this fact.[3]

NATO was willing to allow a token Yugoslav presence at some border points as a sop to the notion that, in some loose way, Kosovo was still, like Montenegro, part of Yugoslavia. The justification offered for this was that the key issue was the replacement of Serb occupation by an international security force that would allow refugees to return and would lay the basis for some new political structure. If it were not for the fact that NATO insisted that such a process required a NATO protectorate, the proposal for a purely transitional, face-saving formula would be a reasonable compromise, permitting an orderly withdrawal of Serb forces.

The UN or OSCE alternative to a NATO-led security force would almost certainly have included a large contingent from some NATO states, but it would also have had significant Russian and neutral participation. If the European powers were prepared to pay the greater part of the cost of such a force, which is only fair considering their large contribution to the escalation of the Yugoslav wars, there is every reason to suppose that such a broader security force would do a more disinterested job than a NATO-led force. So long as their wages are paid armies are structured to obey orders; this is as true for the Russian, Irish, and Finnish armies as it is for NATO forces. And because it would not provoke the Russians, it would contribute to regional security rather than undermining it. In terms of the practicality of inserting such a force into Kosovo it should be borne in mind that in February 1999 there were already a few thousand OSCE monitors in place; instead of withdrawing them, an act which undoubtedly encouraged the Serb paramilitaries to do their worst, the number of monitors could have been sharply increased as the occupation force was assembled.

Some saw any countenancing of a Russian role as naïve or treacherous; it was to ignore Russia's brutal attempt to suppress the Chechen republic or to underestimate how reckless and bloody Russian politicians and the Russian military can be. The fact is that a very similar objection could be made to the leading NATO states. For example in 1998 the U.S. appointed William Walker, a man responsible for working with a murderous military regime in Guatemala, to lead the OSCE monitoring force in Kosovo; on a recent trip to Central America President Clinton publicly apologized for the U.S. contribution to the campaign of military terror unleashed by Rios Montt and the Guatemalan military and paramilitary forces in the 1980s. The British government has publicly apologized for the Bloody Sunday shootings, and its soldiers in Northern Ireland have been found guilty of torture of suspects. The French security services blew up the "Rainbow Warrior" and actively collaborated with the Hutu militia in Rwanda. And so on. In all these cases the misdeeds of the Western security forces and advisers primarily reflected the character of the mission entrusted to them by the politicians. Likewise in Chechnya. In the Chechen case the Russian political authorities were eventually persuaded that enough was enough and allowed General Lebed to negotiate a settlement and military withdrawal in 1996. This episode represented a major shift in Russian politics, with President Boris Yeltsin only narrowly escaping impeachment on the issue.[4] The West itself has not banned Russia from any military role outside its borders. Indeed it allowed a token Russian contingent in the Bosnia security force. The Primakov government formed in 1998 was committed to peace in Chechnya, but it was also regarded as unreliable by the West, and this is why it was cold-shouldered in the Kosovo negotiations of 1998–1999. If the Kosovo security force had excluded all NATO powers then it could certainly have excluded Russia as well without aggravating the already lop-sided military stand-off in east-central Europe, but this has never been proposed.

The prolonged occupation of Kosovo by troops of any foreign power—Russian, U.S., or for that matter Finnish and Irish—will be likely to lead to abuse, corruption, and repression, which is why any such arrangement should be strictly limited to the period of time required to allow self-determination for the people of Kosovo to become a reality. At all times it was clear that the negotiated withdrawal of the Serbian paramilitaries, police, and army units was the precondition for lifting the afflictions of the Kosovar Albanians. The unleashing of the bombardment and the wave of Serb reprisals made the task of peace and reconciliation vastly more difficult. But a Serb withdrawal was still required to create the best conditions for a return of refugees and for recuperation from the ordeal of occupation and war. A large force of mixed foreign troops would then be needed to keep the peace, and this force would undoubtedly face the very difficult task of preventing further revenge attacks. The UN or the Council of Europe would have been a far more suitable sponsor of such an occupation than NATO, but even it should have had the urgent goal of recruiting and training a local police force drawn from all sections of society. Advocates of the war sought to discredit any UN role by intoning the word Srebrenica, as if the deployment of a UN force in Kosovo *after the withdrawal of Serbian forces* would invite the disasters that attended UN "peacekeeping" efforts in Bosnia, where there were large Serb military formations and where, unlike Kosovo, the Serbs were the largest national group. The group most at risk in Kosovo after a Serb withdrawal was obviously going to be the local Serbs, a fact which the war party wilfully ignored.

I have argued that the war was unleashed, and was allowed to become a protracted assault on the whole social infrastructure of Yugoslavia, for one reason, and one reason only: that nothing less than a NATO-led solution and NATO-protectorate status for Kosovo was acceptable to the United States and Britain, and that other alliance members went along with this, whatever their public or private reservations. In other words the war had a strategic dimension which blighted early prospects of settlement, precipitated a humanitarian catastrophe and is likely to continue to poison East-West relations.[5]

When former President Mikhail Gorbachev visited King's College, Cambridge, in March he expressed astonishment that the West was prepared to follow up the expansion of NATO by making a bonfire of all the international accords and organizations that had been put in place to safeguard peace and human rights. Those who went to war treated the Helsinki agreements as a scrap of paper and shunted aside the OSCE. They denied Russia a real say in the crisis, notwithstanding the obvious contribution which the Russian government could make to a settlement. Those who heard Gorbachev and had the opportunity to speak with him could not fail to be impressed by his alarm nor fail to be shocked by the failure of many commentators even to address the wider issues raised by the war. On this issue Gorbachev was evidently speaking for nearly every strand of Russian opinion.

From the outset the Russian government denounced unilateral NATO military action, warning that it would provoke a new Cold War, bring instability to a wide arc of countries and lead to the final burial of both nuclear and conventional disarmament. It saw the insistence that Kosovo become a NATO protectorate as part of a wider scene of encirclement.

Advocates of a NATO-led ground war proposed a further escalation of the provocation. Given the huge difficulties of landing a significant force in Kosovo the NATO commanders would be tempted to move against Belgrade directly from their bases in Macedonia, Bosnia and Hungary, with the help of allied local forces. A military plunge into Serbia could well have detonated the political mine fields in Macedonia, Bosnia, and Montenegro. If Hungary, Romania, or Croatia had been given any role then territories such as the Voyvodina and Moldova could also be dragged in, as could Russia, the Ukraine, and their respective borderlands. A NATO-occupied Yugoslavia would complete Russia's encirclement.

So, had the NATO leaders forgotten about Russia's possession of 3,500 intercontinental ballistic missiles, with their nuclear warheads? Did the fragility of the political order in Russia need to be pointed out to them? Did it require the Chinese reaction to the bombing of their Belgrade embassy to notice that Russia, the military giant, and China, the rising economic power, are exploring economic and military cooperation?

For whatever reason most Western commentators rarely refer to such matters preferring to maintain the comfortable illusion of an end to the Cold War. But it would be absurd to suppose that Pentagon or State Department strategists do not think about them the whole time. The Kosovo operation is a further evolution of the new policy of enlarging NATO, projecting NATO power and containing Russia. U.S. Secretary of State Madeleine Albright and National Security Adviser Sandy Berger, with encouragement from veteran Cold Warriors such as Zbigniew Brzezinski and Senator Jesse Helms, have certainly focused on the global strategic dimension, even if the U.S. president, Congress and public were engrossed in the Lewinsky affair. When justifying the size of the U.S. military budget complicated formulas have been put forward about the need to confront two major regional crises at the same time; thinly veiled hints then make it clear that the U.S. military establishment is designed to be able to confront and contain Russia and China. Two former senior officials at the Defense Department recently noted: "For obvious reasons, the administration would like to avoid having to explain why it regards these countries [i.e., Russia and China] as potential adversaries in its defense analyses."[6] But is a new show-down with Russia inevitable or could it be avoided by constructive engagement? Should the emphasis be upon carrying through already-negotiated disarmament agreements, such as START-II, or should these be abandoned in favor of discreet preparations for a new confrontation with what William Cohen, the defense secretary, has called the potential "global peer competitor"? Should Russia be invited to join NATO or should the alliance give Russia a demonstration of the fate that awaits it if it steps out of line?

In their book *Preventive Defense*, Ashton Carter and William Perry, who stepped down as secretary of defense in early 1997, explained their own fears that the U.S., in overreacting to manageable problems such as Kosovo, may actually re-create a mortal threat to U.S. security. Paraphrasing their argument in a review of this work Lawrence Freedman writes:

> Unfortunately the fund of goodwill between Washington and Moscow with which the 1990s started has now largely been spent, and has not been replenished. A large part of the problem is economic as the Russians blame the West for the failure of their bowdlerised version of capitalism to deliver the goods. The major strain in political relations, however, has come from NATO enlargement, a policy that was bound to be seen in Moscow as reneging on past pledges not to take advantage of the collapse of the Warsaw Pact to strengthen the Western Alliance. The authors make it clear as delicately as they can that they opposed the advocates of this move in the Clinton administration, precisely because of the negative Russian reaction it predictably generated.[7]

Other opponents of enlargement have included George Kennan, Jeff Matlock, and many other senior diplomats and former ambassadors, including virtually all of those who have been posted to Moscow. The fullest statement of the case against by a U.S. strategic analyst was Michael Mandelbaum's book, *The Dawn of Peace in Europe*.[8]

Brzezinski on the other hand consistently claimed that NATO expansion was not only a wise but also an essential policy. In 1996 he was quoted as saying that the Russian Federation was "redundant." He explained: "Russia is viable as a nation state. I don't think, however, it has much future as an empire. I don't think the Russians can re-establish their empire. If they're stupid enough to try, they'll get themselves into conflicts that'll make Chechnya and Afganistan look like a picnic."[9] He believes that Russia is menacing and overcentralized: "Given the country's size and diversity, a decentralized political system and free-market economics would be most likely to unleash the creative potential of the Russian people and Russia's vast natural resources." He looks forward to a "loosely confederated Russia—composed of a European Russia, a Siberian republic and a Far Eastern republic."[10] Brzezinski advocates economic and military measures to boost the independence of each of the states on Russia's borders. Indeed, he has himself helped to promote the formation of a new alliance between Georgia, Ukraine, Azerbaijan, and Moldova (GUAM). Following the financial crisis in Russia in August 1998 Brzezinski observed that the events in Moscow signaled "the end of this rather naïve spin . . . namely that Russia has been successful at privatizing and that Russia has been successful at democratizing. I'm afraid neither is true."[11]

As a former national security adviser, Brzezinski, who is still based in Washington, gave needed strategic weight to the policy of NATO enlargement. For his part Clinton adopted the policy prior to the last presidential election, having found that it would play well with many Polish Americans, Baltic Americans, Czech Americans, and so forth, as well as enhancing his image as a tough leader. NATO enlargement was one more issue on which the incumbent could wrongfoot the Republicans. This was politics rather than thoroughgoing backing for the Brzezinski vision, and efforts were still made to help Yeltsin, including a very mild response to the repression in Chechnya. For its part the Russian government was almost pathetically anxious to do the West's bidding. Brzezinski discounts this on the grounds that it is the power structure that matters; for him the Russian Federation is a chip off the old block and its politics and armed forces are insufficiently de-Sovietized. The secretary of state is obliged to be more cautious, but basically Madeleine Albright remains in thrall to the outlook of her old mentor and contemptuous of those who would indulge Russia. In an article published in November she curtly observed that "Russia is wrestling with severe economic and military challenges" and lectured its leaders on the need for disarmament.[12]

With Kosovo, and with the president distracted, NATO enlargement moved from diplomacy and budget planning to fait accompli and unilateral military initiative. It is unlikely that Tony Blair, Britain's callow and histrionic prime minister, grasped the larger picture or understood that he was helping the hawks to prevail. On the eve of the war *Foreign Affairs* published articles by Garry Wills and Samuel P. Huntington expressing alarm at the course of events. Wills proclaimed that it was a great error for the U.S. to play the role of the "bully of the

free world" while Huntington urged that "the core state of a civilization can better maintain order among the members of its extended family than an outsider."[13]
But such advice had already been flouted by the time it appeared.

It was at U.S. insistence that Russia was cut out of the process that led to the
war and excluded from its implementation. The humiliation of the Russians was
the more intense because they had played a central role in diplomatic contacts
before and during the Rambouillet conference. The notion that bombing would
be effective, even without Russian support, and that Milosevic would quickly
crumble, was sold to the lesser allies by the Anglo-Saxon powers. But the dominant faction in Washington was anyway persuaded that the best way to deal with
the Russian threat was by encircling that country with military bases, client states
and NATO protectorates. Some British foreign policy advisers urged that it was
unwise to forego the possible contribution of Russian good offices in the attempt
to impose an agreement on Milosevic, but they were told that Russian involvement was not acceptable to the Americans. The crassly provocative exclusion
of Russia eventually had its opponents in NATO counsels, but to begin with they
tamely followed where the United States and Britain led, sending out pathetic
little signals of concern as the military juggernaut headed for the abyss.

The rigorous exclusion of Russia from any other than a messenger-boy role
represented a clear departure from previously announced doctrine. Javier Solana,
the NATO secretary general, declared in a speech on June 23, 1998, that it was
essential that "Russia must be on board" if the West was to tackle the critical
issue of Kosovo.[14] At this time it was obvious to Solana that Russia should be
involved, both because that would maximize the chances of a successful settlement and because to leave Russia out would be a colossal strategic snub. The
financial collapse of August that led to the advent of the Primakov government
may help to explain a hardening of the U.S. position and the eventual abandonment of the position so recently adopted by Solana.

The reading offered here might seem to be at odds with the well-informed
account written by Tim Judah in the *New York Review of Books* in its issue dated
June 10. After discussions with Chris Hill, the U.S. ambassador to Macedonia.
Judah wrote:

> What of the then-current theory that Milosevic was prepared to accept a military
> force so long as it was not overtly a NATO one? Hill says that this is simply not
> the case. The Rambouillet negotiators—Hill himself, Wolfgang Petritsch for the
> EU and Boris Mayorski for Russia—would have been happy to agree to any suit-
> able disguise for the force, but the Serbs simply "would not engage" on the ques-
> tion. He adds: "If the Serbs had said yes to the force but no to the independent
> judiciary—and insisted on all sanctions relief (i.e., on the West dropping all sanc-
> tions)—do you think we could have bombed?"

This account at least takes us to the crux of the question. But the direct and
indirect quotes from Ambassador Hill only seem to allow for a "suitable disguise"

not for a genuinely non-NATO force. It is also certainly the case that the Russian government expected to participate in implementation, notwithstanding the view curiously attributed to the Russian negotiator here—Ambassador Mayorski boycotted the Kosovar signing ceremony because of the NATO-led formula. Naturally Russia resents its exclusion just as keenly as Serbia, if not more keenly. And the purpose of getting it on board would always have been to maximize the pressure on Serbia.

If the United States rather than Russia had been excluded from the negotiating process then the chances of a peaceful outcome would have been much greater. United States involvement may gratify the hawks in Washington but overseas military adventures, with limitless prospects of further entanglements, are of no interest to the great mass of U.S. citizens. It serves to distract the U.S. public from such alarming problems as the growth of its prison population, and the expense of NATO enlargement and the sustenance of a string of protectorates could erode those budget surpluses which make possible Clinton's surprisingly bold approach to the problem of social security retirement funding. No country should arrogate to itself the role of global bully, and the United States is particularly unsuited to it because the structure of its politics makes it so vulnerable to special-interest lobbies.[15] The reluctance of U.S. political leaders to envisage casualties to their own forces might be a gain for restraint but it is largely canceled out by Washington's ability and preparedness to launch destruction from afar.

On May 24, Clinton used the columns of the *New York Times* to restate U.S. terms, to signal a small change, and backhandedly to acknowledge criticism of the policy adopted. After reiterating that the security force for Kosovo should "have NATO command and control and NATO rules of engagement, with special arrangements for non-NATO countries, like our force in Bosnia," he added: "Our military campaign will continue until these conditions are met, not because we are stubborn or arbitrary but because they are the only conditions under which the refugees go home in safety and the KLA will have any incentive to disarm— the basic requirements of a resolution that will work." In point of fact the United States's roles in Bosnia and Somalia simply did not bear out this claim; many refugees had not returned to Bosnia, and in Somalia U.S. troops under U.S. command proved very bad at handling a difficult and delicate situation.[16] Whoever entered Kosovo after a Serb withdrawal was going to have a difficult task of preventing new communal conflicts and a new wave of refugees. There was no basis for claiming that only NATO had the answer. Obliquely referring to critics of the dump-on-Russia approach, Clinton continued: "this strategy gives us the best opportunity to meet our goals in a way that strengthens, not weakens, our fundamental interest in a long term relationship with Russia. Russia is now helping to work out a way for Belgrade to meet our conditions. Russian troops should participate in the force that will keep the peace in Kosovo, turning a source of tension into an opportunity for cooperation, like our joint effort in Bosnia." No doubt the new willingness to contemplate a Russian role in both mediation and implementation—under NATO command and control—reflected Yeltsin's willingness to accommodate Washington and his success in removing Primakov. But an item on the front page of that day's *Herald Tribune* showed the damage being done—it reported that the START-II disarmament agreement had completely stalled, since it needed the approval of the Duma. Far from being ready to implement either conventional or nuclear disarmament the Russian high command had taken the decision to modernize their nuclear arsenal.

Public opinion in the NATO countries only gradually became aware of the costs of the air war, to the many refugees still inside Kosovo, to Yugoslav civilians and to regional tension. The Italian and German governments came out against a ground offensive. Unhappy coalition partners called for an immediate cessation of the air bombardment and encouragement for Russian mediation efforts. Some realized that NATO's supposed objective of "degrading" the "command and control" function of the Yugoslav forces only made sense to those bent on a wider war since, if successful, it would prevent Belgrade from ordering its forces to withdraw and release Serb units in Kosovo from any remaining restraint. And the relentless air assault actually strengthened Milosevic's control over his own population. Only the advent of peace could expose Milosevic to the attacks of all those Serbs who had good cause to rue his long history of disastrous leadership. (Significantly, the strong Serb opposition movement of 1996–1997 occurred during a time of peace.)

The principles enunciated by the Council of Europe, the Organization for Security and Cooperation in Europe, and the United Nations could have furnished the appropriate basis for conducting negotiations with Yugoslavia. Past and present Yugoslav governments have subscribed to them, as have the NATO powers. Intervention by these bodies would have a legitimacy which NATO lacked and would thus have subjected the Serbian leader to greater pressure. Right up to the end the method of NATO diktat simply prolonged the agony. The bodies to which I have referred were established by arduous international agreement, and subsequently ratified by parliaments and assemblies, for the very purpose of regulating relations between states and monitoring their observance of human and civil rights. When the new Yugoslav Federation was established it vociferously insisted that it assumed all the international obligations of the old Federation. Of the previously mentioned organizations the Council of Europe, a body specifically established to safeguard human rights and civil liberties, would have been by far the most appropriate for dealing with the Kosovar crisis, so long as it was given appropriate facilities by its member states. The Council represents the region threatened by the crisis and, as a body, had no responsibility for the recent chapter of disasters. It would also be a suitable vehicle for channelling much-needed economic assistance from the EU to the whole region.

The international organizations referred to are far from perfect and their modes of operation are open to improvement. Both in principle and in practice the Western powers, as important member states, have had every opportunity to obtain improvements to the operating principles of these organizations. In the past they have used their influence to block the emergence of more effective systems for making and executing decisions, notably Russian proposals for an OSCE secretariat and security council. The OSCE and the Council of Europe do include Russia and would ensure its participation in both negotiation and implementation of any agreement.

In 1998 and early 1999 the Albanians of Kosovo were beginning to resist a structure of oppression that had been tightened over the previous decade and a half. The European countries, who allowed this to happen, had a special responsibility for taking up the Kosovar cause in appropriate and helpful ways. For two decades the West ignored or even aggravated the plight of the Kosovars. In the seventies it had seemed that the people of Kosovo were at last emerging from a semicolonial condition, but following Tito's death, the growing strength of the racist variant of Serbian nationalism led to a worse subjugation than before. The Western powers aided and abetted the disorderly disintegration of the old Federation, which had acted as a restraint on the Serb authorities. The IMF greatly aggravated a desperate economic crisis and denied the last Yugoslav government the money to pay its soldiers.[17] Without a squeak from the West Milosevic imposed a brutal and arbitrary regime on the so-called province.[18] Kosovar self-determination was a more justified and urgent cause than the secessions of Slovenia, Croatia, or Bosnia, which were so precipitately and fatally recognized by the Western powers. The Kosovar cause should have been supported throughout the nineties in appropriate diplomatic and material ways, much as, say, Sweden, the Soviet Union, and, belatedly, the United States supported the cause of the African National Congress in South Africa. The armed actions by the KLA in 1998 created a situation with all the elements of a classic anticolonial struggle, as in Algeria, with guerrilla attacks and military repression, with some localized massacres, but not on a big scale, up to Rambouillet.

According to NATO up to February 1998 about one thousand Serb soldiers and functionaries had been killed and two thousand Albanian Kosovars; two hundred thousand Kosovars had left their homes but, up to this point, most remained in Kosovo.

The bombing transformed a vicious colonial conflict into ethnic cleansing on a large scale, a phenomenon which in the twentieth century has so often required the cover of war to carry through—as the wartime fate of Armenians, Jews, Palestinians, Germans, Bosnians, and, most recently, Serbs in the Krajina demonstrates.[19] The glib analogy that has been so often made between Hitler and Milosevic forgets that Britain and France did not declare war on Nazi Germany because of its practice of genocide; the Holocaust was the product of war not the casus belli. War was declared against Germany because it broke treaties and invaded neighboring countries in the name of defending German minorities from persecution.

According to the classic Augustinian theory of the "just war" the means should be proportionate to the ends; the decision for war should be made only after all prospects of mediation have been exhausted and as an act of legitimate authority. A war which causes massive harm to those on whose behalf it is undertaken, where a vital prospect of mediation has been shunned, which is in violation of treaties, and not put to the prior sanction of elected bodies, cannot be a just war. Those who brandish crusading causes, such as Tony Blair, can be the most dangerous militarists of all. There is a world of difference between a just war and a holy war. The carnage of the First World War was held to be justified by the wrong done to Belgium. The colonial partition of Africa was undertaken in the name of suppression of the slave trade. In pursuing a justified cause we should always be alert to the ulterior motives and vested interests which might distort it, seeking, so far as may be possible, to favor approaches which stymie those interests and motives. Thus the more principled and effective abolitionists found it quite possible to support resistance to slavery and international covenants against the slave trade without endorsing wars of colonial conquest.

Both the UN and the OSCE have been involved in the peaceful and/or negotiated resolution of difficult cases of national oppression, decolonization, and conflict containment in the past. They have had their failures, but the U.S. has contributed to these, too. The Council of Europe and European Union could have aimed to improve on their records. They would at least have been able to do better than NATO, which furnished a dangerous precedent of unilateral action, shed much innocent blood, and stoked local and global tensions.

But would not such a negotiated approach have delivered the Kosovar cause to cynical exploitation by great power interests? An alert public opinion and active peace movement could have acted as one safeguard against such an outcome. But potentially so does an inclusive network of international and regional agreement. The pressures of international negotiation, agreement and military disengagement can help to neutralize or restrain both great power interests and reckless emotional spasms. It obliges participants to justify themselves in terms of international norms and public opinion. In a context of structured negotiation and cooperation the whole is just a bit better than the parts since the participating states hold one another in check. We should not forget or discount the appalling role of Serb security forces in Kosovo or much of former Yugoslavia, nor of Russian forces in Chechnya, nor of Turkish forces in Kurdish areas, nor of U.S.-backed and advised military regimes in Central America. We should press for a world where the special military units responsible for death squads are disbanded. But faced by the Kosovo crisis we cannot ignore the reality that Western military power acts as a potential check on Serbia and that Russian military capacity acts as a check on NATO. Without endorsing either military establishment we should be able to see the merit of pressing for a pacific accommodation between them, one that leads to a further program of disengagement and disarmament.

And without romantic illusions about the KLA we can see that it offered a means of self-defense to the major national group in Kosovo and that its armed methods drew away support from the pacific parties which had previously won elections there. It accordingly deserved a measure of recognition but not a monopoly of de facto control. In any settlement there had to be a transitional role for the Yugoslav armed forces—though not for the paramilitaries and police battalions which were specially created to carry out the lawless terror and ethnic cleansing which the regular army found distasteful. If it was always true that only an agreement could produce a peaceful Serbian withdrawal from Kosovo, as actually happened, then the cooperation of the Yugoslav armed forces was essential to this. Those who wish for peace in the Balkans and in Europe cannot simply wish away the various bodies of armed men that are in contention but must rather seek to disengage them in the most effective way possible.

The Council of Europe should have been convened to consider action on Kosovo in March 1998 when the armed struggle commenced, or at any later time. It was then, and remains now, the best body to convene a wider conference to consider the fate of the region and to furnish security guarantees. At such a conference there should have been a range of representatives of the people of Kosovo, including the party of Ibrahim Rugova, the KLA, and representatives of minority groups. The KLA might well have demanded full and immediate self-determination for the people of Kosovo. While the KLA should have had every right to put forward its point of view, the conference would not have been bound to accept it. Given the situation in Kosovo an immediate vote on the future of this territory was not possible anyway. As it was NATO used its huge leverage to manipulate Kosovar organizations—for example by excluding the veteran Kosovar leader Adem Demaci and by promoting a former Croatian general, who participated in the cleansing of the Krajina Serbs, to a key position in the KLA structure in April 1999. After June the NATO occupation forces gave great leeway to the KLA while denying them the immediate self-determination they demanded—indeed the June agreement did not even contain the promise of a referendum in three years time which had been part of the Rambouillet accords.

While the Albanian Kosovars have suffered greatly we should be wary of understandable but misguided attempts to absolutize their cause. The exercise of self-determination by the people of any state should itself be pursued by proportionate means and with due account taken of wider implications of the action. While large nations are given to hegemonism small ones can also be, in their own way, oblivious, and self-centred. Thus the precipitate haste with which Slovenia exited from the Yugoslav Federation in 1991 actually assisted Milosevic in his oppression of the Kosovars. The European Community of the time should have delayed recognition of the break-up of the Yugoslav Federation until the Kosovars had been conceded their own republic. That Slovenian leaders gave overwhelming priority to Slovenian interests—regardless of the consequences—was, no doubt, as inevitable as it was unfortunate. The real culpability here resided with those Western powers, above all Germany and Britain, who went along with Slovenian secession despite the warnings they had received.[20] Another case of small nation egoism would be the response of Fidel Castro and Che Guevara to the Cuban missile crisis of 1962. The defense of Cuba against the United States was an entirely just cause, but risking nuclear war was not justified; fortunately Khrushchev was prepared to back down. As it turns out Cuba was secured from direct invasion by the results of the crisis. Some Kosovar leaders have insisted—very much at Western prompting—that only a NATO-led force is acceptable to them. But even if all Kosovars agreed, it would still not be right to ignore the larger context. And some Kosovars are aware that NATO's tutelage may be indefinite. An international occupation force is, and was, needed to ensure the evacuation of the Serb forces and to ensure the safety of all inhabitants of Kosovo—including the Serb minority. But its aim should always have been to make itself redundant as speedily as possible.

Those who rightly called for an immediate halt to the bombing knew that Belgrade would still have an incentive to settle to prevent any resumption. Does this mean that the policy of the doves was covertly complicit with that of the hawks and thus prove that the latter were right all along? No, because the situation would have been better for the Kosovars at every stage if their case had been strongly pressed by all means short of war—in 1991–1992 at the time of the break-up, in 1995 at Dayton, and in 1998–1999 when hostilities began. If the Western governments who now pose as champions of human rights had been genuinely concerned with the fate of the Kosovars on any of these occasions they could have achieved a decent settlement and avoided the humanitarian catastrophe we face. On each of these occasions it would have been better to act with Russia and without the United States.

In the end settlement was reached with Russia's good offices. Indeed the Chernomyrdin-Ahtisarri mission that produced the basis for the agreement was the first joint Russian-European approach to Belgrade. By this time, after much arm-twisting, the Russians had been brought to accept a mainly NATO occupation force. However it, would still be better for the Kosovars, and better for Europe and the world, if NATO announced a schedule for its withdrawal from Kosovo and encouraged the Council of Europe to convene a conference to address the need for a new and democratic Balkan settlement.

John Lloyd, reporting from Moscow in the *Financial Times* for May 27, 1999, explained two important points relating to the Russian role, whether military or diplomatic, in a solution. First, Chernomyrdin was seen as a corrupt, compromised, and pro-Western figure in Russia, and consequently a settlement endorsed only by Chernomyrdin and Yeltsin would have little credibility. On the other hand, Lloyd also reported that the plan for a settlement proposed by Igor Ivanov, the foreign minister, envisaged a complete Serb withdrawal and not a partition of Kosovo.[21] Not surprisingly, the concern of Russian political circles was always with whether there was to be a huge NATO force in Kosovo and not with any other details of the settlement. The inclusion of a token force of Russian soldiers in a NATO-led operation was the eventual price of the settlement but was so modest and grudging that it will not allay this concern and will simply store up problems for the future.[22]

The dramatic Russian seizure of the airport at Pristina helped to highlight the dangers courted by Western policy. Later reports indicated that General Wesley Clark ordered General Jackson to contest this action, with the latter declining to do so. In fact a more assertive Russian government could have used control of the airport to fly in a sizeable force—after all Russia still has very capacious troop-carrying aircraft and no shortage of oil. The British commander of K-FOR and the British chief of the defense staff also gave it as their opinion that the Russian mediation had been decisive in ending the conflict and that, by implication, the air war had been misconceived. General Jackson told the *Sunday Telegraph*: "The event of June 3rd (when Moscow urged Milosevic to surrender) was the single event that appeared to me to have the greatest significance in ending the war." Asked about the air war he replied: "I wasn't responsible for the air war; you're talking to the wrong person." A *Guardian* interview with General Sir Charles Guthrie, chief of the defense staff, also acknowledged that the war ended "thanks to the Russian intervention."[23]

The eventual decision to settle with Milosevic, rather than send NATO's forces smashing into Yugoslavia, was welcome, cheating the Western ground assault party of the reckless further slaughter and provocation they craved. In allowing many refugees to return it has at least undone some of the damage inflicted in late March. But despite many months of notice, no police forces were on hand to prevent looting and revenge killing, or to prevent gangsterism or to begin training a mixed, locally recruited force. Those Kosovar Albanians who still support Ibrahim Rugova, perhaps a majority, were also treated with hostility by the KLA. The continuing danger of Albanian revenge attacks is now held to justify protectorate status and effectively denies the rights of Kosovars to run their own affairs. It seems likely that, before long, Kosovo will become one more ethnically cleansed statelet, joining such other shards of former Yugoslavia as Croatia and the three Bosnias. And as the Bosnian statelets show, protectorate status encourages criminal networks rather than the capacity for self-government.[24] More generally, the reluctance to engage constructively with the Russia of Premier Primakov set the scene for the rise of Putin and an invasion of Chechnya, preceded by a protracted aerial bombardment.

In the short run NATO's war for NATO expansion is being claimed as a huge success for the hawks. Not only is its Balkan sphere of action greatly enlarged—probably permanently—but the intimidation of war has assisted a reordering of regional and global politics. In Germany Oskar Lafontaine has been ousted and the Social Democrat-Green coalition bloodied by combat. Lionel Jospin has declared himself happy with the new order of things, and José Borrell, the Spanish Socialist leader, has been induced to resign. Hungary, the Czech Republic, and Poland have been kept in line, and Romania and Bulgaria are prepared for the next round of expansion. Last, but not least, NATO itself, after some bad moments, looks set to preside over a world in which it can act more freely than ever before. If they were unwise the hawks might add Primakov's scalp to their trophy list, notwithstanding the fact that that he was brought down thanks to a new yellow/brown alliance of Yeltsin, Zhirinovsky, and Chernomyrdin, men who were the architects of the first Chechen war and who have, with Western help, imposed on the Russian people a dreadful toll of misery. We are told that those who sow the wind reap the whirlwind. In this case the first to be hit by the whirlwind were the inhabitants of Chechnya, while Tony Blair rushed to exchange visits with Russia's new Man of Destiny, declaring that Putin was a man he "felt comfortable with." The poisonous legacy of the Kosovo war contrasts strikingly with the negotiated evacuation of East Timor just a few months later, which was accomplished by the UN with the help of regional forces and the consent of China, and done in such a way as to weaken General Wiranto, the Indonesian military leader. In contrast to this successful, if belated, example of international action, the "humanitarian" war to get NATO into Kosovo has fostered distrust among the victors, hatred between the victims, and contempt for cant about human rights and international norms in Moscow.

NOTES

1. Jonathan Steele, a knowledgeable and seasoned observer of the prewar diplomacy, later argued that "NATO has achieved its aims in Yugoslavia but the war need never have been. The deal extracted from Milosevic last week could probably have been obtained twelve months ago without the horror of bombing at all." "NATO's Russian Roulette," *The Guardian*, June 9, 1999. The strapline on this piece read: "The West's contempt for its former Cold War enemy caused estrangement during the Kosovo crisis just when they needed to work together."

2. This emerges even from an account written by the legal adviser to the Kosovar delegation, Marc Weller, "The Rambouillet Conference," *International Affairs* 75 (April 1999).

3. See Weller, "The Rambouillet Conference."

4. See the conclusion to Anatol Lieven, *Chechnya, Tombstone of Russian Power* (New Haven: Yale University Press, 1998). It is worth noting, though, that the assault on Yugoslavia, along with everything else it did, created new problems in Chechnya by

upsetting the tenuous status quo established there by early 1999. The air strikes against Belgrade allowed a tacit deal to be struck with Russia, to the effect that if Moscow allowed NATO to pound Serbia, the West would not complain if the bombing of Chechnya was resumed.

5. How things might have been handled differently, in a manner that more effectively detaches human rights concerns from the pursuit of geopolitical agendas in a campaign of intervention, is indicated by the recent case of East Timor. There, matters have been handled quite differently: no bombs have fallen on Jakarta, an agreement with China has been reached, and the leading role in intervention has been taken by a regional power. The result has been largely successful pressure on Indonesia to withdraw.

6. Zlamy Khalilzad and David Ochmanek, "Rethinking U.S. Defense Planning," *Survival* (IISS London) 39, no 1 (Spring 1997): 49, quoted Gilbert Achcar, "The Strategic Triad: the United States, Russia and China," *New Left Review*, no. 228 (March-April 1998): 91–128, 102–103.

7. Lawrence Freedman, "On the C List," *TLS*, April 30, 1999. This is a review of Ashton B. Carter and William J. Perry, *Preventive Defense: a New Security Strategy for America* (Washington, D.C.: Brookings Institute, 1999).

8. Michael Mandelbaum, *The Dawn of Peace in Europe* (New York: Twentieth Century Fund Press, 1996). I cite this work and that by Carter and Perry because they show that the recklessness of current U.S. policy arouses disquiet even within the political establishment. For an informative critique of NATO enlargement see *The Expansion of NATO*, Campaign Against the Arms Trade, London 1999, available from 11 Goodwin St, London N4 3HQ.

9. *Transition*, November 15, 1996.

10. Zbigniew Brzezinski, "A Geostrategy for Asia," *Foreign Affairs* (November-December 1997).

11. Interview, CNBC, "Power Lunch," 27 August 1998. Sternly critical of Russia's democracy Brzezinski is, however, known for favoring close links to Azerbaijan. He is a consultant to Amoco and the Azerbaijan International Operating Company, a cartel whose projected oil pipelines and agreements help to cement the GUAM alliance. Freedom House, of which Brzezinski is a board member, recently pronounced that political conditions in Geidar Aliev's Azerbaijan were improving (Aliev was a member of Brezhnev's Politburo and responsible for the ethnic cleansing of Armenians from Nagorno-Kabarak). For material on Brzezinski and Azerbaijan see the web site of counterpunch (www.counterpunch.org) and the article by Christopher Hitchens in the web magazine *Salon*, September 29, 1997 (www.salon.com). While Brzezinski's links with the oil companies are evidently close it is not necessarily the case that he is doing their bidding; some observers believe that the oil concerns are being dragged into Brzezinski's politically inspired machinations through a combination of naiveté and greed.

12. Madeleine Albright, "The Testing of American Foreign Policy," *Foreign Affairs* (November/December 1998): 50–68.

13. Garry Wills, "Bully of the Free World," *Foreign Affairs* (March-April 1999): 50–60; and Samuel P. Huntington, "The Lonely Superpower," *Foreign Affairs* (March-April 199): 35–49.

14. Tariq Ali, "Springtime for NATO," *New Left Review*, no. 234 (March-April 1999).

15. See Daniel Lazare, *The Frozen Republic* (New York: Harcourt Brace, 1996).

16. For an authoritative discussion of this issue, see Alex de Waal, "U.S. War Crimes in Somalia," *New Left Review*, no. 230 (July-August 1998): 131–144, 135.

17. Robin Blackburn, "The Break-up of Yugoslavia," *New Left Review*, no. 199 (May-June 1994). For the role of economic "landslides" in precipitating ethnic violence, see Tom Nairn, "Reflections on Nationalist Disasters," *New Left Review*, no. 230 (July-August 1998).

18. See Branka Magas, "The Balkanization of Yugoslavia," *New Left Review*, no. 174 (March-April 1989).

19. See Michael Mann, "The Darkside of Democracy: the Modern Tradition of Ethic and Political Cleansing," *New Left Review*, no. 235 (May/June 1999): 18–45.

20. For a trenchant indictment of Western policy towards Yugoslavia see Susan Woodward, *The Balkan Tragedy* (Washington: Brookings Institution, 1995). As Woodward points out most Western statesmen and diplomats gave absolute priority to self-determination within each of the republics of the Federation, neglecting the ways in which this prejudiced the rights of individuals and nationalities within the republics.

21. John Lloyd, "Russians Doubt Chernomyrdin's Kosovo Chances," *Financial Times*, May 27, 1999.

22. Brzezinski's comment on June 15 on the CSIS web site was "It is really the strategic task of the U.S. to create a situation through its relationships with Europe and China whereby Russia really has a single, constructive option, that is to say, accommodation with Europe and the West." He also pointed out:

In the last several days, three countries in southeastern Europe [Romania, Bulgaria, Hungary], one of which is a member of NATO [Hungary], have refused overflight rights to the Russians, and they have been and remain the object of intense pressure to yield these rights, including now some threats. We have actually encouraged Romania and Bulgaria to refuse these rights. That de facto creates a special security relationship with them, which introduces a new element into the NATO enlargement process. Romania and Bulgaria are now in a relationship with NATO which is quite special, and puts them in a special category as candidates for membership.

23. See Richard Norton-Taylor, Analysis and Comment page, *The Guardian*, August 3, 1999; interview with General Jackson, *Sunday Telegraph*, August 1, 1999.

24. The dismal record of the Bosnia protectorate is surveyed in David Chandler, "Rise of the Balkan Protectorate," *New Left Review*, no. 235 (May/June 1999): 124–134.

13

The Strange Career of Radical Islam

Timothy McDaniel

For liberals committed to the priority of the individual and the inviolability of individual rights, religion and revolution are both suspect. Such defenders of individual choice could easily agree with Khomeini's dictum (referring to the United States and the Soviet Union) that "each is worse than the other," for both religion and revolution relativize the value of the individual by placing him or her in the context of a much vaster canvas: the will of an almighty God who demands absolute obedience or the logic of a historical process that will culminate in the good society. In *Exodus and Revolution* the political philosopher Michael Walzer has made the parallels between monotheistic religion and revolutionary vision into a historical connection. He believes that the logic of "Exodus politics"—the sequence of consciousness of oppression, liberation, social contract, political struggle, and new society—has decisively shaped secular revolutions as well. "The Exodus, or the later reading of the Exodus, fixes the pattern."[1]

The idea of an Islamic revolution must be, from this point of view, doubly dangerous. It fuses the demands for absolute submission to God's will—we recall that Islam has the literal meaning of submission—with the conviction that God's purpose for humanity will find fulfillment in history. It thus links individual commitment, politics, and divine injunction. Jihad, religious struggle in the service of the faith, is the human embodiment of God's will in history. For such reasons, some observers contend that contemporary Islamic movements that want the faith embodied in all aspects of social life are totalitarian, insensitive to the priority of a set of inalienable individual rights over and above any social and political vision.[2]

Contemporary international events throughout the Islamic world offer lamentably strong support for the liberal indictment of radical Islamic movements.

211

Whether we turn to the murder of innocent tourists in Egypt, to the slaughter of tens of thousands of people of every description in Algeria, to the enforcement of restrictions of women in public life in countless places, or to the recent order by the Afghan taliban for people to destroy their television sets, the conclusion seems inescapable: The combination of Islam and revolution is one of the major threats to human rights in our time, as dangerous in its own way as was communism.

However, as tempting as it may be to emphasize the compatibility between Islam and revolution, and thus to use the term "Islamic revolution" as a unified concept, in fact the relationship between Islam, revolution, and human rights is more complex than might appear. Islam may indeed animate a revolutionary assault against human rights, but it may also, even in Khomeini's Iran, provide protections for the individual against the claims of revolutionary movements. As compared with Jacobin or communist movements unalloyed with religion, there appear to be certain checks to totalitarian politics in Islamic revolutions. These checks stem in large part from the fact that an Islamic vision of the world cannot avoid certain conservative—conservative from a characteristically revolutionary point of view—Islamic principles, including an emphasis on the sanctity of private property, the private sphere, and revealed legal norms. These cannot simply be obliterated by revolutionary ideology. Of course, Muslim revolutionaries have in practice violated religiously defined human rights in sometimes horrifying ways, but it is not enough merely to point to the joint dangers of religion and revolutionary vision as an explanation. Instead, to understand the complex links among Islam, revolution, and human rights, we must analyze the key terms in pairs: Islam and human rights; revolution and human rights; Islam and revolution. Only in this way can we begin to understand the special features of Islamic revolutions both within the history of Islam and within the history of revolutions.

ISLAM AND HUMAN RIGHTS

Contemporary advocates of moral universalism have sought to develop a universal ethic on the basis of shared human values. One important result has been the Universal Declaration of Human Rights, which has had truly worldwide impact. But the search for and espousal of universal moral standards is not simply the product of modern liberal thinking rooted in Enlightenment values, for moral universalism in different forms makes up an important part of all the world religions. In Buddhism this universalism extends beyond humanity into the world of animals as well.

It is a tragic paradox, however, that no matter how international in scope the roots of a universal morality may in fact be, in the contemporary world the very idea of a shared and binding set of human rights calls forth cries of ethnocentrism and cultural imperialism. For example, in the Middle East the Universal Declaration has been attacked on the grounds that it violates the cultural integrity of the Muslim community. Muslims have also countered with a potent counter-argument: Not only are such "universal" documents seen to be not at all universal, but Muslim culture is said to be far more universal and respectful of human rights than that of the West, past or present. Here are the words of a member of Morocco's Council of Religious Scholars: "Human rights may be something new for the West, but we in Islam have had it [sic] since the beginning. We have no differences between whites, blacks, Jews, Muslims—everyone is free. We never persecuted the Jews here the way they did in France and England. In England and in the U.S. you fight against the blacks—why just the other day there were news items about fighting between the police and blacks in London."[3] Typically, this statement immediately places current issues in the context of cultural heritages. Thus, the problem of human rights cannot be addressed merely through abstract philosophical or legal reasoning but must be placed in the context of "the beginning"—fundamental cultural principles.

Ironically, then, the very concept of "human rights" provokes battles over the relative worth of different civilizations despite its universalizing intent. Perhaps there is no more poignant evidence for a central paradox of twentieth-century history: Although greater contact among cultures and a certain degree of convergence of aspirations and values among peoples are undeniable, these cosmopolitan and universalizing elements have often served to exacerbate xenophobic and exclusionary tendencies. Just as too much openness to the international market can give rise to economic protectionism, especially in the weaker economies, so can emphatic moral universalism create moral protectionism, especially among societies preoccupied with their cultural authenticity.

If we are to understand the claim that the Islamic world has recognized and protected human rights from the beginning, we must clarify some essential conceptual issues, for we have already been warned that our concept of human rights may not be as universal as we think. First, if we look behind any of the fundamental statements on human rights, we find the assumptions that rights inhere in the individual and are shared by all individuals, at least by all adults. In certain essential senses, then, any concept of human rights implies that human beings are seen to be both capable and in some essential respect equal. In this lies the universalistic element in the principle of human rights—if there were no universalism, the adjective "human" would not be suitable.

The opposite of a universalistic concept of human rights is absolute exclusion: the denial that the individual as such has any rights whatsoever. It is only the individual as believer or as a member of a race or class who is worthy of respect. People become defined in terms of categories inherently opposed to each other. It is unfortunately true that religions have proved to be as potent as ideologies in creating such absolute dualisms. In a fundamental sense, the very idea of rights is thus obliterated, for even the rights of the accepted categories are only

contingent. Further, as the philosopher Hannah Arendt emphasized, such exclusion of whole categories destroys the very idea of personhood, for the rightless
person loses his or her place in the world and in essential respects ceases to be
an individual. For Arendt the stateless person and the concentration camp in-
mate both suffer from the denial of their status as individuals imbued with rights;
and any practice that utterly denies rights to individuals is totalitarian.

There is a third possibility, an alternative to universalism or exclusion, that
is often inadequately recognized in debates on human rights: Rights can be—
not denied—but defined hierarchically. According to such hierarchical ascrip-
tion of rights, the individual is not an isolated atom but a social being defined
through participation in webs of social relations. He or she does not cease being an individual, but individuality is inseparable from social relations, which
thereby become the matrix for defining an individual's relative rights, for hierarchical rights are always relative to one's place in social relationships.

These, then, are the three alternatives: universalism, which always departs
from the individual; exclusion, which denies to the individual a place in society on the basis of group membership; and hierarchy, which, while not denying
the individual, regards him or her also in terms of social roles and relationships.

These simple but important distinctions will help elucidate the paradoxical
fact that the very concept of universal human rights gives rise to conflicts over
civilizational values between Islam and the West. For although it is true that both
Christian and Islamic religio-cultural traditions include elements of universalism, exclusion, and hierarchy, Islamic culture has for much of its history embodied a more strongly hierarchical view of rights based on a rich appreciation of
the individual in his or her socially defined roles. Unlike early Christianity, Islam became a society and a state very early: thus the much greater attention to
social roles and relations. Christianity, by contrast, has been more universalistic, less socially oriented, in its claims; ironically, this very universalism has posed
a greater danger of exclusion, for there was no subordinate place for the outsider.
However, despite the centrality of a hierarchical view of rights throughout Islamic history, in the twentieth century, and especially after World War II, Islamic movements with a much more dualistic stance based on exclusion have
emerged, a product of wrenching social changes that have called into question
the Islamic heritage. A revolutionary form of Islam has challenged what militants label as a hollow religious tradition that in their view has violated the
authentic values of Islam for centuries.

To say that Islam has devoted great attention to the definition of hierarchical relations among people is not to downplay the strong exclusionary elements
that have plagued it, as they have the other monotheistic religions. The bitter
experience of crusades and jihads, of inquisitions and religious massacres,
throughout the centuries bears ample witness to the dualistic, exclusionary elements in both Christianity and Islam, these most explicitly universal of the

world's creeds. The very affirmation that there is a single transcendent God ruling over all peoples has been the source of division among those who accept this universal affirmation in different ways. Tragically, it is in some measure the universal claim on people's consciences that has created such hostility to those who have not accepted the revealed faith. Given that God has spoken to all people through his prophets and messengers, people are all the more culpable for refusing to believe.

In what, then, is the shared universalism of the monotheistic, prophetic religions? First and foremost, they begin with a rejection of all purely local gods identified with a particular group of people. Since the one creator God is the Lord of all, all are subject to his will and his demands and are in this sense alike in his sight. For the creator God is a moral God who makes demands on the individual as responsible actor, and the individual has the capacity and duty to obey. Moral conduct according to God's will is incumbent on all, whether high or low. Unlike the Confucian tradition, in which there is no sense of the people's responsibilities, there is no essential distinction in moral capacities made among individuals.[4] Further, all individuals should be both subject and object of moral action; this enlarged moralism therefore embodies an imperative for social justice. Thus, not the promise of individual self-awareness (as in many forms of Eastern religion) but the imperative of individual moral conduct as the basis for collective morality lies at the center of the prophetic religions.

Accordingly, these religions all embody a powerful individualistic and contractual element. The covenant is not between a faceless collectivity led by a wise leader with a monopoly on a uniquely close relationship to God, but between a community of individual moral agents and a God who requires just actions and dealings from all of them. In Christianity the teachings of natural law imported from classical philosophy buttressed this individualistic and universalistic element. In Islam the tradition of natural law and philosophy did not acquire the same salience as in Western Europe, but there were other sources of individualistic universalism that were more conspicuous than in the West—particularly the highly developed contractualism rooted, according to Marshall Hodgson, in the centrality of merchants and trade in Islam.[5]

The Islamic monotheistic emphasis on the individual, his rights and choices, finds a powerful echo in modern radical Islamic thought, from Banna and Mawdudi to the more militant Qutb. For such leaders, Islam guarantees a wide variety of what contemporary political sociologists would classify as civil, social, and even political rights. There is much emphasis on the political contract between ruler and ruled based on religious norms and the Islamic imperative of consultation. For Banna, the founder of the Muslim Brotherhood, Islam since its inception has emphasized individual rights, which were designed "to raise the standards of individuals, permit their participation in activities which would serve the welfare of society, safeguard human dignity, nurture individual talents, and aid in the exploitation of their physical and intellectual resources."[6] The universal rejection of Marxist-Leninism by Islamic radicals is grounded in this doctrine's submersion of the individual and his rights in the collective.

Before turning to the hierarchical elements in Islam, I should stress that the universalism of the monotheistic religions affirms a human right of the greatest significance to believers, even if not taken seriously by nonbelievers or ratified in liberal declarations: the universal possibility of salvation. So significant was this "human right" in the mind of Paul and other early Christians convinced of the immanence of the kingdom of God that they devoted little attention to the question of the nature of a Christian society and Christian ideas of social justice.

The situation was of course otherwise in Islam. In the Quran it is asserted that "to each of you We have given a law and a way and a pattern of life" (5:48). Indeed, whereas the New Testament hallows love and freedom, but is relatively inattentive to social relations, the Quran speaks of justice perhaps even more than of love. Justice is anchored in the responsibility of believers as defined by their social roles and relationships. These social relationships, in turn, are not egalitarian, although the universal element is never entirely lacking. Men are stronger and more powerful than women; free individuals are above slaves; and members of the Muslim community have rights not accorded to the nonbeliever. Accepting the hierarchy of relationships seen to be ordained by God in society, Islam seeks to define and regulate inequalities in accord with a revealed vision of justice. As the influential Iranian religious leader Nuri bluntly declared during the debates on a constitution at the turn of the twentieth century, "In Islam there is no equality between the mature and the immature, the sane and the insane, the healthy and the ill, the slave and the free, wife and husband, the learned and the ignorant, the Muslim and the non-Muslim and so on."[7] Does such a statement contradict Banna's insistence on the centrality of equality in Islam? Not at all, say Muslim spokesmen. For example, with respect to gender relations: "What discrimination exists (in inheritance, legal hearings, prayer) is a function of the greater responsibility devolving on men and of the difference in the mental and emotional attributes of the sexes."[8]

We now see why the Western concept of human rights as attaching solely to the individual is seen to be both partial and ethnocentric. It is partial because it fails to take account of individuals in their social roles as members of a religiously defined community, and it is ethnocentric because, without recognizing its own assumptions, it elevates one concept of rights above another. We also see a certain justice in the assertion that Islam endorsed and supported "human rights" before the West; by recognizing hierarchy and developing religious norms about the responsibilities of superiors to inferiors (dowries, alms, protection of orphans, acceptable treatment of nonbelievers) Islam extended a measure of justice to groups who in Christendom were largely ignored by religious norms.

A further observation is in order about the partial nature of the liberal concept of human rights from an Islamic perspective. Precisely because it sought to
define a pattern of life, Islam did not restrict itself to individual civil and political rights, but affirmed a broad range of responsibilities that the privileged and
powerful have with respect to the weak. The giving of alms is, of course, one of
the five pillars of Islam; and throughout the Quran there are injunctions to protect orphans and widows. It is not without reason, then, that advocates of Islamic values in the modern world express their sympathy for the broad range of
economic and social rights affirmed, at least in principle, in communism. In their
view such a broadened conception of human rights provides the foundation for
both equality and a richness of community unknown in the capitalist West.

The fact that hierarchy can indeed define rights can be seen in the differen-
tial treatment of Jews in medieval Christianity and Islam. According to the historian Mark Cohen, Jews in thirteenth-century Europe came to be "assaulted as
aliens, persecuted collectively for alleged crimes against Christians and Christianity, increasingly isolated in their Jewish quarters, soon to be confined to legal ghettos, and all too often expelled."[9] No such extreme exclusion occurred
in the Islamic world of that time, where the rights of Jews were encompassed
within Islamic law. Certainly not the bearers of equal rights—they were subject
to such forms of discrimination as dress codes, special taxes, and formal prohi-
bitions on holding public office—they were yet embraced within that "law" and
"pattern of life" of which the Quran spoke. In Islam, the dualistic element within
confessional religions was more tempered by the hierarchical emphasis of an
encompassing religious law.

REVOLUTION AND HUMAN RIGHTS

The emergence of apocalyptic religious movements throughout the history of
monotheistic religions demonstrates that these religions have the potential to
promote dualistic visions that separate the true believer and the corrupt world
of unbelief. And yet there can be no easy identification between religion and
dualism; the relationship between them must be treated as a historical and so-
ciological problem of great complexity. By contrast, dualism is of the essence of
revolution, whether religious or secular in inspiration. Thus, revolutions always
threaten human rights because they do not envision people as individuals but
only as members of ideologically defined categories.

If the ultimate truth of the Western monotheistic religions is the reality of a
transcendent God in intimate relation with individual human beings, the truth
of modern revolution is an ideal social and political vision that demands realization in this world. Certain uniform consequences of such ideological commitment in modern revolutions can be identified across a broad spectrum of cases.

For example, as different from each other as are revolutionary Marxism and radical Islam, they nonetheless share a certain number of common emphases stemming from a uniform revolutionary logic. In the same vein, the core similarities between the two major secular twentieth-century revolutionary ideologies, communism and fascism, have received exhaustive attention in classic works of modern social thought. The following generalizations about revolutions and human rights thus apply to all the major cases.

Modern revolutionary visions are integral, embracing all aspects of social life. If, despite their dramatic claims on the conscience, religions have tended to allow some distinction between the realm of God and the realm of Caesar, revolutionary ideologies are totalistic. The economy, politics, all key social institutions, indeed, even the individual conscience: All must be remade in accord with the ideology. The totalistic emphasis of Marxism-Leninism is well-known, at least in principle, although it is by no means clear from Marx's own work what even a Marxist economy, let alone a Marxist culture, would look like.

It is perhaps somewhat surprising that Islamic revolutionary visions intend to be equally comprehensive. Their concepts and theories about the Islamic economy or the Islamic state bear the marks of modern integral ideologies rather than the stamp of tradition.[10] Islam in the eyes of Islamic radicals is both all-embracing and a coherent system. For them it has an answer for everything, even for questions that could not have been posed in the seventh century. Thus, while the idea of an Islamic state in the medieval period merely meant a state that embraced Islam and protected it from its enemies, for Islamic radicals the authentic Islamic state must be based on a set of comprehensive Islamic principles with practical consequences.

If Islam can thus be systematized, then it also becomes clear, as it was not in "traditional" Islam, which practices and institutions are *not* Islamic. (Note that it would be impossible to systematize a religion in such a thorough way; indeed, throughout Islamic history even the specific sphere of Islamic religious law could not be clearly systematized, for there were always a plurality of traditions and interpretations that largely cohabited with each other despite fundamental tensions.) Radical Islamic thinkers thus conceive of themselves as an alternative to the other twentieth-century "systems," communism and capitalism (often failing to observe that Western capitalism has rarely been as thoroughly systematized as its more transcendental rival). Their system, they claim, offers a superior pattern of social life in all spheres than does the model of its rivals.

Certain consequences all too familiar from the history of twentieth-century communism follow from this commitment to an ideal integral system. A dualistic ethical stance emerges, with its corresponding mythology and demonology. Since the truth has been revealed, everyone has access to it; those who do not accept it are thus guilty. Revolutionary morality separates the pure from the impure, and since the pure must be active in the struggle for the ideal society, passivity is not neutrality. Those who do not engage in jihad—not merely for the protection of the faith, but for the pursuit of the ideal—display their unworthiness. Active engagement is incumbent on all. The parallels between this activist vision of jihad and the campaigns for socialist construction in communist societies are rooted in their systematic character and in their shared embrace of a dualistic vision.

Dualism is also expressed in the ideal of the revolutionary vanguard destined to lead and transform the masses. It may come as a surprise to those unacquainted with the literature of Islamic radicalism that the apotheosis of the enlightened elite is as central to the vision of Islamic revolution as it is to Marxism-Leninism. And the demands on this elite are almost equally high. For Lenin, as expressed in *What Is to Be Done*, the revolutionary elite was separated from the masses in part by the former's possession of ideological knowledge, which was necessary to guide the movement in all its tactical and strategic decisions. But Lenin was also convinced that only a small minority would possess the necessary moral qualities of revolutionary commitment and dedication. Since both correct ideological understanding and moral purity were rare, the party should constitute a select elite.

For the Islamic vanguard the challenges are somewhat different, though the overarching logic is the same. For Islamic revolutionaries ideological knowledge was not so rarefied, since God had chosen to reveal his message clearly to all those willing to hear it. The significance of superior knowledge is not entirely denigrated, for it is necessary for the elite to understand how Islamic tradition has distorted the truths of Islam, which must be discovered anew as for the first generation.

Yet the key requirement for the Islamic vanguard is not superior knowledge but moral purity as exemplified by the Prophet and his companions. The revolutionary elite should emulate the model of what Qutb, the Egyptian Islamic radical executed by the Nasser regime, called "the sole Quranic generation," so that they in turn can serve as models for the masses. Extravagant claims are made for the potential of this enlightened elite, particularly with respect to the man who is to be the authoritative leader of the Islamic community, the amir—in accord, it would seem, with Islam's lack of emphasis on original sin. There is even talk of the "Perfect Man" to whom unquestioning obedience is due, a clear echo of Sufi traditions now transposed to a quasi-modern mass movement. Characteristically, in Egypt the Muslim Brothers' oath includes the following words, entered into by "contract with God": "to have complete confidence in its [the organization's] leadership and to obey absolutely, under all circumstances."[11]

There is thus no single and shared concept of the vanguard in all revolutionary tradition. It can base itself on ideological knowledge or moral authority, and its leadership can be primarily defined as an organizational elite, or its basis can be almost entirely personal qualities. Further, the vanguard may be called upon to do many different things, to direct the revolution strategically, to organize a mass party, or to inspire the inner self-transformation of the masses. Whatever the differences, however, the question of the role of the vanguard is always posed in a distinctively revolutionary way: The key actors envisioned are a vanguard and a broad public, so that the arena of activity is modern mass politics; and the vanguard is utterly separated from the masses through its possession of rare qualities that validate its revolutionary leadership regardless of the views of the masses themselves.

Islamic revolutionaries have thus largely transformed what might otherwise be an amorphous religious tradition into an ideology. And although ideologies can be based upon religious values and religions can have ideological elements, there are nonetheless critical distinctions between religion and ideology. Ideologies in their modern sense (and ironically, this would even include radical Islam, so obviously shaped by other ideological traditions) are products of the Enlightenment. No matter how unrealistic they may seem, they embody the rationalist idea that human beings can understand and control history and society. They therefore provide a vision of a desired end state as well as concrete mechanisms for reaching it. Ideologies are future oriented, teleological, and inherently dualistic. Although the monotheistic religions emphasize God's justice and the community of moral individuals acting in history, the religious mainstream in all of them has been more modest in offering promises to transform human life from top to bottom. Nor can anything like a program for an ideal society or an explicit model of a vanguard party be found in any of the monotheistic scriptures. Although Walzer is certainly right that foreshadowings of such ideas can be found in the Exodus model, the monotheistic religions' emphasis on humanity's weakness and God's omnipotence undermines such expressions of human self-confidence.

All of the preceding themes are exceedingly familiar from the history of twentieth-century secular revolutions, which, in accord with their exclusionary dualism, grant little respect to the concept of human rights inherent in the individual. Islamic revolutionary movements recapitulate this same pattern of thought and model of political leadership. In thus departing from more traditional Islamic ideas, in which a hierarchical conception of rights played a more central role, the experience of radical Islam gives added weight to the hypothesis that revolution embodies a common ideological and political logic despite immense differences in content. In large part, then, radical Islam threatens human rights because of its revolutionary nature rather than its religious content.

But what, then, is the content of the Islamic revolutionary ideology, and why did Islam become transformed into a dualistic vision of radical transformation? To address these questions is also to illuminate the peculiar features of Islamic revolutionary movements.

ISLAM AND REVOLUTION: THE MODERN TRANSFORMATION

Contemporary radical Islamic movements are defined above all by the conjunc-
tion of two exclusions: the dualism of Islamic belief versus the threatening outside world and the dualism of Islamic ideology versus all who do not live according to its ideal model. Consequently, the enemy within the Islamic world is
identified with the external enemy, and against both of them any form of struggle
is legitimate and necessary.

A crucial concept for revolutionary Islam is *jahiliyya*. In traditional Islam the
term denotes the state of ignorance in pagan Arabia before the Quranic revela-
tions. In radical Islam it becomes an ideological term of rejection for everything
that does not correspond to the totalistic vision of the Islamic good society. If
the watchword of traditional Islam is justice in accord with law, radical Islamic
activists seek a society suffused with goodness. Thus, for the Iranian Islamic radical Ali Shariati, the Shariah is not just the body of Islamic law but a "complete
scheme of life and all-embracing social order," which will guarantee that nothing—whether "legal, class, social, political, racial, ethnic, territorial, cognatic,
genetic, intrinsic and even economic"—will hamper "the development of
Man."[12] Given such an exalted standard, everything is condemned: for Qutb,
"everything around is jahiliyya; perceptions and beliefs, manners and morals,
culture, art and literature, laws and regulations, including a good part of what
we consider Islamic culture."[13] The extraordinary implication of this doctrine is
that the so-called Muslim world is no more Islamic than those obvious enemies
of the faith, the West and communism. From this standpoint, almost all spheres
of existing Middle Eastern societies have already been infected by these hostile
forces.

But almost all of Islamic history has also been the realm of *jahiliyya*. Here we
touch another of the central points of revolutionary Islamic ideology: the choice
of principle over tradition. Radical Islamic activists reject any form of society
that is not thoroughly penetrated with religious ideals, as no historical Islamic
society ever was. It was never enough only to structure social relations through
religious law without changing the overall context within which law operates.
This kind of "fundamentalist" Islam, basing itself only on the Quranic revelation and the lives of the Prophet and his companions, is necessarily at odds with
an Islam that accepts the validity of the historical development of the community. No wonder that a favorite assassination target of Islamic radicals has been
conservative clerics who affirm the fundamentally Islamic nature of both Islamic
history and the status quo in the Middle East!

The root causes of the appeal of such a dualistic vision in the contemporary
Middle East are varied and profound. The view of the world as *jahiliyya* makes
sense in a civilization victimized by Western imperialism and by oppressive states
seeking to modernize under Western or communist sponsorship (for example,

Iran under the last shah, Egypt under Nasser). Thus, it would be a mistake to think that Islamic revolutionaries are alone in the Middle East in embracing a dualistic view of the world, for a rejection of the status quo has been an extremely common response to the weight of historical experience in the period of Islamic decline. Even pro-Western secularists can feel a sense of polar opposition between their world and the world of the threatening dominant powers. Thus, the cultural building blocks of Islamic radicalism pervade the contemporary Middle East, giving a penumbra of legitimacy to radical movements even when radical goals are not shared.

Further, the threat to the Islamic world, everywhere palpable, gives to radical Islam a large part of its appeal among the masses. As Richard Mitchell's account of the Muslim Brotherhood in Egypt shows, the experience of humiliation by the Western powers was not just an abstract experience felt at a distance. Many ordinary people recruited to the Muslim Brotherhood had directly experienced the sting of haughty attitudes and discrimination. And what was it like for a devout Egyptian Muslim to watch President Nasser ingratiate himself with the Soviet leadership, knowing that the Soviet government did not allow Islam to develop freely within its own borders? Another kind of experience was even less abstract and tragically widespread: time spent in torture chambers and concentration camps, an ordeal guaranteed to generate a dualistic view of the world. As a major scholar of radical Egyptian Islam remarked, "Islamicist thought was reconstructed after 1954 primarily in the concentration camps."[14]

Recent Islamic radical thought has given increasing weight to the dangers of Western cultural penetration. Behind bravura statements about the inevitable victory of their ideals—inherent in any highly ideological mind-set—there is a pervasive sense of the immense threat of Western culture, with its promise of liberation of the individual from traditional values and social institutions. Qutb's view that "everything around is jahiliyya" exemplifies a crucial difference between the Christian exclusion of Jews at the time of the Crusades and the shift toward revolutionary dualism in the recent history of the Islamic world. In medieval Europe the Jew became less necessary economically and more repellant culturally as the Christian world entered a period of increased power and expansion. By contrast, in the contemporary Muslim world the situation is the reverse: The transformation toward dualism is especially full of pathos because of the devastating decline of the Muslim world, which made the external world not just repellant but menacing.

In this context of a perceived struggle to the death, for people who feel that pernicious outside forces threaten their authenticity as individuals as well as the survival of a meaningful world, there can be no politically neutral idea of human rights based on the individual. The liberal freedoms, so facilely propounded in international documents by foreign lawyers and politicians, are seen to play into the hands of the opponents of the only true way. Thus, why should the militants of Islam respect that hypocritical weapon of their opponents, the appeal for tolerance and human rights? After all, these too are part of the world of *jahiliyya*, for under their banner every kind of subversive cultural message can pollute people's minds. The same goes for other forms of cultural interchange, such as tourism. According to one Muslim militant ("disappeared" subsequent to this late 1993 interview), "tourism in its present form is an abomination: it is a means by which prostitution and AIDS are spread by Jewish women tourists, and it is a source of all manner of depravities, not to mention being a means of collecting information on the Islamic movement. For these reasons we believe tourism is an abomination that must be destroyed."[15] As a pernicious example of a radically Manichaen worldview, this statement is worthy to stand beside any Stalinist diatribe of the 1930s.

When radical Islamic militants brand capitalism, communism, and all existing Muslim societies as *jahiliyya*, they conform to the logic of revolution, which always makes an absolute distinction between the sphere of revolutionary purity, represented by the revolutionary movement, and the outside world of corruption. At the very least, then, radical Islam is revolutionary in "form"—in its emphasis on ideology, on the vanguard, on a dualistic world view. But, to return to a famous Stalinist distinction, what is the relationship between revolutionary form and revolutionary content? What, concretely, is the essence of this revolutionary vision which "is destined to liberate all humanity from man's domination upon man"?[16] In Marxism-Leninism there was a certain correspondence between revolutionary form and revolutionary content; the revolutionary party acting on the basis of a dualistic ideological stance promises to abolish private property and social classes, eliminate the division of labor, and create a harmonious society based on a nonantagonistic mode of production. The content of the revolutionary vision is obviously utopian, an utter break with all previously existing societies.

In revolutionary Islam there is certainly utopian rhetoric about the final goals of the revolution: The abolition of all domination and exploitation according to the model of the golden age of Islam, which can still be discerned across the centuries despite the distorting lens of tradition. But *in fact* was this primordial Islamic society anything like a utopia? Clearly not: orphans, the poor, and abandoned women continued to exist. Islam urged that they be treated with justice; it did not promise that the conditions responsible for their plight could be eliminated. Rivers flowing with wine would only be encountered in paradise, not in this imperfect world of wayward human beings. Although it was certainly incumbent on the believer to promote justice, in the world of Muhammad and the companions just actions could not bring about the revolutionary millennium.

And so we come to a strange irony. In their abstract statements about the perfection of the Islamic model of society, Muslim revolutionaries strike a utopian note familiar from the literature of Marxism. However, when writers such as Qutb, Shariati, or Mawdudi actually describe the nature of economic or political institutions in an authentically Islamic society their goals seem rather prosaic. Ideologists of radical Islam certainly go further than traditional legal scholars who, often wished for nothing more than a ruler who acted according to Islamic norms and promoted the expansion of Islam. For radicals, Islamic society should be headed by a wise ruler who acts in consultation with a council of sages (*shura*). The precise qualities necessary for this exalted ruler have been discussed endlessly in their theoretical writings and polemics, but the key requirement is always superior moral character based on religious commitment. The composition and nature of the *shura* have also aroused much interest: how it should be chosen; its sphere of competence; and the like. In Islamic Iran the general model of the Islamic state has been embodied in the special constitutional position of the *faqih*, the guardian of Islamic law (until his death, Khomeini), whose authority was seen by many to be virtually infallible. Sunni Islamic militants are more likely to use the term *amir* for this exalted leader, to whom qualities of perfection are also ascribed. It also follows from this theory that the people owe the *faqih* or amir absolute obedience.

Although the ideal of leadership is certainly more elevated than in historical Islamic regimes, such a political framework hardly promises the end of domination so favored by Islamic radicals. The *faqih*, if he has the requisite personal qualities, may be able to render just (though hardly perfect) decisions, but he cannot transform the nature of modern political life, where a multiplicity of interests, factions, and parties compete for power quite apart from any rhetoric of unity based on transcendent wisdom. The exclusively moralistic vision of leadership, based on the example of the Prophet and his companions, virtually ignores real institutions and processes of power. The contrast with communist regimes, where revolutionary form and revolutionary content coincided to a much greater degree, could not be starker. Thus, despite considerable personalism of their own, the communist leadership knew that a revolution required revolutionary organization and they understood how to make use of revolutionary organizations for radical social change.

In a certain sense, there is nothing really surprising in this disjunction between the ideology of Islam and actual proposals for the nature of political rule in a thoroughly Islamic society, for in fact the ideology of Islamic radicals has little to do with the realities of Islamic history even during the pristine rule of the Prophet. Thus, their return to basic Islamic principles, if the slightest bit authentic, cannot be truly revolutionary. If one is to extract a political lesson from the earliest Muslim political community, it cannot be about the possibility of ending domination and creating perfect harmony. In his famous treatise on Islamic government Khomeini was clearly much closer to the mark than more consistent Muslim revolutionaries, who are caught in a web of contradictions. For Khomeini, Islamic government based on the Prophet's model meant leadership by religious authorities according to divine law—and not the coming of the Millennium to earth.

A utopian tone also pervades the radicals' discourse about the Islamic economy. Both Western capitalism and communism are attacked as extreme systems incapable of properly balancing the interests of the individual and society. Both are therefore unjust and immoral. And, as in the political sphere, revolutionary Islam is resolutely moralistic in its approach to the economy. As the influential Iranian religious leader Taleghani declared, Islamic economics is "inseparable from an intellectual and moral orientation and training and from religious and social ordinances."[17] Following the Prophet's example, the individual should curb his appetite for consumption, exercising self-control and moderation. Further, the community has the moral responsibility to guarantee that the exercise of private property rights does not infringe upon the moral development of other individuals, for freedom from pressing material needs is a prerequisite for moral freedom. Thus, according to the same authority, Islamic government "has priority in disposing property and exists, moreover, to establish equity."[18]

With such a moral foundation, it is claimed that the Islamic economy can provide a "third way" in the contemporary world, one which, like all such chimerical theories of the third way, is designed to provide an alternative to rapacious capitalism and totalitarian communism. Apart from such high-blown claims, however, the actual content of the ideal of the Islamic economy seems rather trite. At their most radical the proposals do not go much beyond a rather typical social democratic vision of capitalism, with much Islamic window dressing on issues such as Islamic taxation (*zakat*), luxury taxes, and the Islamic government's right to redistribute. Occasionally there are more disturbing pronouncements: For Taleghani, Islamic government "is empowered to limit individual ownership to a greater degree than the law may authorize,"[19] for the wisdom of the religious leader is ultimately superior to law.

However, when one gets to actual policies the pronounced emphasis on property rights and considerable freedom of contract in Islamic law generally takes precedence. For example, the Iranian Council of Experts has played a distinctly conservative role, opposing land reform legislation that would infringe upon the clergy's property rights and in general upholding Islamic rights of private property. There have been a plethora of conflicts between such conservative voices and radical groups who advocate more social democratic policies—but even the most far-reaching proposals are not especially radical! Such endemic conflicts are inherent in such "third ways," which eclectically combine different principles. Thus, moralistic in "form," the ideal and also the embodiments of the Islamic economy are distinctly lacking in coherent content. A few radical exceptions aside, they are certainly not revolutionary in any classical sense of the term. They will thus disappoint any deeply held revolutionary convictions.

CONCLUSION

It has become apparent that the fit between Islam and revolution is far from perfect. Islamic revolutionary movements and regimes are neither consistently revolutionary nor consistently Islamic. With respect to the first, they embrace many elements from the traditional Islam that they deride, such as a respect for private property, a hierarchical view of many social relations (especially gender), and limitations on the role of the vanguard party. Thus, no thoroughgoing revolutionary assault on society will be conducted by Islamic revolutionary regimes; despite the charges of many Western scholars, Islamic revolutions cannot be totalitarian. It is symptomatic that nothing like collectivization or the great purges of the Soviet 1930s has occurred in Iran, in many ways the bellwether Islamic revolutionary regime.

Revolutionary Islam is also in certain fundamental ways not really Islamic. Islamic radicals mythologize the golden age of the Prophet and his companions and reject the rest of Muslim history, including the whole development of the Islamic legal tradition, as a distortion of basic principles. But ultimately radicals like Shariati and Qutb cannot win their battle for an ideologized, and thus ahistorical, religion. It is no doubt true that aspects of Islam are compatible with a totalizing ideology, as are aspects of Judaism and Christianity. For example, they all claim a special relationship to God which will be brought to fulfillment in the future, and so the promise of individual and collective moral purity always exists, even if in abeyance. For such reasons it is warranted to find an intimate connection between religion and revolution.

Despite such connections, both the theory of radical Islam and the historical experience of the Iranian revolution show the ultimate contradictions between monotheistic religion and total revolution, for Islam has strong conservative and also democratic elements connected, respectively, to its hierarchical and universalistic features. These cannot easily be swept aside in favor of a doctrine of "revolutionary ethics"— that is, the conviction that whatever is good for the revolution is right. Nor, in the context of Islamic law, is it so simple to justify a radical vanguard's efforts to purify the society and create absolute harmony. Radicals in Iran argued that the thoroughgoing application of Islamic law would only be appropriate if the individual and society already lived according to the authentic principles of Islam. Until that time, they said, revolutionary logic, including the use of state terror and infringements on private property rights, superseded religious legalism. There certainly *was* a radical moment in the Iranian revolution. But basic Islamic values could only be disregarded so far in the name of revolutionary purity, and ultimately even Khomeini himself, after a period of flirtation with social radicalism, came down firmly on the side of such values as private property and the respect for privacy, including the inviolability of the home. For, unlike communism, at the heart of Islam is a pronounced individualism—the individual as moral agent, as responsible actor in contractual relations with other people and with God. If Hannah Arendt is right that the fundamental idea of totalitarianism is the conviction that anything is possible, we can hope that the inhuman and potentially totalitarian elements in contemporary radical Islam can be tempered by the limits inherent in Islam, not as a set of abstract principles, but as historical experience based on revelation.

The political system that emerged out of the Iranian revolution shows as clearly as do the economic principles that Islam cannot provide a firm basis for an autonomous revolutionary vanguard. As noted earlier, in accord with the elitist spirit of Shiite Islam, the constitution of Islamic Iran gave pride of place to a religious elite, in the form of an esteemed religious guide (the *faqih*) and a Council of Experts not subject to the popular will. Yet, at the same time it endorsed the principle of popular sovereignty, created an elected legislature, and gave broad guarantees of civil and political rights, including the legal equality of men and women. These latter constitutional principles could be grounded in traditional Islamic principles such as consultation and consensus. Although the resulting political system certainly had dictatorial elements, it also provided for an array of institutions expressing the interests of diverse social groups and allowed for a degree of political pluralism and conflict inconceivable in a polity run purely by an ideological vanguard model. After Khomeini's death a revised constitution gave more power to both state officials and the popularly elected president at the expense of strictly religious authorities, thus further undermining the vanguard model. Still a system based on mixed principles, in part on the commitment to Islam and in part on the ideals of popular sovereignty and representation, there is no prospect in sight of a permanent revolution that will sweep away all elements of moderation. (Nor of course can the complete triumph of the moderates be expected.)

How, then, to characterize revolutionary Islam, and what are its implications for human rights? I have already hinted at a formula that expresses the eclectic nature of both theory and practice: Revolutionary Islam is revolutionary in form, moralistic in content. It is revolutionary in form because there is a theoretical commitment to the end of injustice and domination in human societies, and this commitment finds expression in vanguard politics and a dualistic mentality. It is moralistic in content because Islamic principles, even as reinterpreted, do not permit a truly revolutionary transformation of society. Thus, the emphasis in theory and practice comes to be the moral qualities of individuals and leaders in the economic and political spheres (the amir, the shura, the obedient subject, the moral consumer, the generous donor). Without a model of new institutions, the realm of revolutionary transformation becomes restricted to the sphere of individual conduct.

Despite these limitations, both form and content have important implications for human rights. Even if the primal revolutionary vision will never be fully realized, revolutionary dualism as expressed in the vanguard mentality will continue to shape the relations between Islamic revolutionary movements and the outside world. Those who do not adhere to the radical vision of Islam, whether Muslim or foreigners, will be seen as corrupted by the world of jahiliyya. As outcasts of the authentic Islamic community, Islamic law does not apply to them. And without the protection of law, there is, in practice, no respect for rights.

As de facto substitute for revolutionary transformation, Islamic moralism will also continue to shape social behavior and relationships on the daily level, as seen in matters of dress and personal conduct, even though the moralism of contemporary Islamic movements is not really revolutionary. Indeed, such moralism can substitute for revolutionary radicalism or even attempt to compensate for the failures of the revolutionary vision. Not nearly as esoteric as revolutionary Islam, and requiring no absolute withdrawal from the world of jahiliyya, moralism has great appeal both in terms of its resonance with Islamic tradition and as a response to the cultural threats of the outside world. As well as operating at the societal level as a substitute for real institutional change in economics and politics, it is flourishing at the local level throughout the Muslim world— grass-roots party organizations, neighborhood groups, religious associations. At this popular level, the strict enforcement of Islamic moral codes of personal behavior is a major threat to human rights as defined by liberal individualism. But in contrast to the revolutionary party state, which reshapes all institutions and imposes itself everywhere, human beings have a relatively effective weapon against moralism: hypocrisy, the contradiction between public and private behavior. Hypocrisy clearly has a bright future in the Islamic world, for it will grow apace with the attempts of militant—if not consistently revolutionary—Muslims to purify their worlds in the face of failure and corruption.

NOTES

1. Michael Walzer, *Exodus and Revolution* (New York: Basic Books, 1985), p. 134.
2. Charles J. Adams, "Mawdudi and the Islamic State," in *Voices of Resurgent Islam,* ed. John L. Esposito (New York and Oxford: Oxford University Press, 1983), pp. 119–120.
3. Quoted in Kevin Dwyer, *Arab Voices* (Berkeley: University of California Press, 1991), p. 38.
4. See William Theodore de Bary, *The Trouble with Confucianism* (Cambridge, Mass.: Harvard University Press, 1991), pp. 12–13.
5. Marshall Hodgson, *The Venture of Islam,* vol. 1 (Chicago: University of Chicago Press, 1974), pp. 128–130.
6. Quoted in Richard Mitchell, *The Society of the Muslim Brothers* (New York and Oxford: Oxford University Press, 1993), p. 249.
7. Quoted in Homa Omid, *Islam and the Post-Revolutionary State in Iran* (London: St. Martins Press, 1994), p. 16.
8. Quoted in Mitchell, *Muslim Brothers,* p. 255.
9. Mark Cohen, *Under Crescent and Cross* (Princeton: Princeton University Press, 1994), p. 194.
10. See Olivier Roy, *The Failure of Political Islam* (Cambridge, Mass.: Harvard University Press, 1994), pp. 132–133.
11. Mitchell, *Muslim Brothers,* p. 165

12. Quoted in Hamid Enayat, *Modern Islamic Political Thought* (Austin: University of Texas Press, 1982), p. 156.

13. Quoted in Emmanuel Sivan, *Radical Islam. Medieval Theology and Modern Politics* (New Haven: Yale University Press, 1985), p. 25.

14. Gilles Kepel, *Muslim Extremism in Egypt. The Prophet and Pharaoh* (Berkeley: University of California Press, 1985), p. 27.

15. "What Does the Gama'a Islamiyya Want?" in *Political Islam*, ed. Joel Beinin and Joe Stork (Berkeley: University of California Press, 1997), p. 320.

16. Book of the Muslim Students' Association published in Cairo, quoted in Sivan, *Radical Islam*, p. 48.

17. Ayatullah Sayyid Mahmud Taleghani, *Society and Economics in Islam* (Berkeley: Mizan Press, 1982), p. 26.

18. Taleghani, *Society and Economics*, p. 28.

19. Taleghani, *Society and Economics*, p. 28.

Suggestions for Further Reading

There is an enormous—and rapidly growing—literature on human rights as well as on the revolutionary events discussed in individual chapters in this volume, though attempts to bring these subjects together continue to be relatively rare. Here, rather than provide a comprehensive bibliographical overview of either or both topics, we focus on providing citations to three kinds of works: First, ones dealing with human rights that our contributors found particularly stimulating or provocative when preparing their chapters; second, ones that these contributors wrote themselves, which explore in much more detail subjects brought up in their chapters; and third, ones that contain information that may prove helpful in placing into fuller context key human rights texts or specific political events dealt with in earlier sections of this book. We begin with a section on general works that provide useful information on varied topics, including reference works and collections of essays that focus on revolutions or on human rights discourse. We then move on to specific periods and themes.

We should note at the outset that almost all of the citations to come are to books, even though many journal and magazine articles covering similar ground have also appeared in recent years. We draw attention to a few special issues of particular periodicals, but for the most part we stick to monographs, document collections, and conference volumes. Readers should be aware, however, of several magazines and journals that fairly regularly publish pieces that address the themes raised in this book. Two very different publications stand out here: *INDEX on Censorship*, each issue of which is likely to have several short pieces on issues related to human rights, and *Human Rights Quarterly: A Comparative and International Journal of the Social Sciences, Humanities and Law*. Many reviews and politically oriented magazines—*Dissent, New Left Review, London Review of*

Books, New York Review of Books, The New Republic, In These Times, and *The Nation* among them—sometimes carry pieces on human rights in theory and practice.

There are also a variety of newsletters specifically devoted to human rights issues. Some of these focus on specific parts of the world (*Human Rights in China,* for example), while others are global in purview (e.g., *Human Rights Dialogue,* which is distributed by the Carnegie Council on Ethics and International Affairs). A useful place for information on all these sorts of publications as well as related ones—such as law reviews and annual reports issued by UN groups and other NGOs that deal with human rights—is the website <http://www.hrw.org/>. Maintained by Human Rights Watch, this site is helpful both for the information it provides and for its links to other web resources. See also <http://www.amnesty.org/>, which is maintained by Amnesty International. And see as well, for a wealth of information on human rights issues and specific contemporary crises provided by an organization that is further to the left politically than either Human Rights Watch or Amnesty International, <http://www.lbbs.org/ZMag.htm>. This last site is directly linked to *Z Magazine,* which carries a large number of reports on human rights issues. It is also associated with the *Noam Chomsky Archive,* which contains essays on the subject of human rights and American foreign policy, an issue raised in the preface to this collection and in some of its final chapters as well.

One thing to note about the sources of information and analysis just mentioned, as well as many of the books to be discussed below, is that few are explicitly historical in orientation. Journals devoted to human rights issues tend to be interdisciplinary and hence showcase works by diverse types of authors. Usually, however, whichever field they come from,whether political science or philosophy or journalism, the contributors have a contemporary orientation. There has been of late a historical turn of sorts in the debate on human rights, to which our book is designed as a contribution, but a survey of the periodicals alluded to above indicates that most of the discussion of the topic remains very presentist. This is understandable. Nevertheless, if the preceding chapters have succeeded, they will have suggested to the reader the need to take historical roots and trajectories seriously even when wrestling with the human rights issues that are currently making headlines. This is one reason why we believe that works such as ours, and a few other recent ones cited below that pay as much attention to historical paradoxes as to contemporary dilemmas, are such meaningful contributions to what is already a massive literature.

Two final introductory notes are needed. First, we have limited ourselves here to works in English, even though in many cases there are large literatures in other languages. The English-language works provided will, via their bibliographies, point interested readers with other linguistic skills in appropriate directions. Second, in general, we are very selective in what we address here, especially when it comes to background works on the best known of the revolutionary case studies at hand such as those associated with the dates 1789 and 1917. For background information on specific revolutionary events that are not discussed here and for additional information and citations for those that are, see the excellent *Encyclopedia of Political Revolutions* edited by Jack Goldstone (Washington, D.C.: Congressional Quarterly, 1998). Useful earlier works include John Dunn, *Modern Revolutions: An Introduction to the Analysis of a Political Phenomenon* (London: Cambridge University Press, 1989); David Close and Carl Bridge, eds., *Revolution: A History of the Idea* (Totowa, N.J.: Barnes and Noble Books, 1985); Mark Almond's richly illustrated and accessibly written coffee-table book, *Revolution: 500 Years of Struggle for Change* (London: Di Agostini, 1996); and James De Fronzo's textbook-style survey, *Revolutions and Revolutionary Movements*, 2d ed. (Boulder, Colo.: Westview Press, 1996).

Influential model-building works include Crane Brinton, *The Anatomy of Revolution* (Englewood Cliffs, N.J.: Prentice Hall, 1952); Barrington Moore, *Social Origins of Dictatorship and Democracy: Lord and Peasant in the Making of the Modern World* (Boston: Beacon Press, 1966); and Theda Skocpol, *States and Social Revolutions* (Cambridge, Mass.: Harvard University Press, 1979). For a wide-ranging overview of recent controversies associated with theory and method in the study of major and minor revolutionary movements, see Nikki Keddie, ed., *Debating Revolution* (New York: New York University Press, 1995).

DOCUMENT COLLECTIONS AND COLLECTIONS OF ESSAYS: HUMAN RIGHTS ISSUES

One of the most wide-ranging document collections is Walter Laqueur and Barry Rubin, eds., *The Human Rights Reader*, rev. ed. (New York: Meridian, 1989), which includes both the texts of international agreements and famous statements by political figures and philosophers. Whereas Laqueur and Rubin's work covers a broad stretch of time, another important resource, Edward Lawson, ed., *Encyclopedia of Human Rights*, 2d ed. (New York: Taylor and Francis, 1996), has a much more comprehensive focus. There are also a variety of works that showcase and interpret documents from particular eras. Two of the most useful of these are recent contributions to the Bedford Books series, which is designed to make short, reasonably priced primary source-driven volumes available for classroom use in colleges. These are Lynn Hunt, *The French Revolution and Human Rights: A Brief Documentary History* (Boston: Bedford Books, 1996), and Jack N. Rakove, *Declaring Rights: A Brief History with Documents* (Boston: Bedford Books, 1998). A much more compendious consideration of influential documents from the twentieth century as opposed to the eighteenth is Johannes Morsink's carefully put together volume on *The Universal Declaration of Human Rights: Origins, Drafting, and Intent* (Philadelphia: University of Pennsylvania, 1999).

Several provocative and interesting collections of essays that, like our volume, move back in time and across space are worth citing here as well. One is Olwen Hufton, ed., *Historical Change and Human Rights: The Oxford Amnesty Lectures 1994* (New York: Basic Books, 1995), nearly all the contributors to which are historians by training, the sole exception being historical sociologist Orlando Patterson. A second is Carla Hesse and Robert Post, eds., *Human Rights and Political Transitions: Gettysburg to Bosnia* (New York: Zone Books, 1999), which is more interdisciplinary in approach and combines pieces by scholars with essays by activists and legal professionals involved in truth commissions. A third, with a more specific regional focus, is Joanne R. Bauer and Daniel A. Bell, eds., *The East Asian Challenge for Human Rights* (Cambridge: Cambridge University Press, 1999), the contributors to which range from economist Amartya Sen to philosopher Charles Taylor to political scientist Dorothy Solinger. Some of the same issues explored in that volume are the focus of attention as well in William Th. de Bary and Tu Weiming, eds., *Confucianism and Human Rights* (New York: Columbia University Press, 1998), which includes a chapter by Jeremy Peltiel that is particularly germane to the argument in some sections of our book. For insights on how political scientists interested in international relations, as opposed to members of other disciplines, approach the subject, finally, see Thomas Risse et al., eds., *The Power of Human Rights: International Norms and Domestic Change* (Cambridge: Cambridge University Press, 1999).

THE ORIGINS OF HUMAN RIGHTS IDEAS WITHIN THE WESTERN TRADITION, 1600–1800

One of the most important books that bears on the Western intellectual and cultural history of human rights is Charles Taylor, *Sources of the Self: The Making of Modern Identity* (Cambridge, Mass.: Harvard University Press, 1989). There are also several noteworthy works that trace the development of concepts of rights in the West up to the start of the 1800s. Two of these are Brian Tierney, *The Idea of Natural Rights: Studies on Natural Rights, Natural Law and Church Law, 1150–1625* (Atlanta: Scholars Press, 1997); and Richard Tuck, *Natural Rights Theories: Their Origin and Development* (Cambridge: Cambridge University Press, 1979). See also Knud Haakonssen, *Natural Law and Moral Philosophy: From Grotius to the Scottish Enlightenment* (Cambridge: Cambridge University Press, 1996).

Turning to country-by-country case studies of the human rights traditions up to the nineteenth century, much of the best writing on the English case has been by Christopher Hill. Several pieces on related themes can be found in his *Collected Essays* (Amherst: University of Massachusetts Press, 1986) and a more recent book of short pieces, *Liberty against the Law: Some Seventeenth-Century Conflicts* (New York: Penguin, 1998). See, as well, Robert Ashton, *Counter-*

Revolution. The Second Civil War and Its Origins, 1646–8 (New Haven: Yale University Press, 1994), and a new book by David Zaret, a contributor to this volume, *Origins of Democratic Culture: Printing, Petitions, and the Public Sphere in Early-Modern England* (Princeton: Princeton University Press, 2000).

One of the best overviews of the American case is likewise provided in a book written by one of the authors whose chapter appears in this volume, Michael P. Zuckert, in his *Natural Rights and the New Republicanism* (Princeton: Princeton University Press, 1994). See, as well, Bernard Bailyn, *The Ideological Origins of the American Revolution* (Cambridge, Mass.: Harvard University Press, 1968), the Rackove collection on *Declaring Rights* already cited above, and Linda Kerber, *No Constitutional Right to Be Ladies: Women and the Obligations of Citizenship* (New York: Hill & Wang, 1998).

For the French case, see the work by Hunt mentioned above under "Document Collections and Collections of Essays," as well as the introduction to the Hesse and Post collection, *Human Rights and Political Transitions*, that is cited in that same section. The events leading up to and accompanying the French Revolution are treated in passing as well by several contributors to Hufton's already cited *Historical Change and Human Rights*. For scholarly disagreements over the meaning of 1789, see Gary Kates, ed., *The French Revolution: Recent Debates and New Controversies* (London: Routledge, 1997), and for alternative treatment of some of the concepts Hunt discusses, see various entries in François Furet and Mona Ozouf, eds., *A Critical Dictionary of the French Revolution* (Cambrdige, Mass.: Belknap Press, 1989).

EUROPEAN REVOLUTIONS AND CONFLICTS: THE 1870s–1990s

Major scholarly works on the Paris Commune include Susanna Barrows, *Distorting Mirrors, Visions of the Crowd in Late Nineteenth Century France* (New Haven: Yale University Press, 1981), and Robert Tombs, *The War against Paris, 1871* (New York: Cambridge University Press, 1981). See also the influential analyses of the events provided at the time by Karl Marx and several decades later by V. I. Lenin, which are brought together in *The Civil War in France: The Paris Commune* (New York: International Publishers, 1989). An important recent reassessment of the Commune, as well as of labor activism during the preceding decades, can be found in Roger V. Gould, *Insurgent Identities: Class, Community, and Protest in Paris from 1848 to the Commune* (Chicago: University of Chicago Press, 1995). See also, for detailed discussion of the actions of female Communards, Edith Thomas, *The Women Incendiaries* (New York: G. Braziller, 1966). A more comprehensive analysis of issues associated with the Commune brought up in Alice Bullard's chapter can be found in her *Exile to Paradise: Savagery and Civilization in Paris and the South Pacific, 1790–1900* (Stanford: Stanford University Press, 2000).

Many of the points made about the Russian case in the chapter by Yanni Kotsonis are elaborated upon in his book, *Making Peasants Backward* (New York: St. Martin's, 1999). Extended discussion of the major events and personalities of the period can be found in works cited above, as well as in syntheses such as Orlando Figes, *A People's Tragedy: The Russian Revolution, 1891–1924* (New York: Penguin, 1998). For the origin of ideas about the "Eastern" and "Asiatic" as "backward" in eighteenth-century European philosophy, see Larry Wolff, *Inventing Eastern Europe: The Map of Civilization on the Mind of the Enlightenment* (Stanford: Stanford University Press, 1994). And for the ambiguities of the Enlightenment and the concept of the "human" in Europe and the Americas in the eighteenth and nineteenth centuries, another theme raised in the chapter by Kotsonis, see Michel-Rolph Trouillot, *Silencing the Past: Power and the Production of History* (Boston: Beacon Press, 1995).

To place the discussions of late twentieth-century Eastern European upheavals and crises found in some of our chapters into historical perspective, two books written by Misha Glenny and two collections either edited or coedited by Vladimir Tismaneanu are very useful places to start. Glenny's books are *The Fall of Yugoslavia: The Third Balkan War*, rev. ed. (New York: Penguin, 1996), and *The Rebirth of History: Eastern Europe in the Age of Democracy*, 2d ed. (New York: Penguin, 1993). The Tismaneanu collections are *The Revolutions of 1989: Rewriting Histories* (London: Routledge, 1999), which he edited on his own, and *Between Past and Future: The Revolutions of 1989 and Their Aftermath* (Budapest: Central European University Press, 2000), which he coedited with Sorin Antohi. Each of these volumes has a chapter by Adam Michnik, a contributor to this volume. In addition to these works, see also, for the upheavals in Europe at the end of the twentieth century, Robin Blackburn, ed., *After the Fall: The Failure of Communism and the Future of Socialism* (London: Verso, 1991).

For Kosovo in particular and the issues of humanitarian intervention and/or new varieties of imperialism they raise, see the following two very different sorts of collections: Roy Gutman and David Rieff, eds., *Crimes of War: What the Public Should Know* (New York: Norton, 1999); and Tariq Ali, ed., *Masters of the Universe: NATO's Balkan Crusade* (London: Verso, 2000), which contains a slightly different version of the Robin Blackburn piece included in our volume and other works that advance related arguments. See also the special section on Kosovo in *Big Science and Little White Lies*, the March 1999 issue of *INDEX on Censorship*, and Noam Chomsky, *The New Military Humanism: Lessons from Kosovo* (Monroe, Maine: Common Courage Press, 1999).

LATIN AMERICAN, AFRICAN, AND ASIAN SETTINGS

Of the various countries discussed in our book, the ones about which there are the least developed scholarly literatures are Burma, New Caledonia, and Peru, so these will be taken up first. After that, we will move on to China, Vietnam, Africa, and the Islamic World—in that order.

Some basic background on the situation in Burma, which was collected by the Asia Watch Staff of the organization Human Rights Watch, is provided in *Human Rights in Burma (Myanmar)* (New York: Human Rights Watch, 1990). See also, for the views of Aung San Suu Kyi, the political leader and human rights activist that Adam Michnik alludes to, the collection edited by Michael Aris, *Freedom from Fear and Other Writings by Aung San Suu Kyi*, rev. ed. (New York: Penguin, 1995). In addition, some of her more recent writings from her continuing position under house arrest can be found in Aung San Suu Kyi, *Letters from Burma* (New York: Penguin, 1998).

Turning to New Caledonia, though much of the best scholarship is in French, several significant works in English do exist. These include Dorothy Shineberg, *They Came for Sandalwood; A Study of the Sandalwood Trade in the South-West Pacific, 1830–1865* (Melbourne: Melbourne University Press, 1967); Myriam Dornoy, *Politics in New Caledonia* (Sydney: Sydney University Press, 1984); and Bronwen Douglas's recently published *Across the Great Divide; Journeys in History and Anthropology* (Amsterdam: Harwood Press, 1998). See also Maurice Leenhardt's path-breaking ethnography of the Kanak, *Do Kamo, Person and Myth in the Melanesian World* (Chicago: University of Chicago Press, 1979), which was originally published in 1947. A good complement to this is James Clifford's biography of Leenhardt, *Person and Myth, Maurice Leenhardt in the Melanesian World* (Berkeley: University of California Press, 1988). The legal history, which to date has only been discussed in French works, will be covered in English in Alice Bullard's forthcoming Stanford University Press monograph.

Four other works that deal with issues raised in Bullard's chapter on New Caledonia are worth mentioning. The first, which deals with missionaries in the western Pacific, is Hugh Laracy's *Marists and Melanesians: A History of Catholic Missions in the Solomon Islands* (Honolulu: University Press of Hawaii, 1976). The second, which deals with British experiments in penal colonization, is Robert Hughes, *The Fatal Shore: The Epic of Australia's Founding* (New York: Vintage Books, 1988). The third, which provides a theoretical perspective on racist attitudes and the state in colonialist contexts is Pierre Clastres, *Society against the State* (New York: Urizen Books, 1987). The fourth, which contains a series of essays on the concept of governmentality, is Graham Burchell et al., eds., *The Foucault Effect: Studies in Governmentality* (Chicago: University of Chicago Press, 1991).

Switching now to Latin America, there have been many works on human rights issues and the revolutionary traditions of specific countries. Here, however, we will focus solely on the nation that is discussed in detail in our volume: Peru. The most useful work on this country is the edited volume in which the piece included here on Shining Path first appeared: Steven J. Stern, ed., *Shining and Other Paths: War and Society in Peru, 1980–1995* (Durham, N.C.: Duke

University Press, 1998). A general overview of the Left in Latin America toward the end of the twentieth century, which is very useful in helping to put Peruvian events into continental perspective, is Jorge G. Castaneda, *Utopia Unarmed: The Latin American Left after the Cold War* (New York: Vintage, 1994).

There is, not surprisingly, a much more compendious literature on China than on Burma, New Caledonia, or Peru, including many works that focus on the actions and ideas of revolutionaries and a smaller but still considerable number that concentrate on the issue of human rights. In the former category, good starting points are provided by the still very useful Lucien Bianco, *Origins of the Chinese Revolution, 1919–1945* (Stanford: Stanford University Press, 1973), and Jonathan Spence, *The Gate of Heavenly Peace: The Chinese and Their Revolution, 1895–1980* (New York: Penguin, 1982). These two works can be supplemented by a pair of volumes that cover more recent developments: Elizabeth J. Perry and Mark Selden, eds., *Chinese Society: Change, Conflict and Resistance* (London: Routledge, 2000), and Jeffrey N. Wasserstrom and Elizabeth J. Perry, *Popular Protest and Political Culture in Modern China*, 2d ed. (Boulder, Colo.: Westview Press, 1994).

When it comes to human rights concerns, two comprehensive general works by Anne Kent are very useful: *Between Freedom and Subsistence: China and Human Rights* (Hong Kong: Oxford University Press, 1993), and *China, the United Nations, and Human Rights: The Limits of Compliance* (Philadelphia: University of Pennsylvania, 1999). To supplement these works, there is a provocative discussion of human rights abuses in Michael Dutton, *Streetlife China* (Cambridge: Cambridge University Press, 1998), which focuses on acts of state repression directed at socially and economically marginal groups. A valuable window onto recent developments in China is provided by *Hong Kong Goes Back*, a special issue of *INDEX on Censorship* published in January 1997. Despite its title, this work does not focus exclusively on Hong Kong, and it includes short essays by Liu Xiaobo, Wang Dan, and other Chinese dissidents. See also, on contemporary developments, several chapters in Timothy Weston and Lionel Jensen, eds., *China beyond the Headlines* (Lanham, Md.: Rowman & Littlefield, 2000). On the processes of dehumanization alluded to in Jeffrey Wasserstrom's chapter on China, see Michael Schoenhals, *"Non-People" in the People's Republic of China: A Chronicle of Terminological Ambiguity*, an *Indiana East Asian Working Paper on Language and Politics in Modern China*, # 4 (Bloomington, Ind.: Indiana University East Asian Studies Center, 1994). See also Marina Svensson's 1996 Lund University doctoral dissertation, *The Chinese Conception of Human Rights: The Debate on Human Rights in China, 1898–1949*, which is being revised and expanded into an academic monograph and is an important addition to the literature on the topic. Svensson has done more than any other scholar to show just how much discussion of human rights issues there was by Chinese political figures in various camps long before the 1980s—when the story of China's engagement with this discourse is often presented as starting.

Connections between China and Vietnam, the next country we take up, can be found in Stephen B. Young and Nguyen Ngoc Huy, *The Tradition of Human Rights in China and Vietnam* (New Haven: Yale University Council on Southeast Asian Studies, 1990). This work suggests that precolonial Vietnam contained important values and resources that are conducive to the establishment of the rule of law and a vision of human rights—a position with which Alexander Woodside, who contributed the chapter on Vietnam to this volume, is in sympathy. There are other works, however, that present the country's tradition as marked primarily by authoritarianism. See, for example, Gareth Porter, *Vietnam: The Politics of Bureaucratic Socialism* (Ithaca: Cornell University Press, 1993), which presents the repressive dimensions of Vietnam's revolutionary regimes as continuing, not breaking with, precolonial patterns. For additional discussion by Woodside of this and other related issues, see his contribution to David Kelly and Anthony Reid, eds., *Asian Freedoms: The Idea of Freedom in East and Southeast Asia* (Cambridge: Cambridge University Press, 1993). An important work on the legal environment in contemporary Vietnam is Carlyle A. Thayer and David G. Marr, eds., *Vietnam and the Rule of Law* (Canberra: Australia National University Research School of Pacific Studies, 1993). See also, for an insider-turned-critic-and-then-exile's account of dissent and repression within the Vietnamese revolutionary movement, Bui Tin, *Following Ho Chi Minh: Memoirs of a North Vietnamese Colonel* (Honolulu: University of Hawaii Press, 1995).

Turning to Africa, we find a well-developed literature on human rights as well as a variety of important works on the political situations within the various countries that are discussed in Florence Bernault's chapter. A good place to start, where human rights issues are concerned, is Abdullahi Ahmed An-Na'im and Francis M. Deng, eds., *Human Rights in Africa: Cross Cultural Perspectives* (Washington, D.C.: Brookings Institution, 1990). Another noteworthy collections is Ronald Cohen et al., eds., *Human Rights and Governance in Africa* (Gainesville, Fla.: The University of Florida Press, 1993). See also Rhoda E. Howard, *Human Rights in Commonwealth Africa* (Totowa, N.J.: Rowman & Littlefield, 1986), a work that deals primarily with Anglophone Africa. Patrick Chabal, ed., *Political Domination in Africa: Reflections on the Limits of Power* (Cambridge: Cambridge University Press, 1986), analyzes the idea that there is very limited revolutionary potential in African civil societies, while the role of NGOs in the contemporary struggle for human rights is the focus in Claude Welch, *Protecting Human Rights in Africa: Role and Strategies of Non-Governmental Organizations* (Philadelphia: University of Pennsylvania Press, 1995). On the constitution of Africa as the "Other" in Europe during the nineteenth century and this idea's resilience late in the twentieth century, which Bernault alludes to, see Edward Said, *Orientalism* (New York: Pantheon, 1978). See also the more specific treatment of Africa in Valentin Mudimbe, *The Invention of Africa: Gnosis, Philosophy, and the Order of Knowledge* (Bloomington: Indiana University Press, 1988).

An important new study of the "civilizing mission" ideology is Alice L. Conklin, *Mission to Civilize: The Republican Idea of Empire in France and West Africa, 1895–1930* (Stanford: Stanford University Press, 2000).

Valuable case studies of human rights issues in individual African countries include Gérard Prunier, *The Rwanda Crisis. History of a Genocide* (New York: Cambridge University Press, 1995), and Lorenzo Togni, *The Struggle for Human Rights: An International and South African Perspective* (Kenwyn, South Africa: Juta and Co., 1994). See also Gwendolen M. Carter and Patrick O'Meara, eds., *African Independence: The First Twenty-Five Years* (Bloomington, Ind.: Indiana University Press, 1985), for an overview of the political trajectories of nation-states that emerged out of what were once French or British colonies. A concise discussion of the Atlantic Charter, the Universal Declaration of 1948, and African decolonization is provided in John Hargreaves, *Decolonization in Africa* (London: Longman, 1988). See also, for the 1981 Banjul Charter, *The African Charter on Human and People's Rights* (New York: UN, 1990).

For the issues raised in Tim McDaniel's chapter on radical Islam, two works are particularly useful: John Esposito, ed., *Voices of Resurgent Islam* (New York and Oxford: Oxford University Press, 1983), and Kevin Dwyer, *Arab Voices: The Human Rights Debate in the Middle East* (Berkeley: University of California Press, 1991). See also Mark Cohen, *Under Crescent and Cross* (Princeton: Princeton University Press, 1994); Olivier Roy, *The Failure of Political Islam* (Cambridge: Harvard University Press, 1994); Gilles Kepel, *Muslim Extremism in Egypt: The Prophet and Pharaoh* (Berkeley: University of California Press, 1985); and McDaniel's own *Autocracy, Modernization, and Revolution in Russia and Iran* (Princeton: Princeton University Press, 1991).

Index

About the Contributors

Florence Bernault teaches African history at the University of Wisconsin, Madison. A specialist of contemporary central Africa, she was trained in France and received her Ph.D. at the University of Paris, Diderot. She is currently conducting research on the history of witchcraft in colonial and postcolonial Gabon. The author of *Démocraties ambigües en Afrique centrale* (Karthala 1996), she has also edited special issues of three journals: *Africa Today*, the *Revue Française d'histoire d'outre-mer*, and *Politique Africaine*.

Robin Blackburn is editor of *New Left Review* and professor of sociology at the University of Essex. In 1998–1999 he was Visiting Senior Research Fellow at King's College, Cambridge. His most recent book is *The Making of New World Slavery* (Verso 1997). His contribution to this volume first appeared, in a slightly different form, in *New Left Review*, no. 235, May-June 1999, and is reprinted here with the permission of New Left Review LTD.

Alice Bullard is assistant professor of history in the School of History, Technology and Society at Georgia Institute of Technology. She is the author of *Exile to Paradise, Savagery and Civilization in Paris and the South Pacific, 1790–1900* (Stanford University Press 2000) and is currently writing a gendered history of psychiatry as practiced in the French colonies. Her articles include "Le théâtre des plages en Nouvelle-Calédonie: La Présentation du corps et l'art kanak feministe," *Journal de la société des océanistes* (1999).

Lynn Hunt is Eugen Weber Professor of Modern European History at the University of California, Los Angeles. She has written several books on the French Revolution, is one of the coauthors of *Telling the Truth about History*

251

(Norton 1995), and is the editor of *The New Cultural History* (University of California Press 1989). Her most recent book, coedited with Victoria Bonnell, is *Beyond the Cultural Turn* (University of California Press 1999).

Carlos Basombrío Iglesias is the subdirector of the Instituto de Defensa Legal, an NGO based in Peru devoted to the defense and promotion of human rights. His writings on oppression and resistance in Peru have appeared in periodicals such as *Nueva Sociedad* as well as *Shining and Other Paths: War and Society in Peru 1980–1995* (Duke University Press 1998), a collection edited by Steven J. Stern in which the essay by Iglesias contributed to this volume first appeared. That piece, which has retained its original title, is reprinted here with the permission of Duke University Press.

Yanni Kotsonis teaches Russian history at New York University. A specialist in the study of agrarian social relations and the development of political parties, he is one of the coeditors of *Russian Modernity: Politics, Knowledge, Practices* (St. Martin's 1999) and the author of *Making Peasants Backward: Agricultural Co-operatives and the Agrarian Question in Russia, 1861–1914* (St. Martin's 1999).

Tim McDaniel is professor of sociology at the University of California, San Diego. He has written *Autocracy, Modernization, and Revolution in Russia and Iran* (Princeton University Press 1991) and *The Agony of the Russian Idea* (Princeton University Press 1996); he is currently working on a comparative study of radical ideals and social change in the twentieth century, especially with respect to communism and radical Islam.

Adam Michnik is a critical intellectual and the editor of *Gazeta Wyborcza*, a newspaper that he helped to found in 1989. His essays have been translated into many languages and appeared in a wide variety of periodicals. Two collections of them have also been published in English: *Letters from Prison and Other Essays* (University of California Press 1985) *and Letters from Freedom: Post-Cold War Realities and Perspectives* (University of California Press 1998). Jacek Dalecki of Indiana University translated his contribution to this volume.

David Rieff is deputy editor of *World Policy Journal* and the author of works on topics ranging from American cities to international wars. His recent publications include *Slaughterhouse: Bosnia and the Failure of the West* (Touchstone 1995) and *Crimes of War: What the Public Should Know* (Norton 1999). His contribution to this volume first appeared under the same title in *World Policy Journal* (vol. 26, no. 2, Summer 1999) and is reprinted here with permission of the author and the World Policy Institute.

Jeffrey N. Wasserstrom teaches Chinese history at Indiana University. His publications include *Student Protests in Twentieth-Century China: The View from Shanghai* (Stanford University Press 1991) and *Popular Protest and Political Culture in Modern China* (Westview 1992), the latter of which he coedited with Elizabeth J. Perry. A regular contributor to the *Times Literary Supplement* (London) and *Dissent* magazine, he is currently working on a book-length study of Old and New Shanghai as global cities and serving as acting editor of the *American Historical Review*.

Alexander Woodside is professor of East and Southeast Asian history at the University of British Columbia. His books include *Vietnam and the Chinese Model: A Comparison of Vietnamese and Chinese Government in the First Half of the Nineteenth Century* (Harvard University Press 1998), *Community and Revolution in Vietnam* (Houghton-Mifflin 1976), and *Education in Late Imperial China* (University of California Press 1994), the last of which he coedited with Benjamin Elman.

Marilyn B. Young teaches history at New York University. Her books include *Rhetoric of Empire: U.S. China Policy, 1895–1901* (Harvard University Press 1969) and *The Vietnam Wars, 1945–1990* (HarperCollins 1991). A coeditor of *Promissory Notes: Women in the Transition to Socialism* (Monthly Review 1989), she is currently writing a book about the Korean War.

David Zaret is professor of sociology and executive associate dean of the College of Arts and Sciences at Indiana University. His essays on citizenship, the politics of communication, and the English Civil War have appeared in the *American Journal of Sociology* and various edited volumes. His most recent book is *Origins of Democratic Culture: Printing, Opinion and the Public Sphere in Early-Modern England* (Princeton University Press 2000).

Michael Zuckert is Nancy Reeves Dreux Professor of Government at the University of Notre Dame, is the author of *Natural Rights and the New Republicanism* (Princeton University Press 1994) and *The Naturtal Rights Republic* (Notre Dame University Press 1996). He has also written many articles and essays on the American founding period and early modern political philosophy.